SELECTED LETTERS, 1523–1546

The Other Voice in Early Modern Europe:
The Toronto Series, 88

Vittoria Colonna, ca. 1490–1547. 16th century. Samuel H. Kress Collection. 1957.14.1079.

VITTORIA COLONNA

Selected Letters, 1523–1546: A Bilingual Edition

~

Edited and annotated by
VERONICA COPELLO

Translated by
ABIGAIL BRUNDIN

Introduction by
ABIGAIL BRUNDIN *and* VERONICA COPELLO

Iter Press
NEW YORK | TORONTO

2022

978-1-64959-028-2 (paper)
978-1-64959-029-9 (pdf)
978-1-64959-039-8 (epub)

Library of Congress Cataloging-in-Publication Data

Names: Colonna, Vittoria, 1492-1547, author. | Colonna, Vittoria, 1492-1547. Correspondence.
Selections. | Colonna, Vittoria, 1492-1547. Correspondence. Selections. English. | Copello,
Veronica, editor. | Brundin, Abigail, translator.
Title: Selected letters, 1523-1546 : a bilingual edition / Vittoria Colonna ; edited and annotated by
Veronica Copello ; translated by Abigail Brundin.
Description: New York : Iter Press, 2022. | Series: The other voice in early modern Europe: the Toronto
series; 88 | Includes bibliographical references and index. | Summary: "English translation of
forty selected letters, with Italian text and critical commentary, by sixteenth-century poet and
evangelical Vittoria Colonna, illustrative of her political, financial, and religious commitments"--
Provided by publisher.
Identifiers: LCCN 2021048975 (print) | LCCN 2021048976 (ebook) | ISBN 9781649590282
(paperback) | ISBN 9781649590299 (pdf) | ISBN 9781649590398 (epub)
Subjects: LCSH: Colonna, Vittoria, 1492-1547--Correspondence. | Women poets, Italian--Early
modern, 1500-1700--Correspondence.
Classification: LCC PQ4620 A83 2022 (print) | LCC PQ4620 (ebook) | DDC 856/.3--dc23/
eng/20211110
LC record available at https://lccn.loc.gov/2021048975
LC ebook record available at https://lccn.loc.gov/2021048976

Cover Illustration

Anonymous Neapolitan painter, Madonna del Soccorso: detail of Vittoria Colonna, Ischia Ponte,
Church of S. Antonio da Padova. Photo credit: John Palcewski.

Cover Design

Maureen Morin, Library Communications, University of Toronto Libraries.

Contents

Acknowledgments

We are very grateful to the following institutions and individuals for their support and assistance during the preparation of this book.

The Faculty of Modern and Medieval Languages and Linguistics, University of Cambridge, kindly provided funding to support this publication. The University of Cambridge, the American Academy in Rome and the Istituto Nazionale di Studi sul Rinascimento (Florence) funded periods of sabbatical leave during which we were able to complete work on the manuscript. The Archivio di Stato in Modena generously gave permission for the reproduction of Colonna's letter to Ercole II d'Este.

Roberto Vetrugno gave valued assistance in the analysis of Colonna's epistolary language.

The feedback from the Press's readers helped improve the text in numerous ways. We are also very grateful to Margaret King for her steady steering of this text to submission (via a rather long and convoluted route, and finally in the midst of a pandemic).

We finished work on this book during the Covid-19 lockdown, one of us in Italy and one in England, and while we did not actually communicate by letter during this period, we were intensely reliant on more modern forms of epistolography. Thus we were acutely and personally reminded of the importance of networks and our enduring need to stay connected, especially during times of peril, lessons that are at the core of Colonna's letters.

Illustrations

Abbreviations

Libraries, archives and museums

AAM	Archivio dell'Abbazia, Montecassino, Italy
AAV	Archivio Apostolico Vaticano, Vatican City
ABF	Archivio Buonarroti, Florence, Italy
ACDF	Archivio della Congregazione per la Dottrina della Fede, Vatican City
AGSc	Archivio Gallarati Scotti, Milan, Italy
ASF	Archivio di Stato, Florence, Italy
ASL	Archivio di Stato, Lucca, Italy
ASM	Archivio di Stato, Mantua, Italy
ASMo	Archivio di Stato, Modena, Italy
ASN	Archivio di Stato, Naples, Italy
ASR	Archivio di Stato, Rome, Italy
BAM	Biblioteca Ambrosiana, Milan, Italy
BAP	Biblioteca Augustea, Perugia, Italy
BAV	Biblioteca Apostolica Vaticana, Vatican City
BCV	Biblioteca Capitolare, Verona, Italy
BFF	Biblioteca Federiciana, Fano, Italy
BL	Bodleian Library, Oxford, UK
BLL	British Library, London, UK
BMF	Biblioteca Moreniana, Florence, Italy
BNCR	Biblioteca Nazionale Centrale Vittorio Emanuele II, Rome, Italy
BNMV	Biblioteca Nazionale Marciana, Venice, Italy
BPP	Biblioteca Palatina, Parma, Italy
BQB	Biblioteca Queriniana, Brescia, Italy
BSSS	Biblioteca di Santa Scolastica, Subiaco, Italy
ISGM	Isabella Stewart Gardner Museum, Boston, Massachussetts, USA
PML	Pierpont Morgan Library, New York, USA
RAH	Real Academia de la Historia, Madrid, Spain

Editions

Colonna 1544	*Litere della divina Vetoria Colonna Marchesana di Pescara alla Duchessa di Amalfi sopra la vita contemplativa di santa Caterina et sopra de la activa di santa Madalena non più viste in luce.* Venice: Alesandro de Viano Venetian, ad instantia di Antonio detto el Cremaschino, 1544.
Colonna, *Carteggio*	Vittoria Colonna, *Carteggio*, edited by Ermanno Ferrero and Giuseppe Müller. Turin-Florence-Rome: Loescher, 1889.

Colonna,   Vittoria Colonna, *Sonnets for Michelangelo. A Bilingual Edition*,
Sonnets   edited and translated by Abigail Brundin. Chicago & London:
             University of Chicago Press, 2005.

LSA 1551   *Lettere scritte al signor Pietro Aretino da molti signori, comunità,
             donne di valore, poeti et altri eccellentissimi spirti, divise in due libri
             sacre al R.mo Cardinal di Monte.* Venice: per Francesco Marcolini
             di luglio, 1551.

Ve 42   *Lettere volgari di diuersi nobilissimi huomini et eccellentissimi in-
             gegni scritte in diuerse materie. Libro primo.* Venice: [eredi di Aldo
             Manuzio il vecchio], 1542.

Ve 45   *Nuovo libro di lettere de i più rari autori della lingua volgare ita-
             liana di nuovo, et con nuova additione ristampato.* Venice: Paolo
             Gherardo, 1545.

Ve 56   *Lettere di diuersi autori eccellenti. Libro primo. Nel quale sono i tre-
             dici autori illustri, et il fiore di quante altre belle lettere si sono uedute
             fin qui. Con molte lettere del Bembo, del Nauagero, del Fracastoro, et
             d'altri famosi autori non piu date in luce.* Venice: appresso Giordano
             Ziletti, all'insegna della Stella, 1556.

Ve 65   *Lettere di XIII huomini illustri. Alle quali oltra tutte l'altre fin
             qui stampate di nuovo ne sono state aggiunte molte da Thomaso
             Porcacchi.* Venice: presso Giorgio de' Cavalli, 1565.

Introduction

Vittoria Colonna: *"in foemineo sexu rara"*[1]

The poet Vittoria Colonna, marchioness of Pescara (1492–1547), was greatly lauded in her day as an accomplished writer and exemplary model of pious widowhood. Pietro Bembo (1470–1547), author of the seminal work on the written Italian language, *Prose della volgar lingua* (*Discussions of the Vernacular Language*, 1525) and expert practitioner of the genre of Petrarchism, in which Colonna also wrote to great acclaim, went so far as to declare that "among the women who practice this art [poetry] you are much more excellent than it seems possible that nature would allow those of your sex to be."[2] Bembo's critical judgement of Colonna's literary work, which carried great weight among his contemporaries, was entirely sincere. Only a few years after he expressed his glowing opinion of her poetic talents, Colonna became the first woman to have collections of her poetry and letters published in print, the first living poet to be honored with a critical commentary on her collected poetry, and the first to found a new literary genre, that of *rime spirituali* or spiritual Petrarchism.[3]

---

1. "A rare example of the female sex": Emperor Charles V described Colonna in a letter as a woman provided with "singulares virtutes et eruditionem non vulgarem—rem in foemineo sexu raram" ("singular virtues and excellent erudition, which is a rare thing in the female sex"): see Giovanni Rosalba, "Un episodio nella vita di Vittoria Colonna," in Nicola Zingarelli, ed., *Nozze Pércopo-Luciani: 30 luglio 1902* (Naples: L. Pierro, 1903), 140.

2. "Tra le donne in quest'arte [la poesia] sete assai più eccellente che non pare possibile che al vostro sesso si conceda dalla natura": Colonna, *Carteggio*, no. XL. Two years later, Bembo returned to his praise of Colonna: in poetry "a me pare che voi di gran lunga superiate et vinciate il vostro sesso" (Colonna, *Carteggio*, no. LII). And in a letter to Vittore Soranzo, Bembo wrote that a sonnet by Colonna was "bello e ingenioso e grave, più che da donna non pare sia richiesto: ha superato la espettazion mia d'assai": Pietro Bembo, *Lettere*, ed. Ernesto Travi (Bologna: Commissione per i testi di lingua, 1987–1993), 3:126.

3. Vittoria Colonna, *Rime de la divina Vittoria Colonna marchesa di Pescara novamente stampate con privilegio* (Parma: [A. de Viottis], 1538); Colonna 1544; Rinaldo Corso, *Dichiaratione fatta sopra la seconda parte delle* Rime *della divina Vittoria Collonna* [sic] (1542). The only extant example of this first edition of Corso's commentary is damaged and missing its final pages, thus lacking information about the printer and place of publication: see Sarah Christopher Faggioli, "Di un'edizione del 1542 della *Dichiaratione* di Rinaldo Corso alle *Rime spirituali* di Vittoria Colonna," *Giornale storico della letteratura italiana* 634 (2014): 200–210. A second edition of Corso's work was published as *Dichiaratione fatta sopra la seconda parte delle* Rime *della divina Vittoria Collonna* [sic] *marchesana di Pescara* (Bologna: Gian Battista de Phaelli, 1543). A year before the Corso commentary on Colonna's collected poems, Alessandro Piccolomini had published a commentary on a single sonnet by Laudomia Forteguerri. See Alessandro Piccolomini, *Lettvra del S. Alessandro Piccolomini Infiammato fatta nell'Accademia degli Infiammati, M.D.XXXXI* (Bologna: Bartholomeo Bonardo e Marc'Antonio da Carpi, 1541); and

Colonna is often typecast, and indeed she herself actively contributed to this image, as a pious widow, shut away from society and immersed in literary and spiritual conversations with illustrious Catholic reformers.[4] This image, while containing much that is true, does not, however, represent the whole story. In the first place, her noble status, in combination with various historical developments of her era, prevented her from adopting the enclosed life that she so desired, dedicated to the silence of meditation: instead she was forced to struggle throughout her life for tranquility and a space of her own.[5] What is more, she frequently found herself caught in the midst of fraught political disputes and was forced to take sides, revealing both the strength and the considerable decisiveness of her character. It is from a perusal of Colonna's letters, rather than from her literary works, that a reader gains a clear sense of the range of her voices and attitudes, the strength of her personality and the effectiveness of her actions and advice in dealing with the complex world in which she made her way.

Striking epistolary evidence of Colonna's often fiery and dynamic character, completely at odds with the image of the pious widow projected in her literary works, is revealed in the events of 1525, when her husband Francesco Ferrante d'Avalos (1490–1525), who had recently been nominated governor of Benevento, was occupied with fighting in the north of Italy and delegated his wife to act as his lieutenant in the new territory. When her authority was questioned on the grounds of her sex, Colonna wrote in almost menacing tones to the papal datary, Giovan Matteo Giberti (1495–1543), asking him to seek a *breve* from the pope reconfirming the validity of her role as governor in her husband's stead.[6] Once she had obtained the document, Colonna wrote again to thank Giberti in ironic tones: he had with his light illuminated her "lowly merit," as well as that of the whole "disadvantaged female condition."[7]

Konrad Eisenbichler, *The Sword and the Pen: Women, Poetry and Politics in Sixteenth-Century Siena* (Toronto: University of Toronto Press, 2014), 10, 121, and 144.

4. On her own image creation, see Abigail Brundin, *Vittoria Colonna and the Spiritual Poetics of the Italian Reformation* (Aldershot, UK: Ashgate, 2008), 15–36; and Virginia Cox, "The Exemplary Vittoria Colonna," in Abigail Brundin, Tatiana Crivelli, and Maria Serena Sapegno, ed., *A Companion to Vittoria Colonna* (Leiden-Boston: Brill, 2016), 467–500.

5. See, for instance, Colonna's request to Pope Clement VII to retire to a house in Naples and hold mass there (Colonna, *Carteggio*, no. XXVII); on this episode, see Ramie Targoff, "La volontà segreta di Vittoria Colonna: Una lettera smarrita a Clemente VII," in Maria Serena Sapegno, ed., *Al crocevia della storia: Poesia, religione e politica in Vittoria Colonna* (Rome: Viella, 2016), 217–24; Ramie Targoff, *Renaissance Woman: The Life of Vittoria Colonna* (New York: Farrar, Straus and Giroux, 2018), 54–55.

6. A *breve* or brief is a papal document, generally simpler and less official than a more formal papal bull.

7. "Basso merito," "depressa condition feminile": letter to Giberti, 8 November 1525, in Pier Desiderio Pasolini, *Tre lettere inedite di Vittoria Colonna, marchesa di Pescara* (Rome: Ermanno Loescher & C. [Bretschneider e Regenberg], 1901), 28–30. On this whole episode see Veronica Copello, "'Locum gerit

Another revealing example of Colonna's character, this time translated into action rather than words, dates from the period after her widowhood when she returned to the Castello Aragonese on Ischia, an island in the Bay of Naples. On 28 April 1528, she heard from that island the cannons firing at the Battle of Capo d'Orso, during which the French fleet encountered imperial ships in the Gulf of Salerno. Colonna's few remaining living relatives were on board the Spanish ships, and she did not wait passively for the battle to end; instead, she began to organize the shipment of supplies to the imperial troops and to instruct spies to penetrate the enemy ranks and bring back information to the authorities in Naples.[8] The devout poet knew how to transform herself into an authoritative and resourceful leader when circumstances required.

While these historical events were exceptional, it is also the case, as her letters reveal in fascinating detail, that Colonna administrated land and goods throughout her life and occupied herself daily with the reality of taxes, payments, arguments between vassals, undisciplined priests, hereditary rights, boundary disputes and many other such worldly matters. As one reads her collected letters, it becomes clear how she embodied a conflict between the desire for a cloistered life and the demands of the real world, between *otium* and *negotium*, or the contemplative and the active life.[9] A better understanding of this ongoing conflict in her life and personality, which her correspondence lays out for us, casts important new light on her literary work. While Colonna's poetry projects one persona to her reading public, defined by piety, contemplation and inner spirituality, her letters add an important worldly dimension to her character and indicate the careful work of strategic selection and omission that went into building the image implied in her poems. It is particularly interesting to note how, while the literary persona was seemingly required to conform to the strict gender expectations of the period, in her letters, and by extension her worldly activities, Colonna's gender was less relevant, while her nobility was a key factor in the high degree of agency and authority that she commanded. Although Colonna's literary voice pushed far in completely new directions, thus recalibrating literary gender norms in a profound way, she achieved this outcome through a carefully orchestrated and gradual process of shifting and negotiation of the established canon. In her letters, on the other hand, even the early letters written while she was a young

---

et tenet authoritate': Il volto politico di Vittoria Colonna tra lettere e documenti inediti," *Rinascimento* 61 (2021): 237–82.

8. The information about Colonna's actions is contained in the imperial privilege of 16 January 1534: see Rosalba, "Un episodio," 140.

9. See Peter Armour, "Michelangelo's Two Sisters: Contemplative Life and Active Life in the Final Version of the Monument to Julius II," in *Sguardi sull'Italia: Miscellanea dedicata a Francesco Villari dalla Society for Italian Studies*, ed. Gino Bedani and others (Exeter: The Society for Italian Studies, 1997), 55–83.

married woman, she demands and receives action, obedience, and deference from a range of interlocutors, and rarely excuses or explains her assumed right to act in the world.

Life, Works, and Spirituality

Born in 1492[10] in Marino, south of Rome, where she was raised and educated, Vittoria Colonna was the daughter of Fabrizio Colonna, a famous soldier who worked for the Spanish king, and Agnese di Montefeltro, daughter of Federico, duke of Urbino.[11] In 1495, at the age of three, she was betrothed to Francesco Ferrante d'Avalos, future marquis of Pescara, whom she would come to love sincerely.[12] The marriage contract stipulated a shift in political allegiance on the part of Colonna's father, Fabrizio, who had until that date been in the service of the king of France, but now agreed to change his alliance to the Spanish side.[13] The political element of the contract reminds us how much was at stake in the marriage of the offspring of nobility: the decision made at this early date concerning Colonna's marriage would have repercussions not only for her personally but for the many soldiers and others who worked in service to the Colonna household.[14]

Following her eventual marriage in 1509, Colonna moved to Ischia, where she entered the lively Neapolitan cultural and intellectual circles that were to have a great influence on her life. The Castello Aragonese on Ischia was presided over by Colonna's aunt-by-marriage, Costanza d'Avalos, duchess of Francavilla

---

10. Many sources cite 1490 as Colonna's birth date, but the evidence for 1492 is clearly presented in Domenico Tordi, "Luogo ed anno della nascita di Vittoria Colonna," *Giornale storico della letteratura italiana* 29 (1892): 17.

11. Recent biographies of Colonna include Targoff, *Renaissance Woman*, and Andrea Donati, *Vittoria Colonna e l'eredità degli spirituali* (Rome: Etgraphiae, 2019), the latter containing many previously unpublished documents and sources. Virginia Cox and Shannon McHugh, eds., *Vittoria Colonna (1490–1547): Poetry, Religion, Art, Impact* (Amsterdam: Amsterdam University Press, 2022) presents new work on Colonna from a range of perspectives.

12. See in this volume Colonna's Letter 4 for evidence of the loving relations between her and her husband. One contemporary source, the biography of Francesco Ferrante d'Avalos by Paolo Giovio, instead paints a picture of a less than happy marriage, in which Ferrante spent long periods away from Naples, and when at home, could rarely be distracted from hunting: see Paolo Giovio, *Le vite del gran capitano e del marchese di Pescara*, trans. Lodovico Domenichi (Bari: Laterza, 1931).

13. Tordi, "Luogo ed anno," 15–17.

14. Anthony D'Elia, *The Renaissance of Marriage in Fifteenth-Century Italy* (Cambridge, MA: Harvard University Press, 2004); Tatiana Crivelli, "Fedeltà, maternità, sacralità: Reinterpretazioni del legame matrimoniale nell'opera di Vittoria Colonna," in *Doni d'amore: Donne e rituali nel Rinascimento*, ed. Patricia Lurati (Cinisello Balsamo [Milan]: Silvana, 2014), 171–79; Julius Kirshner, *Marriage, Dowry, and Citizenship in Late Medieval and Renaissance Italy* (Toronto: University of Toronto Press, 2014).

(1460–1541), who gathered a distinguished intellectual circle there.[15] Also residing on Ischia were the three siblings Maria, Giovanna, and Antonio d'Aragona, as well as Alfonso (1502–1546) and Costanza d'Avalos (1503/4–1575), cousins of Colonna's husband Ferrante. These individuals were to become close to Colonna and to remain so for the rest of her life, as her letters testify.

Colonna's life in this period was taken up with parties and other courtly festivities and seems to have been pleasurable, although her husband was frequently absent, increasingly committed to military activities on behalf of the emperor.[16] In 1524, Ferrante was named captain of the imperial infantry in Italy. In 1525, he was victorious at the Battle of Pavia, a decisive victory over the French troops during which the king of France, Francis I (1494–1547), was taken prisoner. Ferrante's death from septicemia[17] on 3 December 1525 was a defining moment for Colonna. Thereafter, her pattern of life changed completely: she abandoned her family's well-appointed palaces and her own sumptuous dress and luxurious habits, and declared that she was ready to abandon all other worldly ties as well.[18] Her intention was to retreat into a state of poverty in a Roman convent, San Silvestro in Capite, but the pope, Clement VII (1478–1534), was not in favor and refused his permission to the nuns of San Silvestro, who were threatened with excommunication if they allowed Colonna to take her vows.[19] Thwarted at the very highest level from taking the veil, Colonna moved instead to her family territories south

---

15. On Ischia and Costanza d'Avalos's role there, see Suzanne Thérault, *Un cénacle humaniste de la Renaissance autour de Vittoria Colonna, châtelaine d'Ischia* (Paris: Librairie Marcel Didier; Florence: Sansoni antiquariato, 1968); Ippolita Di Majo, "Vittoria Colonna, il Castello di Ischia e la cultura delle corti," in Pina Ragionieri, ed., *Vittoria Colonna e Michelangelo: Firenze, Casa Buonarroti, 24 maggio–12 settembre 2005* (Florence: Mandragora, 2005), 19–32; Raffaele Castagna, *Un cenacolo del Rinascimento sul Castello d'Ischia* (Ischia: Imagaenaria, 2007); Maria Teresa Guerra Medici, "Intrecci familiari, politici e letterari alla corte di Costanza d'Avalos," in Maria Teresa Fumagalli Beonio Brocchieri and Roberta Frigeni, eds., *Donne e scrittura dal XII al XVI secolo* (Bergamo: Lubrina-LEB, 2009), 115–62; Veronica Copello, "Costanza d'Avalos (1460–1541): 'Letras' e 'valor guerrero' alla corte di Ischia," *Mélanges de l'école française de Rome: Moyen Âge* 31, no. 2 (2019): 343–60, <journals.openedition.org/mefrm/6397>.

16. See Letter 6 for details of Ferrante's military activities in this period.

17. Donati, *Vittoria Colonna*, 49–51.

18. "Essendo piaciuto al nostro Signor Idio farme priva de quel bene che più prezava in nel mundo, che era il marchese de Pescara, mio Signor marito, patre, fratello, figliolo et amico, et in nel quale io senteva ogni sorte de amoroso vinculo, determinata sequirlo senza offendere l'anima, voglio intrare in uno monesterio per fare ogni officio ad me possibile in salvare l'anima sua e la mia; per il che, essendo da reputare il mundo come persona fora de quello, fin dal presente ho deliberato lassare alcune cose de quella facultà che 'l nostro Signore me concesse in remuneratione delli servitii havuti da amici, servitori et servitrici": Colonna's proxy-will, 12 December 1525: BSSS, III BB 53, 55, ed. Veronica Copello in Donati, *Vittoria Colonna*, 397–404.

19. See Targoff, *Renaissance Woman*, 44–57. The pope's opposition to Colonna's entry into a convent presumably derived from his belief in the possibility of a second, politically favorable marriage.

of Rome. The political climate was growing increasingly fraught, however: on 20 September 1526, Colonna troops attacked Rome and in November the pope, in retaliation, sacked and set fire to their properties. Fleeing the conflict, Colonna moved south again to Ischia, where she remained during the Sack of Rome of May 1527 and the French siege of Naples, followed by an outbreak of plague in 1528.

In the years that followed these traumatic events, Colonna continued to host writers and intellectuals at the court on Ischia. By the end of the 1520s she had also begun an epistolary friendship with Pietro Bembo.[20] These were years of renewed cultural as well as spiritual engagement for Colonna, as we learn from the testimony of a contemporary, the historian and humanist Girolamo Borgia, who wrote of her some time before 1528:

> as she grew older, she dedicated herself entirely to Christ, and aban-
> doning all earthly concerns, she turned to the holy study of the sa-
> cred texts, in which she progressed so far that she would not seem
> inferior to the most learned theologians in either her knowledge or
> her discussion thereof.[21]

Clear traces of the studies described by Borgia can be observed in Colonna's poetry as well as in her letters that deal with philosophical and religious themes, in which the high level of her learning and specialist knowledge is always very much in evidence.[22]

Alongside her increasing immersion in the study of theology in this period, Colonna also became more concretely involved with religious causes. After 1529, when the Order was first founded, she followed the fortunes of the Capuchins with close attention, and she fought on their behalf with the highest ecclesiastical authorities over a number of years, expending both energy and hard cash on the question of their right to grow their Order through the admission of new friars from the Observants.[23] Colonna's letters on behalf of the Capuchins reveal

---

20. On the friendship between Colonna and Bembo, see Letter 9, as well as Carlo Dionisotti, "Appunti sul Bembo e su Vittoria Colonna," in *Miscellanea Augusto Campana* (Padua: Antenore, 1981), 1:257–86; and Abigail Brundin, "Vittoria Colonna in Manuscript," in Brundin, Crivelli and Sapegno, *A Companion to Vittoria Colonna*, 39–68.

21. "Cum interim aetate processisset, sese totam Christo devovit curisque terrenis prorsum omissis ad sanctissima sacrae paginae studia convertit in quibus tantum profecit ut nec eruditissimis theologis et bene sentiendo et disserendo quippiam cedere videatur": Girolamo Borgia, *Historiae de bellis italicis* (before 1528), cited in Elena Valeri, *"Italia dilacerata": Girolamo Borgia nella cultura storica del Rinascimento* (Milan: F. Angeli, 2007), 79.

22. See in particular Letters 25 and 35.

23. See Letter 12. On Colonna's defense of the Capuchins, see Tacchi-Venturi, "Vittoria Colonna e la riforma cappuccina," *Collectanea franciscana* 1 (1931): 28–58; Costanzo Cargnoni, ed., *I frati cappuccini: Documenti e testimonianze del primo secolo* (Perugia: Edizioni Frate Indovino, 1988–1993),

her outrage when she perceived that the Church was acting unfairly. She was an idealist, but also a pragmatist who took action to avert such injustices in every way at her disposal. She also may have had the opportunity during these years to meet directly with the Spanish reformer Juan de Valdés (ca. 1500–1541), who had moved to Naples in 1534 and gathered a circle of like-minded people around him in that city.[24]

In March 1535, Colonna finally returned to Rome, where she attended sermons given by the famous preacher Bernardino Ochino (1487–1564), who would become Vicar General of the Capuchins and who swiftly assumed the role of her indispensable spiritual guide.[25] In Rome, as well, probably in 1536, Colonna made another friendship—a friendship that would be one of the most important of her life—with the renowned artist Michelangelo Buonarroti (1475–1564).[26] In 1537 she left for Venice, with the intention of setting out by boat on a pilgrimage to the Holy Land. En route, she paused in Ferrara where, when her plans for the pilgrimage fell through, she remained for nearly a year.[27] While in Ferrara she had the opportunity once again to hear Ochino preach, as well as to form a close bond with the duchess of Ferrara, Renée de France (1510–1575), who had notable reformist leanings, and to meet the future Jesuits Simón Rodriguez and Claudio Jajo. We can also assign to this period in Ferrara the beginnings of Colonna's important friendship with Marguerite d'Angoulême (1492–1549), the French queen of Navarre and sister of the king of France.[28] Thus, the Ferrara sojourn was

vol. 2; Concetta Ranieri, "'Si san Francesco fu eretico li suoi imitatori son luterani': Vittoria Colonna e la riforma dei cappuccini," in *Ludovico da Fossombrone e l'Ordine dei Cappuccini*, ed. Vittorio Criscuolo (Rome: Istituto storico dei cappuccini, 1994): 337–51; Veronica Copello, "Nuovi elementi su Vittoria Colonna, i cappuccini e i gesuiti," *Lettere italiane* 69, no. 2 (2017): 296–327; Marianna Liguori, "Vittoria Colonna e la riforma cappuccina: Documenti epistolari e un'appendice inedita," *Atti e memorie dell'Arcadia* 6 (2017): 85–104.

24. On Valdés, see Letter 24. There is no documentary evidence to support a meeting between Colonna and Valdés, although some sources suggest that one took place: see for example Concetta Ranieri, "Premesse umanistiche alla religiosità di Vittoria Colonna," *Rivista di storia e letteratura religiosa*, 32 (1996): 531–48, at 537–38.

25. For the exchanges between Colonna and Ochino, see Letters 14, 15, 28, and 31. More broadly on their relationship, see Giovanni Bardazzi, "Le rime spirituali di Vittoria Colonna e Bernardino Ochino," *Italique* 4 (2001): 61–101; Emidio Campi, "Vittoria Colonna and Bernardino Ochino," in Brundin, Crivelli and Sapegno, *A Companion to Vittoria Colonna*, 371–98; Michele Camaioni, *Il Vangelo e l'anticristo: Bernardino Ochino tra francescanesimo ed eresia, 1487–1547* (Bologna: Il mulino, 2018).

26. On this famous friendship, see Letters 33–34, 37, and 40 as well as the bibliography cited in the notes to those letters.

27. See Letter 15, and on the plans for a pilgrimage, Targoff, *Renaissance Woman*, 125–31.

28. See Letter 20, and the bibliography cited in the notes to that letter.

probably key to the progressive development in this period of Colonna's understanding of and engagement with reform theology.

From Ferrara, Colonna traveled further afield in order to hear Ochino preach, attending his sermons in Pisa, Florence and Lucca. She returned to Rome in 1538, where she took up residence at the convent of San Silvestro in Capite and remained there until 1541. Her stay in Rome in these years was the context for the establishment of another key friendship, that with the English Cardinal Reginald Pole (1500–1558), who from about 1540 took over Ochino's position as Colonna's primary spiritual mentor.[29] Other close friends were also to be found in Rome at this time: the reformist bishop Pier Paolo Vergerio (1498–1565), writing from France, described a "school which includes Your Excellency along with my most reverend Cardinals [Gasparo] Contarini, Pole, [Pietro] Bembo and [Federico] Fregoso, all united together."[30]

Over this whole period, relations between Colonna's brother Ascanio (1500–1557) and Pope Paul III (1468–1549) had continued to deteriorate. For some years the pope had been looking for an excuse to invade the Colonna lands south of Rome, while Ascanio refused to be commanded by the pope and rejected any kind of compromise in the dealings between them.[31] In the winter of 1541, Ascanio rejected the pope's new salt tax, at which point the tension reached breaking point and Vittoria was forced to take refuge in the Dominican convent of San Paolo in Orvieto.[32] At the urging of the Emperor Charles V (1500–1558), she tried to mediate between the factions and persuade her brother to accept the terms for peace, but her pleas fell on deaf ears. In March 1541, the so-called Salt Wars broke out between Ascanio and Pope Paul III: the pope seized all the Colonna territories and Ascanio was forced into exile.

Shortly afterwards, Reginald Pole was chosen as legate of the Patrimony of Saint Peter in Viterbo. Colonna followed him there, and took up residence once again in a Dominican convent, that of Santa Caterina.[33] While in Viterbo she joined the discussions of the so-called *Spirituali* or "Spirituals." The Spirituals were a group of prelates and humanists who were active in pursuit of church reform during the middle decades of the sixteenth century. They were particularly sympathetic to the Lutheran doctrine of *sola fide* (justification by faith alone),

29. See for evidence of Pole's growing role, Letters 24, 28, 30–31, 36, and 39. More broadly on Pole, see Dermot Fenlon, *Heresy and Obedience in Tridentine Italy: Cardinal Pole and the Counter Reformation* (Cambridge: Cambridge University Press, 2008).

30. "Schola della Eccellentia Vostra et di Reverendissimi miei Cardinali Contareno, Polo, Bembo, Fregoso, che era tutt'una": Colonna, *Carteggio*, no. CXV.

31. See Letters 21 and 22.

32. See Letter 23 and the bibliography in the notes to that letter.

33. For evidence of Colonna's desire to spend time with Pole while she was in Viterbo, a desire that was mostly thwarted, see Letter 24.

and as a result they questioned the validity of many of the rites and practices of Catholicism. After the death of Juan de Valdés in 1541, some members of the Valdesian circle gathered in Viterbo in the household of Reginal Pole.[34] This group included men such as the humanist poet Marcantonio Flaminio (1498–1550), the Venetian nobleman Alvise [Luigi] Priuli (ca. 1500–1560), Bembo's protégé Vittore Soranzo (1550–1558), the bishop of Modena Giovanni Morone (1509–1580), the humanist and papal secretary Pietro Carnesecchi (1508–1567) and, there in spirit rather than in person, the widowed noblewoman Giulia Gonzaga (1513–1566). During her stay in Viterbo, Colonna's exposure to and understanding of reformed theology, including Lutheran positions, evidently increased exponentially. It was also during this period that she witnessed the preparation of the draft of the reformist book, *Il beneficio di Cristo*, which came out in print in 1542 but was swiftly suppressed by the Inquisition.[35]

In 1542, three of Colonna's close friends were taken from her in quick succession. Gasparo Contarini (1483–1542) died in August of that year.[36] Just a few days later Bernardino Ochino, who had failed to present himself before the Inquisition in Rome, fled instead to Switzerland and definitively abandoned the Catholic Church.[37] In November, Reginald Pole, who had been nominated as papal legate to the Council of Trent, left Viterbo to travel to Trent from where, when the first planned meeting of that body did not eventuate, he rejoined the papal Curia.

In the autumn of 1543, having recovered from an illness that had seriously worried her friends, Colonna returned once again to Rome and took up residence in the Benedictine convent of Sant'Anna. She joined the Compagnia della Grazia (Fellowship of Grace), founded to protect and run Casa Santa Marta, an institution for the rehabilitation of repentant prostitutes that had been set up by Ignatius of Loyola, founder and Superior General of the Jesuit order.[38] Many

---

34. On the Spirituals, and Colonna's relationship to them, see Massimo Firpo, "Vittoria Colonna, Giovanni Morone e gli 'spirituali,'" *Rivista di storia e letteratura religiosa* 24, no. 1 (1988); Massimo Firpo, *Tra alumbrados e 'spirituali': Studi su Juan de Valdés e il valdesianesimo nella crisi religiosa del '500 italiano* (Florence: Olschki, 1990); Brundin, *Vittoria Colonna and the Spiritual Poetics*; and relevant chapters in Brundin, Crivelli and Sapegno, *A Companion to Vittoria Colonna*.

35. On the *Beneficio di Cristo*, see Carlo Ginzburg and Adriano Prosperi, *Giochi di pazienza: Un seminario sul Beneficio di Cristo*, 2nd ed. (Turin: Einaudi, 1977); and Luigi Lazzerini, *Teologia del Miserere: Da Savonarola al Beneficio di Cristo, 1490–1543* (Turin: Rosenberg & Sellier, 2013).

36. See Stephen Bowd, "Prudential Friendship and Religious Reform: Vittoria Colonna and Gasparo Contarini," in Brundin, Crivelli and Sapegno, *A Companion to Vittoria Colonna*, 349–70.

37. Gigliola Fragnito, "Gli 'spirituali' e la fuga di Bernardino Ochino," *Rivista storica italiana* 84 (1972): 777–813.

38. Copello, "Nuovi elementi," 322–23.

contemporaries also record Colonna's considerable charitable activities in this period, in particular her work to build churches and convents.[39]

Three years later, her health once again took a turn for the worse: she died on 25 February 1547 in Rome. At her deathbed were a number of friends from the group of Spirituals: Marcantonio Flaminio, Luigi Priuli, and, in Pole's absence, his secretary Tommaso Maggi. In her will Colonna left Pole a considerable sum of money.[40]

Colonna's corpus of poetry, according to the collection edited and published by Alan Bullock in 1982, consists of 141 poems treating amorous themes (commemorating the death of Ferrante); 217 poems with spiritual subject matter; and around thirty correspondence poems.[41] There is almost no trace of poetry composed before her widowhood in 1525, despite contemporary sources citing her as a known poet in these early years.[42] The exception is a poetic *Epistola* composed on the theme of the rout of Ravenna in 1512 during which her husband was taken prisoner.[43] Colonna's fame as a poet spread rapidly once she was widowed, however: already by 1532 Ludovico Ariosto was singing her praises in the final edition of his epic *Orlando furioso*,[44] and in 1535, a sonnet by Colonna was printed in the second edition of Pietro Bembo's collected *Rime*.[45] Her poetry, as well as her poetic judgement, were sought out by some of the finest writers from across the Italian peninsula.

Sometime around 1535, as her poetry appeared in print via Bembo's mediation, Colonna made known her decision to resume writing after a pause and to turn her literary vocation entirely over to the service of God, narrating her

---

39. Copello, "Nuovi elementi," 309–10 and 317–18.

40. Targoff, *Renaissance Woman*, 252–73.

41. Vittoria Colonna, *Rime*, ed. Alan Bullock (Bari: Laterza, 1982); and Vittoria Colonna, *Sonetti: In morte di Francesco Ferrante d'Avalos marchese di Pescara: Edizione del ms. XIII.G.43 della Biblioteca nazionale di Napoli*, ed. Tobia R. Toscano (Milan: Mondadori, 1998), which identifies a number of new poems by Colonna. Bullock's division of "amorous" and "spiritual" poems has been problematized and nuanced by later critics: see especially Danilio Romei, "Le *Rime* di Vittoria Colonna," review of Colonna, *Rime*, ed. Alan Bullock, *Paragone-Letteratura* 34, no. 404 (1983): 81–84; Giovanna Rabitti, review of Colonna, *Rime*, ed. Alan Bullock, *Studi e problemi di critica testuale* 28 (1984), 230–39; and above all Toscano in Colonna, *Sonetti: In morte*, 22–51. The identification of correspondence poems is also discussed in Brundin, "Vittoria Colonna in Manuscript."

42. Thérault, *Un cénacle humaniste*; and Concetta Ranieri, "Descriptio et imago vitae: Vittoria Colonna nei biografi, letterati e poeti del Cinquecento," in *Biografia: Genesi e strutture*, ed. Mauro Sarnelli (Rome: Aracne, 2003), 123–53.

43. The *Epistola* on the rout of Ravenna appears as poem number A2:1 with the first-line title "Excelso mio Signor, questa ti scrivo," in Colonna, *Rime*, ed. Bullock, 53–56.

44. Ludovico Ariosto, *Orlando furioso* XXXVII.16–21; see Nuccio Ordine, "Vittoria Colonna nell'*Orlando furioso*," *Studi e problemi di critica testuale* 1 (1991): 55–92.

45. See Letter 9.

personal journey of faith for the benefit of her readers.[46] This is the moment when her most original and unprecedented literary activity began, activity that was to give rise to an entirely new genre: the genre of *rime spirituali*, spiritual Petrarchism, effectively established by Colonna and subsequently imitated by many other poets.[47] A key example of her originality in crafting poetry in the new genre can be found in the collection that Colonna personally oversaw as a gift for her friend Michelangelo in 1539 or 1540.[48] The many printed editions of her poetry that begin in 1538 were never, however, officially sponsored or initiated by the author; not even the 1546 Valgrisi edition in which for the first time a substantial collection of *rime spirituali* circulated in print.[49] In 1543, Colonna's poetic influence was acknowledged in the printing of a commentary on her collected verse by the young linguist and scholar Rinaldo Corso, the first time this honor had been conferred on a living writer.[50]

Colonna was also the author of a number of prose works, written in her preferred form of letter-treatises, and all treating spiritual themes. The two works *Pianto sopra la Passione di Cristo* (*Lamentation on the Passion of Christ*), also known as the *Meditatione del Venerdì Santo* (*Good Friday Meditation*), and the

46. See Abigail Brundin, "Poesia come devozione: Leggere le rime di Vittoria Colonna," in Sapegno, *Al crocevia*, 161–76.

47. Gabriele Fiamma wrote that it is "noto a ciascuno, che l'Illustr. Signora Vittoria Colonna, Marchesa di Pescara, è stata la prima, c'ha cominciato a scrivere con dignità in Rime le cose spirituali": Gabriele Fiamma, *Rime spirituali* (Venice: Francesco de' Franceschi Senese, 1570), fol. 4r. There are numerous volumes entitled *Rime spirituali*, following Colonna's example: see Amedeo Quondam, "Note sulla tradizione della poesia spirituale e religiosa (parte prima)," in *Paradigmi e tradizioni*, ed. Amedeo Quondam (Rome: Bulzoni, 2005), 127–211.

48. The manuscript, identified as ms Vat. lat. 11539 in the Vatican Apostolic Library, has been edited and translated in Colonna, *Sonnets*; Vittoria Colonna, *La raccolta di rime per Michelangelo*, ed. and commented by Veronica Copello (Florence: SEF, 2020). The original can be viewed online at <digi. vatlib.it/view/MSS_Vat.lat.11539>. On the manuscript's dating, see Tobia R. Toscano, "Per la datazione del manoscritto dei sonetti di Vittoria Colonna per Michelangelo Buonarroti," *Critica letteraria* 175 (2017): 211–37.

49. On the complex print history of Colonna's verses see Tatiana Crivelli, "The Print Tradition of Vittoria Colonna's '*Rime*'," in Brundin, Crivelli and Sapegno, *A Companion to Vittoria Colonna*, 69–139.

50. The author of the commentary was Rinaldo Corso, a young writer working at the court of Veronica Gambara in Correggio: his work came out in two editions, a partial one in 1542 and a complete one in 1558. For more on the commentary see Giacomo Moro, "Le commentaire de Rinaldo Corso sur les *Rime* de Vittoria Colonna: Une encyclopédie pour les 'tres nobles dames,'" in *Les commentaires et la naissance de la critique littéraire, France/Italie, XIVe–XVIe siècles: Actes du Colloque international sur le commentaire (Paris, 19–21 mai 1988)*, ed. Gisèle Mathieu-Castellani and Michel Plaisance (Paris: Aux amateurs des livres, 1990), 195–202; Monica Bianco, "Le due redazioni del commento di Rinaldo Corso alle *Rime* di Vittoria Colonna," *Studi di filologia italiana* 56 (1998): 271–95; Christopher Faggioli, "Di un'edizione."

Oratione sopra l'Ave Maria (*Oration on the Ave Maria*), which were published together a number of times in the sixteenth century, were probably both composed
originally as letters to Ochino.[51] Her meditations on Mary Magdalene and Saint
Catherine of Alexandria and on the Madonna were composed as letters addressed
to Colonna's cousin-by-marriage, Costanza d'Avalos Piccolomini, and were
also published in sixteenth-century editions.[52] All of these prose works model a
meditative practice for the reader, which the author authoritatively embodies and
teaches to her listener.

Already as early as 1540, given her close links to reformist groups, a whiff of
controversy surrounded Colonna's literary production, such that it was claimed
that in her poetry "there were many things contrary to the faith of Jesus Christ."[53]
More specific accusations against Colonna's orthodoxy came to light during the
inquisitorial trials of Pietro Carnesecchi and Giovanni Morone, although by 1557,
when these prosecutions began, she had been dead for ten years.[54] Accusations
against Colonna concerned, on the one hand, her intimacy with Ochino, Pole,
and other protagonists of Italian reform, and on the other, her alleged belief in
the doctrine of justification by faith alone, or *sola fide*.[55] Her writing does not
clearly reveal Colonna's beliefs on this matter: all too often her words are veiled,
sometimes even contradictory, and she seems to have been unwilling to adopt
any position that was too explicitly heterodox.[56] Nonetheless, the people and en-
vironments that she frequented in her lifetime indicate her developed interest

51. See also the letter on the Gospel of the Adulteress (Letter 27 in this edition), which was also
intended for Ochino. Colonna's prose works are edited in Paolo Simoncelli, *Evangelismo italiano del
Cinquecento: Questione religiosa e nicodemismo* (Rome: Istituto storico italiano per l'età moderna e
contemporanea, 1979), 423–28; and Eva-Maria Jung-Inglessis, "Il *Pianto della Marchesa di Pescara sopra la Passione di Cristo*: Introduzione," *Archivio italiano per la storia della pietà* 10 (1997): 115–47. The
Pianto appears in English translation in Susan Haskins, *Who is Mary?: Three Early Modern Women
on the Idea of the Virgin Mary* (Chicago: University of Chicago Press, 2008), 53–65. For analysis of
these works see Eleonora Carinci, "Religious Prose Writings," in Brundin, Crivelli and Sapegno, *A
Companion to Vittoria Colonna*, 399–430.

52. See Letter 26, on Mary Magdalene and Catherine of Alexandria; and Colonna, *Carteggio*, no.
CLXIX, on the Madonna.

53. "V'erano di molte cose contro la fede di Gesù Christo": Letter from Alberto Sacrati to Ercole II
d'Este, duke of Ferrara, in Colonna, *Carteggio*, 204.

54. See the editions by Massimo Firpo and Dario Marcatto of the Carnesecchi and Morone prosecutions, respectively *I processi inquisitoriali di Pietro Carnesecchi, 1557–1567*, 2 vols. in 4 (Vatican City:
Archivio Segreto Vaticano, 1998–2000); and *Il processo inquisitoriale del cardinal Giovanni Morone*,
new critical ed., 3 vols. (Rome: Libreria editrice vaticana, 2011–2015); the latter being the second edition of the original publication by Firpo and Marcatto, *Il processo inquisitoriale del cardinal Giovanni
Morone: Edizione critica*, 6 vols. in 7 (Rome: Istituto storico per l'età moderna e contemporanea,
1981–1995).

55. See Brundin, *Vittoria Colonna and the Spiritual Poetics*, 37–100.

56. A notable exception to this is Letter 26 in the current edition.

in "reformed" ideas, in the widest sense of that term. As an example, Gasparo Contarini sent Colonna a long letter on the theme of justification, on which topic he was busy seeking agreement with Protestant representatives at the Diet of Regensburg (February–June, 1541). His letter brings Colonna up to date on recent developments, and he seeks her opinion on them as something of value: as Alvise Priuli commented to Monsignor Lodovico Beccadelli, Contarini's letter "greatly pleased the same very Reverend [Cardinal Federico] Fregoso. . . . The Lady Marchioness [i.e., Colonna] also greatly appreciated it."[57] Reform of the institution of the Church was a cause close to Colonna's heart, and she labored to nurture every religious experience that seemed to her to encourage true faith. Alongside her ongoing support for Bernardino Ochino and for the group of Spirituals, as well as the long-term battle she fought on behalf of the new Capuchin Order, she also spoke out in defense of the newly formed Jesuits.[58] Moreover, her close collaboration with leading Capuchins during the 1530s brought her into contact with some of the core texts on which their spirituality was founded, from early Franciscan works to later ones.[59]

While Colonna's opinions on spiritual matters were clearly influenced by her encounters with charismatic religious figures, we should not underestimate the dynamic quality of her own thinking on these topics. After Ferrante's death her faith took on an increasingly significant role in her daily life, but its significance also extended to her political and economic decisions. On her return to Rome, and in particular following her encounter with Ochino, Colonna's contemporaries could not fail to remark on the new depth and authority of her devotion. This increased further from around 1540, under the influence of her friendship with Pole, as her expression of faith grew more intimate and personal, and perhaps less closely shackled to the traditional rites of the Catholic Church.

The ambiguity of her own pronouncements on some of the key doctrinal issues of her day has led some critics to assign to Colonna only a minor role in the circles of reformers that she frequented as a disciple and willing student. Certainly her relations with Reginald Pole were often cool; clearly, she was frustrated by her lack of direct access to him and his inner circle, as her letters make clear. Nonetheless her contribution to the debates on key theological issues of the period seems to have been serious, as Contarini's letter cited above suggests, and

---

57. Letter from Alvise Priuli to Lodovico Beccadelli, Capranica, 15 July 1541, in Simoncelli, *Evangelismo italiano*, 112.

58. On Colonna's defense of the Jesuits, see Pietro Tacchi-Venturi, "Vittoria Colonna, fautrice della Riforma Cattolica, secondo alcune sue lettere inedite," *Studi e documenti di storia e diritto* 22 (1901): 153–79; Copello, "Nuovi elementi," 320–27.

59. One such text was probably Bartolomeo Cordoni, *Dyalogo della unione spirituale di Dio con l'anima* (Milan: Francesco Cantalupo e Cicognara Innocenzo, 1539), the influence of which can be detected clearly in Letter 25.

as Colonna herself asserts. In her mature poetry as well as in her prose works she explicitly claims for herself the role of teacher, modeling the right kind of devotional practices in her own life and, crucially, in her writing. Significantly, her spiritual authority derives much of its power from her gender, as she embraces the emotional connection with Christ represented by the example of Mary Magdalene, and thus channels the kind of raw, emotive spirituality that was traditionally viewed as the preserve of women.[60] Crucially, however, Colonna marries emotion with intellect, represented by the figure of Catherine of Alexandria, and then claims both of these attributes for herself in her passionate devotion to Christ and in the ordered, stylistically complex, and sophisticated writing with which she expresses it.

The Correspondence

The famous poet and writer Ugo Foscolo pronounced a well-known (and notably harsh) judgment on Colonna's epistolary style: "The letters . . . of Vittoria Colonna, the most accomplished of Italian ladies and celebrated for the elegance of her poetry, are letters which seem to have been written by a farmer's wife."[61] Certainly it seems to have been the case that Colonna did not conceive of many of her letters as literary acts. Instead the majority of correspondence is precisely that, the exchange of information by letter relating to specific historical and geographical contexts, teeming with references that were meaningful only to the original recipient. Some of the letters were clearly dashed off at speed, intended to convey a practical message rather than a rhetorical display, and thus scant attention was paid to form and style.[62] In these cases Foscolo's judgement, while extreme, is not without some justification. Other of Colonna's letters, however, in no way match Foscolo's description, especially when we consider that her epistolary style matured greatly over time, and she also clearly adapted it according to the content and destination of each letter. In letters destined for noble readers, of the caliber of Emperor Charles V or Marguerite de Navarre, for example, or for those of high literary standing such as Pietro Bembo, great care is taken over both form and content.[63] And, of course, the exceptional power of Colonna's epistolography emerges from a reading of the letters written to Ochino and Costanza d'Avalos Piccolomini, which are beautifully crafted literary prose works.[64] These latter are

---

60. See Constance Furey, "'Intellects Inflamed in Christ': Women and Spiritualized Scholarship in Renaissance Christianity," *Journal of Religion* 84 (2004): 1–22.

61. Letter to Lord Holland, 13 September 1824, cited in Ugo Foscolo, *Epistolario*, ed. Mario Scotti, in the *Edizione nazionale delle opere di Ugo Foscolo*. vol. 9, part 22 (Florence: Le Monnier, 1994), 434.

62. See Letter 11 as a good example of this informality.

63. See for example Letters 6, 19, and 20.

64. See Letters 25–27.

something of a case apart, however; the majority of Colonna's letters are more valuable as historical documents than as literary works.

In the letters written during the 1520s, the earliest to have survived, one frequently encounters a mannered style, as if each letter were written with the intention to provide proof of rhetorical and intellectual skill by seeking out new ways to thank or congratulate the addressee.[65] The influence of Renaissance treatises on epistolary writing, which prescribed structure and style according to content and addressee, is most evident in these early letters.[66] A complete contrast is found in the brief letters to Michelangelo, in which style and content indicate compelling levels of personal respect for and familiarity with the addressee, which is especially noteworthy in light of the difference in their social status. A sign of the frequency with which Colonna must have communicated with Michelangelo by letter is the lack of any opening address (Letter 34), of any date (Letters 33–34, 37, and 40), or of the name of the recipient, usually only scrawled on the reverse (Letters 33, 34, 40). It is rare to find in any letter Colonna's direct expression of her opinions on art and literature, so the glimpses of such views are to be treasured: notable among them is her judgment of Michelangelo's work that reveals how art functioned for her as the precious medium by which to enter into dialogue with God.[67] Equally valuable are her acute appraisals of literature and her profound grasp of philosophical and theological concepts.[68]

Some of the letters, written when Colonna was oppressed by the menace of war or caught up in the defense of a cause in which she passionately believed, betray the haste with which they were written or the strong emotions at play. They can appear fractured (Letters 21 and 22), or else infused with emotion almost to the point of irony (Letters 12 and 17). Letters about the defense of the Capuchin Order (again, Letters 12 and 17), or Bernardino Ochino's sermons (Letters 14 and 15), or the rightful restitution of the Abbey of Montecassino (Letters 7 and 13), or the negotiation of a peace accord (Letters 21 and 22), all betray Colonna's strong emotional investment in her epistolary work, and allow her combativeness and assertiveness to emerge with full force.

As the years progress, the spiritual content of Colonna's letters grows increasingly prominent. As a result, her style becomes more sustained and intimate, and Latin citations from devotional texts infiltrate the Italian prose with increasing frequency. The letters become the vehicle for deep spiritual reflection, and

---

65. See, for example, Letters 1 and 6.

66. Nicola Longo, "*De epistola condenda*: L'arte di 'componer lettere' nel Cinquecento," in Amedeo Quondam, ed., *Le "carte messaggiere": Retorica e modelli di comunicazione epistolare, per un indice dei libri di lettere del Cinquecento* (Rome: Bulzoni, 1981), 177–201.

67. See Letters 33 and 34.

68. See as examples Letters 5, 9, and 16.

bear witness to her pious life and her continuous search for spiritual guidance.[69] These letters adopt the appropriate themes and lexical range demanded by the discussion of religious topics in the period, and are notably influenced by the strongly Pauline flavor of the language of the Spirituals. Thus we find frequent use of terms such as *fede* (faith), *gratia* (grace), Christ represented as *consolatione* (consolation) or *gaudio* (joy), and Christ's *merito* (merit); the comparison of celestial and earthly man, the annihilation of the self, and the election from eternity that gives the writer certainty of paradise; and the use of numerous metaphors such as the divine light, the way to salvation, the fountain of grace, etc.[70]

While the epistolary language Colonna was using in the 1540s evinces the impact of her proximity to Italian reformers, it seems that she had engaged closely with the linguistic debates of her day from a much earlier point in her literary career. As Helena Sanson has demonstrated in her recent essay on the subject, Colonna writes in a form that equates to the epistolary variety of the *lingua cortigiana*, the diverse and flexible type of vernacular used at the Italian courts and embodied in literary form in the *Libro del cortegiano (Book of the Courtier)* by Baldassare Castiglione (1478–1529), which she praised highly (see Letter 5).[71] Examples of such usage include her choice of orthographic and phonetic Latinisms such as *ct* in *election* (Letter 22) and *actioni* (Letter 28); or the use of *x* in place of *ss* in *peximo* (Letter 12) and *vaxalli* (Letter 13).[72] One also finds in Colonna's letters a general absence of the standard Tuscan form of spontaneous dipthongization (vowel breaking), so that she writes *vole* in place of *vuole* (Letter 7), *novo* in place of *nuovo* (Letter 35), and *core* in place of *cuore* (Letter 15). She often resorts to the article form *el* instead of the Tuscan form *il*, and uses –*el* before an *s* followed by a consonant (such as *nel scrivere* in Letter 9). Where we might expect *er* Colonna instead uses pretonic *ar*, as in *lassarà* (Letter 9) and *restarò* (Letter 10). There is a prevalence of short consonantal forms (*alegro, Ipolita, dificil*, Letter 10), and a tendency to use *ss* or *s* in place of *sc* (for example *lassarà* and *basar* in Letter 9). All these phenomena coexist, however, with elements derived

---

69. See as examples Letters 30, 31, 35, 36, and 39.

70. On the language of reform, see Brian Cummings, *The Literary Culture of the Reformation: Grammar and Grace* (Oxford: Oxford University Press, 2002).

71. Helena Sanson, "Vittoria Colonna and Language," in Brundin, Crivelli, and Sapegno, *A Companion to Vittoria Colonna*, 195–234, at 205. For a discussion of female-authored epistolography, including a discussion of the language used, as well as extensive related bibliography, see Rita Fresu, *L'altra Roma: Percorsi di italianizzazione tra dame, sante, popolani nella storia della città (e della sua regione)* (Rome: Edizioni nuova cultura, 2008), 9–40; and Rita Fresu, "Educazione linguistica e livelli di scrittura femminile tra XV e XVI secolo: Le lettere di Giulia Farnese e di Adriana Mila Orsini," *Cahiers de recherches médiévales et humanistes*, 28, no. 2 (2014): 105–52.

72. All these examples as well as all those that follow in the next paragraph derive from Colonna's autograph letters. The authors are very grateful to Prof. Roberto Vetrugno (Università per Stranieri di Perugia) who provided invaluable assistance in the analysis of Colonna's epistolary language.

from literary Tuscan as laid out by Pietro Bembo and employed by Renaissance typographers. These include the use of the pronoun *egli*, which not by chance appears only once, in a letter to the highly cultured correspondent Paolo Giovio (1483–1552), in the small sample of autograph letters that have survived (Letter 10, in contrast to the more common use of *lui*), or the choice of *vocaboli* in place of *vocabuli* (in the same letter).

Colonna was raised in the central-southern region of Italy, and traces of this different linguistic context are also evident in various places in her letters. So, for example, she replaces –*ss*– with palatal –*sc*– in *nisciuna* (Letter 10), *cascetta* and *prescia* (Letter 11); she drops the letter *v* in *hauto* (Letter 10), and opts for the conditional form *sariano* (Letter 32). Thus in the space of a few short lines, Colonna's epistolary language can range across contrasting linguistic forms. We see this clearly in Letter 10 to Paolo Giovio (*me manca* and *mi par*; *laude* and *lodato*). It is also evident in Letter 32, addressed to Pope Paul III, which mixes on the one hand Latinisms and *koine* typical of courtly epistolography (*voluntà*, *doi*, *dirme de*, *novo*, *charità*, *exspedirla*, *pontifice*, *ultra*), and on the other hand forms deriving from literary Florentine (*ottima* instead of *optima*, *suore* rather than *sore*, *degnata di* in place of *dignata de*).

While many of Colonna's letters treat themes that are of pronounced historical, religious and literary interest, nonetheless some of the texts included in this edition convey a far more familiar and domestic mood. Through these, we meet the writer in different guises: as a shopper for luxury goods (Letter 11); as an advisor on the safe delivery of babies (Letter 10); or even as the concerned friend who organizes a dispatch of wine out of fear that the nuns of Santa Caterina will have to go without (Letter 32). While it is not surprising that Colonna the pious widow was also a friend, neighbor and consumer, it is a pleasure, and perhaps something of a relief, to witness her engaging with worldly and day-to-day affairs in a fluent and unproblematic way.

Even as Colonna's letters establish essential dates and locations that help us to reconstruct her biography, they also occasionally reveal the spirit in which she met some of the most dramatic experiences of her life. They convey, for example, her bitterness at the pirated printing of her poetry, done in Parma without her permission (Letter 18); the profound emotion elicited by her contemplation of the image of the Crucifixion done for her by her friend Michelangelo (Letter 33); her notable calm in the face of the destruction of her natal territories (Letter 23); her longing for absent friends (Letter 36). These are only glimpses, however, and it cannot be assumed that the collection as a whole faithfully reflects Colonna's thoughts and hopes or acts in any way as an unmediated autobiography. While it is true, as noted above, that she never conceived of her letter collection as a literary enterprise, thus never went through the process of editing and correcting the individual letters with an eye to future publication,[73] nonetheless she was always highly aware, as all letter writers of the period were, of the many hands through which these documents would inevitably pass before or after reaching their destination. Letter writing was rarely direct and unmediated, and its status as any kind of autobiographical "truth" is therefore highly fractured.

Sending any document out of one's immediate possession was essentially an act of "publication" to a wider readership that the writer could control only to a limited extent.[74] A contemporary example helps to clarify how far a letter might travel from its original destination. We know from other sources that Pietro Aretino (1492–1556) wrote to Colonna to ask forgiveness for impolite words he had exchanged with Alfonso d'Avalos, in a letter which is no longer extant.[75] On June 2 1536, Giovan Battista Malvezzi wrote to Aretino with the following convoluted narrative:

> I recently promised to send you one of your letters written to excuse yourself to the Marchioness of Pescara for what you had said, not without reason, about the Marquis of Vasto. As soon as I got to Bologna I set about searching in the place where I keep all your things . . . , and when I couldn't find it, I checked in my record of loans and found that I had loaned it to a priest, a friend of mine. Since he was not at the time in Bologna, I waited for him to get back, and once he was back, I thought I would obtain the letter. But he, with the usual priestly discretion, had loaned it to some magistrate from Cento, who had taken it with him to Ferrara, where it had passed through two or three other hands, such that it is tricky now to get it back quickly.[76]

---

73. There were many writers in the period who decided to publish their letters in order to grow their popularity, from Aretino to Bembo: see Quondam, *Le "carte messaggiere"*; Axel Erdmann, Alberto Govi, and Fabrizio Govi, *Ars epistolica: Communication in Sixteenth-Century Western Europe: Epistolaries, Letter-Writing Manuals and Model Letter Books, 1501–1600* (Luzern: Gilhofer and Ranschburg, 2014); and the publications by Archilet (Archivio delle corrispondenze letterarie di età moderna, secoli XVI–XVII): <archilet.it/Pubblicazioni.aspx>.

74. See for a useful discussion of this implicit type of publication, Brian Richardson, *Manuscript Culture in Renaissance Italy* (Cambridge: Cambridge University Press, 2009).

75. Traces of this correspondence are perhaps visible in a letter from Colonna to Aretino of 17 November 1533; see Colonna, *Carteggio*, no. LIX.

76. "Io alli giorni passati le promessi mandarle una sua lettra scritta in sua iscusazione alla Marchesana di Pescara, di ciò che vostra signoria avea con non poca ragione detto dil Marchese dil Vasto. Subito gionto a Bologna, mi messi a cercare, dove tengo tutte le sue cose servate . . . , e non la trovando, mi posi a leggere il mio memorial delle cose prestate, e trovai ch'io l'avevo prestata ad un Prete amico mio, il qual all'ora non essendo in Bologna, ho aspettato, che torni di fuori, e ritornato, credendo riaverla, esso, per la solita pretesca discrezione, l'aveva prestata a un certo Podestà di Cento, il quale

Similarly, when Colonna sent Paolo Giovio a detailed analysis of a sonnet by Bembo, she would have known—and indeed this would have been her specific intention—that her letter containing the poetic commentary would be passed from Giovio to Bembo himself.[77] The use of an intermediary was a form of courtesy, allowing her to praise Bembo in the highest terms, but indirectly: thus Colonna was freed to speak as she wished about Bembo's poem, and Bembo was spared the embarrassment or obligation that might be provoked by a more direct address.

The practice of "attaching" a third party (or more) to a letter exchange between two people was common in the sixteenth century, and also a practical way of disseminating information and literary drafts.[78] It is in this light that we should understand Colonna's concluding instruction in her letter to Emperor Charles V about the very delicate relations between her family and the pope: "I beg your Majesty to have this letter burned."[79] Other readers than the addressee were always lurking in the background of any epistolary exchange, and some were welcome while others were not. Thus Colonna, fearing interception of a politically charged letter to her brother Ascanio, decided to hold off from committing more to paper—"I cannot write more clearly now" (Letter 21); or, on another occasion, she chose to make use of a cipher.[80]

It is a surprising and frustrating fact that few of Colonna's letters have survived the centuries, despite the renown of many of her correspondents and her own place at the center of many of the key historical, religious, artistic and literary debates of the age. Even leaving aside the exceptional case of Isabella d'Este (1474–1539), who left a *carteggio* of more than 28,000 letters,[81] the paucity of Colonna's collection is striking when it is compared to the thousands of letters included in Aretino's collected works,[82] the 1392 extant letters written by Michelangelo, the 1779 by Castiglione, or the 2578 by Bembo.[83] The total number of extant letters

---

di poi se l'ha portata a Ferrara, et è andata in due, e tre mani, di maniera, che è difficile a riaverla così presto": Pietro Aretino, *Lettere scritte a Pietro Aretino*, ed. Paolo Procaccioli, in *Edizione nazionale delle opere di Pietro Aretino*, vol. 9 (Rome: Salerno, 2002–2003), Part 1, no. 292.

77. See Letter 9 for evidence of Giovio's mediation between Colonna and Bembo.

78. See Richardson, *Manuscript Culture*; and Abigail Brundin, "Composition *a due*: Lyric Poetry and Scribal Practice in Sixteenth-Century Italy," in *Renaissance Studies in Honor of Joseph Connors*, ed. Machtelt Israëls and Louis Waldman (Florence: Olschki, 2013), 2:496–504.

79. "Suplyco vuestra Majestad mande quemar esta carta": Veronica Copello, "Vittoria Colonna a Carlo V: 6 dicembre 1538," *Studi italiani* 29, no. 1 (2017): 108.

80. For her use of a cipher, see Colonna, *Carteggio*, no. CXXXV. See also no. XCIV.

81. Isabella d'Este's correspondence is available online at IDEA: Isabella d'Este Archive: <isabelladeste.web.unc.edu>.

82. Pietro Aretino, *Lettere*, ed. Paolo Procaccioli, in *Edizione nazionale delle opere di Pietro Aretino*, vol. 4 in 6 parts (Rome: Salerno, 1997–2002).

83. Michelangelo Buonarroti, *Il carteggio di Michelangelo*, ed. Giovanni Poggi, Paola Barocchi, and Renzo Ristori, 5 vols. (Florence: Sansoni-SPES, 1965–1983); Badassarre Castiglione, *Lettere famigliari*

to and from Colonna currently stands at 267: 181 letters from her, and 86 to her from her correspondents.[84] Certain of her practices and experiences might help to explain this low number. Colonna may not have systematically archived the correspondence she received; she may have been equally negligent in conserving copies of the letters she sent. The archival deficit may well be linked to Colonna's frequent relocations, after her widowhood in particular, from one city to another, across the whole Italian peninsula from north to south: on her death she was in possession of only a single "crate containing all her writings, that is contracts and privileges."[85] She seems to have kept with her only a very few precious documents concerning her family.[86] As a result, of her extant correspondence, the number of letters she sent (181), which were preserved with care by their recipients rather than by the sender, far exceeds the number sent to her (86).

Another significant factor in the survival of Colonna's letters is the manner in which letters from her correspondents are known to us: thirty-three of these survive in drafts, letter copy books (the volumes in which all letters sent out were transcribed), or in other copies preserved by the sender; thirty are known to us via printed editions published in the sixteenth century; twelve are known from other copies from various other sources.[87] Only six letters are conserved in their original form, either because the sender was of the highest noble status (Emperor Charles V); or very close to Colonna (Michelangelo, Bembo); or because they were sent "attached" to a letter for a third party and thus preserved again by that third party.[88]

Assessing the evidence, it is clear that the surviving letters to and from Colonna account for only a tiny portion of her lifetime correspondence. Her contemporaries remarked on the volume and quality of her letter writing and seem to have had access to letters that were circulating at the time. In his dialogue *Notable Men and Women of Our Time*, set on the island of Ischia in 1527, Paolo Giovio makes reference to Colonna's "almost innumerable letters: what authority, what

---

e diplomatiche, ed. Guido La Rocca, Angelo Stella, and Umberto Morando, 3 vols. (Turin: Einaudi, 2016); Bembo, *Lettere*.

84. This total excludes dedications in volumes that were sent to Colonna, as well as administrative documents and the three letters included in Filonico Alicarnasseo's 'Life of Vittoria Colonna' (Colonna, *Carteggio*, no. CLXXXIII; *Supplemento*, no. IV and no. XVI), since it is not possibile to assign them to Colonna with certainty.

85. "Una casetta cum tutte le scritture, cioè contratti et previlegi." Lorenzo Bonorio to Ascanio Colonna, 27 February 1547: BSSS, Archivio Colonna, Corrispondenza di Ascanio Colonna, sottoserie I, anno 1547: Lorenzo Bonorio.

86. See also the letter to Fabrizio Colonna: Colonna, *Carteggio*, no. CLXVI.

87. For example, one was prepared by a copyist working for Ascanio and sent to the emperor: see Francesco Gui, *L'attesa del concilio: Vittoria Colonna e Reginald Pole nel movimento degli spirituali* (Rome: Editoria università elettronica, 1998), 561–62.

88. Five letters that were preserved in their original form have now disappeared from the archives.

manly decorum, and what charm these display, written as they are to the loftiest and most learned men and to the greatest kings, and concerning the most weighty and honorable matters."[89] Colonna herself also drew attention to her activity as a prolific letter writer. In the autumn of 1538 she had to excuse herself from providing a few lines of recommendation that she had promised: she "had been writing continuously already" of other "most important" matters.[90] And yet of the "many letters" that Michelangelo said that he had received from her, only two survive.[91] Similarly, no letter survives from Giovanni Mauro d'Arcano (ca. 1489–1535), who wrote many to her;[92] only two letters survive to Gasparo Contarini, and one from him; only one letter to Carlo Gualteruzzi (1500–1577), and one from him; one single letter from Ochino; one to Alvise Priuli and none from him; no letters at all to or from Francesco Maria Molza (1489–1544) or Marcantonio Flaminio. It is no wonder that for some centuries Colonna's name has been missing from its rightful place at the heart of the literary networks where she clearly operated. The situation with family members is no less patchy: only six letters to Alfonso d'Avalos, and none from him; none to or from his wife Maria d'Aragona (1503/1504–1568), nor to or from her sister Giovanna (1502–1575), wife of Ascanio Colonna; no letter from Costanza d'Avalos Piccolomini; no letter even from Colonna's husband, and only one that she sent to him (this latter almost certainly rewritten by Filonico Alicarnasseo, who transcribed it).[93]

The letters themselves bear the material traces of the archival carelessness noted above: many are written in a disorderly hand, with intensive use of abbreviations. The hand varies in line with the variation of themes and styles: thus a serene letter to Michelangelo containing reflections on the nature and spiritual scope of art does not bear comparison with the lines dashed off to her brother Ascanio on the eve of a catastrophic war. Most of the time Colonna failed even to note the date and place of sending. Emblematic in this regard is the letter to Reginald Pole that signs off "From Santa Anna in Rome, on the . . . ": Colonna failed to insert the day on which the letter was written or sent, leaving the sentence unfinished.[94]

89. Paolo Giovio, *Notable Men and Women of Our Time*, ed. and trans. Kenneth Gouwens (Cambridge, MA: Harvard University Press, 2013), 533.

90. Pietro Rapondo to the Elders of Lucca, 7 December 1538: ASL, Fondo Anziani al tempo della libertà, 546, p. 575. For analysis of this letter, see Copello, "'Locum gerit,'" 279.

91. Michelangelo, *Il carteggio*, 361–62.

92. Concetta Ranieri, "Censimento dei codici e delle stampe dell'epistolario di Vittoria Colonna," *Atti e memorie dell'Arcadia* S. 3, vol. 7, no. 4 (1980–1981), 280; and Mauro D'Arcano Grattoni, "Lettere inedite di Vittoria Colonna, Giulia Gonzaga e Laura Sanvitale Rangoni a Gian Mauro d'Arcano," *Ce fastu?* 2 (1982), 305–6.

93. Colonna, *Carteggio*, no. CLXXXIII.

94. "Da Santa Anna di Roma, a' dì . . . ": in Sergio M. Pagano and Concetta Ranieri, *Nuovi documenti su Vittoria Colonna e Reginald Pole* (Vatican City: Archivio Segreto Vaticano, 1989), 98–99; see Firpo and Marcatto, *Il processo inquisitoriale del cardinal Giovanni Morone* (2011–2015), 3:551–52.

Of the forty letters included in this volume, the only ones in which the year of sending is included are those written by a copyist and those surviving in copies.[95] In the case of Letter 17, addressed to Pope Paul III, we know the year in which it was written only because someone, probably a secretary or other administrator, has added the date to the back of the letter when archiving it. Letters to the highest echelons of society usually guarantee this kind of care: the lack of it in relation to Colonna's own correspondence is rendered more striking as a result. In the absence of annotations of the kind added to the pope's letter, or of internal clues or paleographical evidence, the editor of Colonna's letters is forced to relegate them only to likely spans of time, sometimes rather large ones.[96]

Perhaps the archival carelessness seemingly afforded to Colonna's correspondence during her lifetime, which accounts for the paucity of letters still extant, might encourage us to take more seriously the writer's own claim that after her husband's death she no longer valued worldly matters. A failure to curate her own epistolary voice might be considered part and parcel of a retreat from the affairs of the material realm that she signaled as her life's ambition. This reading of the evidence is problematized by the content of the letters that we do have, which clearly demonstrate the ease and authority with which Colonna continued to deal with that material realm over her whole lifetime. Perhaps, as her devotion to the spiritual life became more intense in her later years, and her possessions were condensed down to the single crate by her deathbed, there was a process of deliberate destruction of the material traces of a worldly life lived.[97] Perhaps the erasure of her epistolary voice is simply a consequence of her gender, responsible over time for the erasure of so many voices—although the case of Isabella d'Este is a compelling counter-example.[98]

Yet the hypothesis of Colonna's deliberate disengagement from epistolography is belied by another factor worth noting: the considerable attachment she seems to have had to writing in her own hand. Three quarters of the letters that survive in their original form are entirely autograph.

---

95. Those written by a copyist are Letters 16, 29, 32, 39; those surviving in copies are Letters 1–6, 18, and 20.

96. See for example Letter 8, in which paleographical evidence has been used to ascertain a date, and Letters 11, 25, 27, 33, 34, 37, 40, in which a single year of composition cannot be identified.

97. Tobia Toscano has suggested that Colonna destroyed her early poetry later in her life: see Colonna, *Sonetti: In morte*, 9.

98. Maria Luisa Doglio, *Lettera e donna: Scrittura epistolare al femminile tra Quattro e Cinquecento* (Rome: Bulzoni, 1993); Gabriella Zarri, *Per lettera: La scrittura epistolare femminile tra archivio e tipografia, secoli XV–XVIII* (Rome: Viella, 1999); Fumagalli and Frigeni, *Donne e scrittura*; Monica Ferrari, Isabella Lazzarini, and Federico Piseri, *Autografie dell'età minore: Lettere di tre dinastie italiane tra Quattro e Cinquecento* (Rome: Viella, 2016).

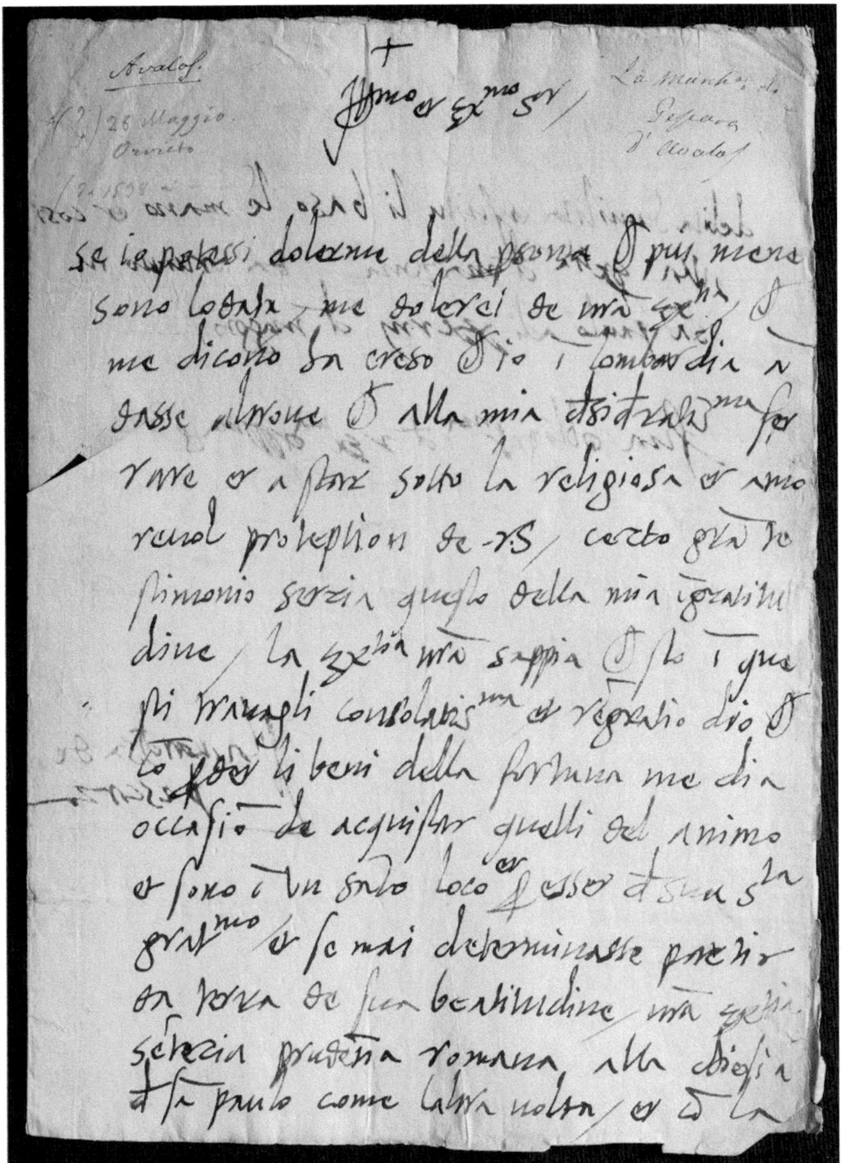

Figure 1. Autograph letter from Vittoria Colonna to Ercole II d'Este, 28 May [1541], fol. 1r.

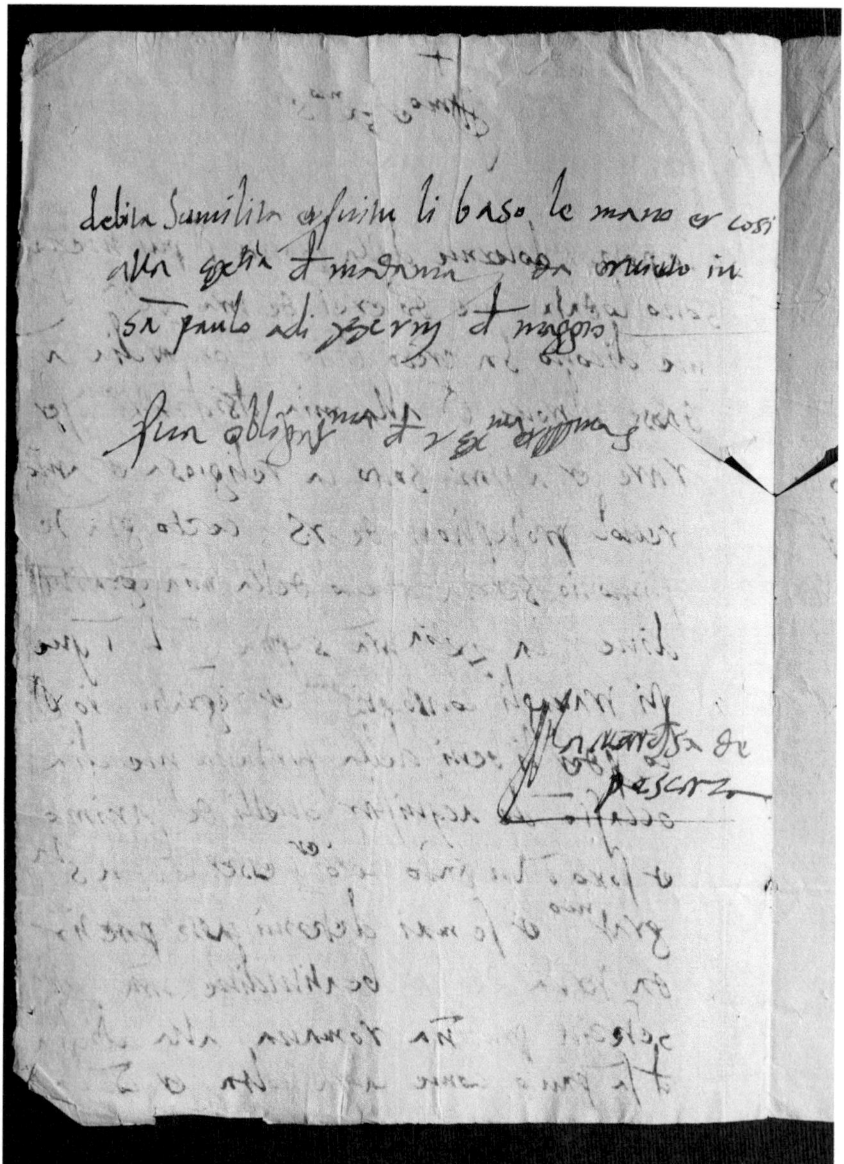
debita humilita et servitu li baso le mano et cosi
alla ex.tia de madama raccomando in
s.to paulo adi xxviii de maggio
Serva obligatissima de v. ex.
La marchesa de pescara

Figure 2. Autograph letter from Vittoria Colonna to Ercole II d'Este, 28 May [1541], fol. 1v.

Figure 3. Autograph letter from Vittoria Colonna to Ercole II d'Este, 28 May [1541], fol. 2v.

The others were dictated to copyists but nonetheless include Colonna's signature and often also an additional postscript in her hand.[99] Moreover, Colonna did not rely on a single copyist, but probably resorted at times to whichever local scribe was available.[100] Her official secretary for some time was Francesco de Caprio,[101] yet few of the documents that have come down to us are written in his hand.[102] The image of Colonna writing letters in her own hand contrasts to that of Colonna the poet whose spiritual muse raised her far above such messy concerns. Carlo Gualteruzzi, who recalls Colonna dictating her poetry as it was taken down in hard copy, portrays her as a poet transported by her spiritual compositions far beyond the realities of pen and paper, which someone else grappled with on her behalf.[103]

In general, for Colonna as for her contemporaries, writing in one's own hand was a sign of familiarity, reserved for relations (recipients such as Ascanio Colonna, Costanza d'Avalos and Eleonora Gonzaga) and friends (Michelangelo, Paolo Giovio). It could also be a signal of the importance or the confidentiality of the message (such as in letters to Pope Paul III and the Cardinals Gasparo

99. For an example of a letter that was clearly dictated, see Letter 4: "I have resolved to have this letter taken down."

100. On Ischia, for example, Colonna made use of the same copyist as Costanza d'Avalos del Balzo: a letter to Charles V dated 30 June 1528 (Colonna, *Carteggio*, no. XXXVII) was sent in another copy, made in the same hand, but signed instead by Costanza (RAH, A-42, fol. 468r); Costanza dictated a letter to the same copyist in July 1528 (RAH, A-43, fol. 7r). In Arpino, by contrast, the same scribe composed a document sent to Juan Vasquez d'Avila on 19 December 1529 (Colonna, *Carteggio*, no. XXXIX) and the letters to Cola Jacobacci and Felice Orsini: see Veronica Copello, "Aggiornamenti sul carteggio di Vittoria Colonna: Parte I," *Nuova rivista di letteratura italiana*, 22, no. 1 (2019): 155–58. From Civita Latina a single hand composed two letters to Fabrizio Peregrino: Colonna, *Carteggio*, LXIII e LXIV.

101. As can be deduced from the proxy-will Colonna dictated in 1525, cited in Donati, *Vittoria Colonna*, 397–404.

102. The documents in Francesco de Caprio's hand are the following: a donation, not autograph but definitely authentic, dated 13 August 1523, now lost (edited in Concetta Ranieri, "Lettere inedite di Vittoria Colonna," *Giornale italiano di filologia* 7 [1979]: 147–48); a receipt for a payment with autograph signature and seal, from Marino on 28 July 1524 (edited in Ranieri, "Lettere inedite," 148); and a letter to Giovan Matteo Giberti from Ischia on 5 October 1525 (edited in Pasolini, *Tre lettere inedite*, 27–28). According to Ranieri, the letters sent by Colonna from Ischia on 13 June 1534 and from Genazzano on 1 June 1535 (Ranieri, "Censimento," S. 3, vol. 7, no. 3, 1979: 267–68), as well as from Genazzano on 17 December 1535 (Ranieri, "Lettere inedite," 143), are all written in the hand of Carlo Gualteruzzi. This hypothesis does not stand up to a paleographical comparison with other autograph manuscripts by Gualteruzzi, however: these include the letter from Gualteruzzi to Colonna edited in Colonna, *Carteggio*, no. LXXIV, now in ASM, Archivio Gonzaga, busta 887, fols. 370r–371v; the autograph document in BAV, Chig., L VIII 304, fols. 202r–203v; and the more italic form of his hand in BAV, Vat. lat. 6412, fol. 56r.

103. See Brundin, "Vittoria Colonna in Manuscript."

Contarini and Marcello Cervini [1501–1555], later Pope Marcellus II). A copyist or secretary would more often deal with the writing of letters to a lower class of recipient (such as Cola Jacobacci in Letter 8), but would also take on the composition of the most formal letters, which required the most ordered and clear text and were addressed to queens and emperors. It is clear, therefore, why Felice Trofino, when he was managing the correspondence of the papal datary Cardinal Giberti in his absence, wrote to Colonna: "My own lowliness is not sufficient to respond to the elegance of your letter nor to satisfy your humanity, as you deigned to write to me in your own hand."[104] For Trofino, Colonna's decision to send him an autograph letter was a clear sign of her benevolence. A letter from Pietro Rapondo, sent from the governors of Lucca to Rome, provides evidence of the added value that the author's own hand could confer upon a document. Rapondo wished to obtain a letter of recommendation from Colonna, addressed to Alfonso d'Avalos and concerning a dispute over land. After meeting her, he wrote to the Elders: "I hope she will carry out this service warmly, since she is doing it by her own hand."[105] In this case Colonna's hand acts as a guarantee of the quality and efficacy of the message.

It was not only in Lucca that Colonna's support was sought to resolve disputes or provide valuable mediation. Cardinal Giovanni Morone claimed that "most of her reasoning was . . . on affairs of State, in which she had great expertise."[106] A reading of Colonna's *carteggio* allows us an unprecedented view of the authority with which she participated in the political developments of her day, not as an observer but as a valued actor, and thus provides further evidence to counter the view that she rejected epistolography in favor of a withdrawal from the world. Her authority was rooted without doubt in the prestige of her noble family name and her ancestry, with its strong imperial links, in addition to the prestige conferred by her marriage. Yet it is also undeniable that over time and with her increasing political engagement, what came to be prized above all by her interlocutors was the compelling combination of intellectual acuity, moral integrity, and Christian charity that Colonna exemplified.[107]

A telling example of the value that others attributed to Colonna's political agency can be found in the correspondence of the poet Francesco Maria Molza. On her arrival in Ferrara in 1537, he wrote to his son of his intention to make use of her mediation in order to resolve a personal issue:

104. AAV, *Segreteria di Stato, Particolari*, 154, fol. 36r–v: edited in Veronica Copello, "Aggiornamenti sul carteggio di Vittoria Colonna: Parte II," *Nuova rivista di letteratura italiana*, 22, no. 2 (2019), 91–92.

105. Pietro Rapondo to the Elders of Lucca, 7 December 1538: ASL, Fondo Anziani al tempo della libertà, 546, p. 575; edited in Copello, "'Locum gerit,'" 279.

106. Firpo and Marcatto, *Il processo inquisitoriale del cardinal Giovanni Morone* (1981–1995), 2:501.

107. See Dionisotti, "Appunti sul Bembo," 274.

Camillo, I believe that the arrival of her ladyship the marchioness of Pescara in Ferrara will have a big impact on our affair, nor could I conceive of anyone who might be of greater benefit to us in this: *with her authority, as well as the good will* that she has always shown towards me, she will perhaps achieve that which neither letters from the pope nor from cardinals have hitherto managed to achieve.[108]

Molza's judgement of the efficacy of Colonna's intervention chimes with what is clearly visible in her letters in defense of the Capuchins (Letters 12 and 17) or on the restitution of Colle S. Magno (Letters 7 and 13): in all matters she holds tenaciously to the ideals of justice and truth. Her autocratic, almost arrogant decisiveness seems at sharp odds with the retiring, nun-like persona implied by her poetry.[109] During a period of great tension between the Colonna family and Charles V, she is reported to have interacted in precisely this decisive manner in her dealings with the Marquis of Aguilar, imperial ambassador to Rome: "she expressed her opinion at times without mincing her words on the coldness with which he treated the affairs of the emperor's servants in matters of such import, as no other ambassador who has been here to attend on His Majesty has ever done."[110] In all these cases, with the sole exception of the Battle of Capo d'Orso when she was able to provide supplies to the soldiers, Colonna's weapons were her words. In private meetings and in letters, even from the convent cells where she often took refuge, Colonna dealt with the wider world: with international politics, the election of cardinals, questions of art and literature, and the reform of the Catholic church. The loss of her correspondence over the subsequent centuries says much more about accidents of history, shaped by gender differentials, than it does about the power and influence of her voice in the sixteenth century.

Reception

In 1889 Ermanno Ferrero and Giuseppe Müller published the *Carteggio di Vittoria Colonna*, an edition containing 184 letters written by Colonna, or sent to her.[111]

---

108. Letter from Francesco Maria Molza to his son Camillo (Rome, 24 May 1537): in Francesco Maria Molza, *Delle poesie volgari e latine di Francesco Maria Molza corrette, illustrate, ed accresciute colla vita dell'autore scritta da Pierantonio Serassi* (Bergamo: Pietro Lancellotti, 1754–1757), 3:65–66.

109. "Vittoria, in contrasto con l'immagine tutta spirituale che ne è stata proposta, sembra spesso comportarsi con arroganza baronale": Gigliola Fragnito, "'Per un lungo e dubbioso sentero': L'itinerario spirituale di Vittoria Colonna," in Sapegno, *Al crocevia*, 195.

110. Letter from Ottaviano Lotti to Cardinal Ercole Gonzaga, Rome, 16 December 1538, in Alessandro Luzio, "Vittoria Colonna," *Rivista storica mantovana* 1 (1885): 25.

111. To the total of 185 letters listed in the *Carteggio* has been added the letter edited in a footnote on p. 145 (confined to a footnote because never sent), while two letters have been subtracted, which the editors only mentioned without transcribing: Colonna, *Carteggio*, no. LXXIII and no. CLXXXIV.

Three years later their edition was republished with a new *Supplemento* containing fourteen further letters edited by Domenico Tordi.[112] A lifelong scholar of Vittoria Colonna's life and works, Tordi had planned to publish a further supplement to the *Carteggio*, but was unable to complete the project.[113] Since that nineteenth-century collection was published, in fact, many new letters have come to light, nearly seventy at the most recent reckoning, which have been published in various locations, while other letters have surfaced in more reliable copies than those relied on for the Ferrero-Müller *Carteggio*.[114]

In general, however, despite the recent upsurge of interest in Colonna and her work in Italy and abroad, only a small number of her letters have attracted much wider attention. Those addressed to Michelangelo Buonarroti (Letters 33–34, 37, 40) have been studied by art historians.[115] Serious literary attention, meanwhile, has been directed most frequently at the three letters addressed to Costanza d'Avalos Piccolomini and published as a discrete edition in the sixteenth century (Letters 25–26).[116] Historians of religion have studied the letters that Colonna

---

112. We are not including in this total the dedicatory letters to literary works which the editor of the *Supplemento* did include.

113. Tordi's plan can be deduced from Domenico Tordi, "Vittoria Colonna in Orvieto durante la Guerra del Sale," *Bollettino della società umbra di storia patria* 1 (1895): 473–533, at 511n, as well as from a number of his letters; see Alan Bullock, *Domenico Tordi e il carteggio colonnese della Biblioteca Nazionale di Firenze* (Florence: Olschki, 1986), 154 and 158. See also the letter from Ermanno Ferrero to Tordi dated 17 November 1895 in Bullock, *Domenico Tordi*, 228.

114. Concetta Ranieri and Alan Bullock have made fundamental contributions to the recovery and editing of Colonna's correspondence.

115. See Alexander Nagel, "Gifts for Michelangelo and Vittoria Colonna," *Art Bulletin* 79 (1997): 647–68; Antonio Forcellino, *La Pietà perduta: Storia di un capolavoro ritrovato di Michelangelo* (Milan: Rizzoli, 2010); Alessandro Rovetta, ed., *L'ultimo Michelangelo: Disegni e rime attorno alla Pietà Rondanini: Milano, Castello Sforzesco, Museo d'Arte Antica, 24 marzo—19 giugno 2011* (Milan: Silvana, 2011); Maria Forcellino, "Vittoria Colonna and Michelangelo: Drawings and Paintings," in Brundin, Crivelli and Sapegno, *A Companion to Vittoria Colonna*, 270–313; Carmen Bambach and others, *Michelangelo: Divine Draftsman and Designer* (New York: Metropolitan Museum of Art; New Haven: Yale University Press, 2017); Donati, *Vittoria Colonna*, 121–74.

116. Maria Luisa Doglio, "'L'occhio interiore' e la scrittura nelle lettere spirituali di Vittoria Colonna," in *Omaggio a Gianfranco Folena* (Padua: Editoriale Programma, 1993), 2:1001–13; Concetta Ranieri, "Vittoria Colonna e Costanza d'Avalos Piccolomini: Una corrispondenza spirituale," in *Cum fide amicitia: Per Rosanna Alhaique Pettinelli*, ed. Stefano Benedetti, Francesco Lucioli, and Pietro Petteruti Pellegrino (Rome: Bulzoni, 2015), 477–90; Michele Camaioni, "'Per sfiammeggiar di un vivo e ardente amore': Vittoria Colonna, Bernardino Ochino e la Maddalena," in *El orbe católico: Transformaciones, continuidades, tensiones y formas de convivencia entre Europa y América, siglos IV–XIX*, ed. Maria Lupi and Claudio Rolle (Santiago de Chile: RIL, 2016), 105–60; Adriana Chemello, "Vittoria Colonna's Epistolary Works," in Brundin, Crivelli and Sapegno, *A Companion to Vittoria Colonna*, 11–36.

wrote in defense of the Capuchin Order (Letters 12 and 17),[117] as well as those letters that surfaced as part of the inquisitional trials of Giovanni Morone and Pietro Carnesecchi (Letters 24, 30, 31, and 39).[118] The lack of attention to her *carteggio* more broadly is a reflection both of the absence of a complete and up-to-date modern edition, as well as of the relatively recent upsurge of interest in Colonna, who has only in the last few decades begun to reclaim her rightful place at the center of the stories we have to tell about the Italian Renaissance.

Note on the Edition

The principal criterion that has guided this selection of forty letters from a much larger corpus has been the desire to present a variety of topics, styles and addressees across the chronological arc of Colonna's life. For each letter we have provided information about all extant copies, citing first, the manuscripts, and second, the sixteenth-century print editions.

The letters are arranged in chronological order. The Italian text is transcribed anew in each case, based on the following transcription criteria:

- The very frequent abbreviations, including those used for titles ("M.^{sa}" for "Marchesa", for example) are resolved in each case. Some doubts occurred over the best way to render the abbreviated "d" with strikethrough, which is used both as a preposition and as an abbreviation within longer words. In Italian this can be resolved as both *di* and *de*: the decision was taken to resolve this uniformly in the Italian texts as *de*, as this is the most common form found in Colonna's wider corpus. Similarly, the abbreviation *mro* (see Letter 4) is resolved as *mastro*, following the usage in Letter 11, which is autograph.
- The use of *j* at the end of words is resolved to *i* in every case.
- Different forms of articulated prepositions – *a la/ala/alla* – are left as they occur in the Italian texts, except in cases where an apostrophe is needed; for example, *al* is changed to *a l'*.

117. Pietro Tacchi-Venturi, "Nuove lettere inedite di Vittoria Colonna," *Studi e documenti di storia e diritto* 22 (1901): 307–14; Tacchi-Venturi, *Vittoria Colonna, fautrice*; Edouard d'Alençon, ed., *Tribulationes Ordinis Fratrum Minorum Capuccinorum primis annis pontificatus Pauli III, 1534–1541: Haec brevis illustratio monumentorum, editorum vel ineditorum, quae ad dicti ordinis historiam spectant, correcta et ampliata secundo prodit* (Roma: Tip. Manuzio, 1914); Cargnoni, *I frati cappuccini*; Liguori, "Vittoria Colonna."

118. Firpo and Marcatto, *I processi inquisitoriali di Pietro Carnesecchi*; Firpo and Marcatto, *Il processo inquisitoriale del cardinal Giovanni Morone*, in first (1981–1995) and second (2011–2015) editions; Pagano and Ranieri, *Nuovi documenti*.

- Pronominal particles – *mello, nello* – are changed to the analytic form using phonosyntactic doubling (*me llo, ne llo*). In the same way, *sesse* and *senne* are resolved to *se sse* (Letter 11) and *se nne* (Letter 10).

- Uppercase letters, punctuation, apostrophes, accents, and paragraphs are conformed to modern standard practice. It should be pointed out that Colonna did not use accents or apostrophes, while her use of punctuation was very variable and unsystematic. The editor has therefore been required to make a number of judgement calls in systematizing and standardizing the texts.

All editorial interventions are listed below. The edited version is cited first, followed by the incorrect version as found in the source text, given in square brackets.

Letter 1: *soverchio recrescevole* [*sovercchio recrescevole*].

Letter 4: *dà relatione*: in the manuscript the text is grammatically incorrect [*danno relatione*]. The copyist has probably transcribed *danno* in place of *dà* because he transcribed *danno colpa* just few lines earlier.

Letter 12: *speranze* [*speranza*].

Letter 13: *Da Roma* [*Ischia*]: *Roma* is a correction in another hand of the autograph word *Ischia*.

Letter 14: *el potente Spirito de Christo* [*el potente Spirito che Christo*].

Letter 18: *spirituale conversatione* [*spirituali conversatione*].

Letter 20: *'l servo Giovanni precedeva*: here the editor prefers the version found in Ve 42, *servo*, rather than the one in the Brescian manuscript, *suo*; this latter probably just a copying error of the abbreviation *s(er) vo*; *alte et regali cure* [*alti et regali cure*], again preferring the version of Ve 42.

Letter 21: *Interim* [*Interimi*].

Letter 22: *che dica* [*che dia*]; *cortessemente* [*cortessmente*].

Letter 25: *domestica* [*dumestica*]; *segreti* [*segretti*]: *visibile a' soi* [*visibile a' soii*]; *perfectione* [*perfectiotie*]; *Verbo ha* [*Verbo*]; *passino* [*possino*].

Letter 26: *amantissima* [*amautissima*]; *che 'l grande* [*ch 'l grande*]; *resurrettione* [*resurretttione*]; *l'intrepido animo* [*l'intepido animo*]; *conveniente al nostro Signore* [*al conveniente nostro Signore*].

Letter 28: *desidera* [*dsidera*].

Letter 30: *mi fa andare* [*mi fare andare*].

Letter 31: *che 'l venir* [*del venir*; the text of AGSc instead reads *quia ch'el*].

Letter 35: *sapientia* [*sapietia*]; *de Aristotile* [*de Aristole*].

Letter 36: *intorno il diluvio* [*intorno il diluvio intorno*]; *solo molestia potevate* [*solo molestia potevi*].

When citing examples of Vittoria Colonna's poetry, we have included the reference from the edition of the *Rime* edited by Alan Bullock in 1982 (in the form A1:1, S1:1 etc.), to allow readers to trace the poems more easily.

Note on the Translation

The translation aims at all times to be as close as possible to the original Italian text while achieving a fluent and readable English style. In some cases this objective has necessitated breaking up extremely long sentences in Italian, and adding a period where the Italian introduces a further sub-clause. It has also necessitated removing "And" and "But" from the beginning of sentences where these seemed stylistically infelicitous in English. Otherwise the translator has tried to intervene as little as possible in rendering the original text in English.

All Bible passages in English are cited from the Douay-Rheims Catholic Bible, which is a translation directly from Saint Jerome's Latin Vulgate (authorized at the Council of Trent).

The names of Catholic institutions that include saints' names have not been translated but left in the Italian form. Otherwise saints' names have been translated into the most common and recognizable English form (e.g., Mary Magdalene). "Signor" has been retained in Italian in the English text, as this is a title that is familiar to Anglophone readers. "Messer" has been translated as "Master".

All translations from other Italian works are the translator's own unless specified in the footnotes and bibliography.

Selected Letters, 1523–1546

1. To Giovan Matteo Giberti: Aquino, 16 December 1523
2. To Giovan Matteo Giberti: Marino, 28 March 1524
3. To Giovan Matteo Giberti: Marino, 15 June 1524
4. To Giovan Matteo Giberti: Marino, 13 August 1524
5. To Baldassare Castiglione: Marino, 20 September 1524
6. To Emperor Charles V: [Ischia], 1 May 1525
7. To Costanza d'Avalos del Balzo: 21 December [1525]
8. To Cola Jacobacci: Arpino, [1529–1530]
9. To Paolo Giovio: Ischia, 24 June [1530]
10. To Eleonora Gonzaga della Rovere: Ischia, 31 October [1531]
11. To Bernardino Rota: Ischia, 9 January [1532–1534]
12. [To Ambrogio Recalcati]: [Genazzano, before 14 August 1535]
13. To Costanza d'Avalos del Balzo: Rome, 10 June [1536]
14. To Ercole Gonzaga: Monte San Giovanni Campano, 22 April 1537
15. To Ercole Gonzaga: Ferrara, 12 June [1537]
16. To Pietro Aretino: Ferrara, 6 November 1537
17. To Pope Paul III: Lucca, 16 September 1538
18. To Pietro Bembo: Rome, 3 December 1538
19. To Pietro Bembo: Rome, 10 April [1539]
20. To Marguerite d'Angoulême, queen of Navarre: Rome, 15 February 1540
21. To Ascanio Colonna: [Rome, early March 1541]
22. To Ascanio Colonna: [Rome, 8 March 1541]
23. To Ercole II d'Este: Orvieto, 28 May [1541]
24. To Giulia Gonzaga: Viterbo, 8 December [1541]
25. To Costanza d'Avalos Piccolomini, duchess of Amalfi: [before 1544]
26. To Costanza d'Avalos Piccolomini: [before 1544]
27. [To Bernardino Ochino]: [1535–1542]
28. To Marcello Cervini: Viterbo, 4 December [1542]
29. To Alfonso de Lagni: Viterbo, 25 August [1542]
30. To Giovanni Morone: Viterbo, 22 December [1542]
31. To Reginald Pole: Viterbo, 15 July [1543]
32. To Alfonso de Lagni: Viterbo, 25 September 1543
33. To Michelangelo Buonarroti: [Rome, Autumn 1543]

34. To Michelangelo Buonarroti: [Rome, 1544]

35. To Antonio Bernardi della Mirandola: Rome, 28 August [1544]

36. To the Mother Superior and the nuns of Santa Caterina in Viterbo: Rome, 2 September [1544]

37. To Michelangelo Buonarroti: Viterbo, 20 July [1545]

38. To Pope Paul III: [before 24 November 1545]

39. To Reginald Pole: [Rome], 25 December [1545]

40. To Michelangelo Buonarroti: [Rome, 1546]

Letter 1: Aquino, 16 December 1523[1]
To Giovan Matteo Giberti

This is one of the earliest surviving letters from Colonna, dating from the period before she was established as a model of pious widowhood, a spiritual guide and a famous poet. The letter reflects the encomiastic style that characterizes all Renaissance letter writing, and stands in stark contrast to some of her later letters (see for example the letters to Michelangelo, 33–34, 37 and 40, which are brief and to the point). Here the author constructs ornate sentences that make repeated use of the rhetorical figure of contrast: "greater" versus "less;" her "leisure time" versus Giberti's "hard work;" her "pleasure" versus his "peace," etc.

The recipient of this letter is Giovan Matteo Giberti, papal datary (a church functionary who dealt with ecclesiastical benefices). In 1524, Giberti became bishop of Verona, a role that he carried out with great diligence. He was later allied with reform groups within the Church which included other members of Colonna's inner circle of friends—men such as Reginald Pole and Gasparo Contarini. Colonna and Giberti maintained a correspondence until the end of the latter's life.

∿

From Aquino,[2] 16 December 1523

Even though my will to serve and honor you cannot grow any greater, I am sure that your equal good will towards me is no less; so I can be sure that just as I delight in writing to you, so you will also delight in replying to me. But since I have such an abundance of leisure time, while you must have a dearth of the same, I fear necessity works in you in opposition to desire, and I often wonder if I should forego my own pleasure in order to leave you in peace. Yet I remember well your addiction to hard work, and the way in which, in order not to leave off your habit, indeed your absolute dedication to courtesy, virtue, and goodness, you would sooner defraud yourself than fail in the duties of true friendship; thus I write and will continue to write to you, wishing you sooner to judge me irritating than neglectful and overly attentive rather than heedless, for the one can be attributed to ignorance, the other to pure malice.[3] Now I will take only the little time needed to declare once again my

1. Copy: BCV, ms 810, fols. 3r–v: Colonna, *Carteggio*, no. IV. On Giberti, see Adriano Prosperi, *Tra evangelismo e controriforma: G. M. Giberti (1495–1543)* (Rome: Edizioni di storia e letteratura, 1969).

2. Aquino was the feudal seat of the d'Avalos family.

3. Encomiastic rhetoric governing Renaissance prose writing required the writer to come up with innovative new forms of praise and thanks in order to prove his or her literary worth. See for comparison the dedicatory letter to the second edition of Baldassarre Castiglione's *Libro del cortegiano*. Castiglione declares that "I have elected rather to be thought imprudent and loving by pleasing you, than wise and lacking in love by failing to please you;" Baldassarre Castiglione, *La seconda redazione del Cortegiano di Baldassarre Castiglione: Edizione critica*, ed. Ghino Ghinassi (Florence: Sansoni, 1968), 3: "Ho eletto

good will towards you, and my long-standing devotion to His Holiness,[4] to whom if you have time I ask you to say that I greatly desire to kiss his worthy feet in person etc.

Most dutiful to Your Lordship,
The Marchioness of Pescara

[Letter 1]
De Aquino, a' XVI de decembre 1523

Ancor che la voluntà mia verso el servitio et honor vostro non possi crescere, tengo per fermo non è la vostra inver me per niente minore; per el che deveria essere secura che come ad me deletta el scriverli, così ad essa el respondermi delettasse. Ma perché io tengo abundantia de otio, dove epso deve haverne carestia, temo la necessità faccia in epso effetto contrario al desiderio, sì che molte volte sto in dubio se devo soprasedere il mio piacer per darli la sua quiete. Pure il ricordarmi quanto assuefatto è alla fatica et che per non manchar de sua consueta anzi totalmente inata cortesia, virtù e bontà vorrà più presto fraudar se stesso che lo ordine de la vera amistà, le scrivo et scriverò, volendo ancor che più presto me iudichi importuna che negligente, soverchio recrescevole che immemore, che quel si pò atribuire ad ignorantia, questo ad malitia chiara. Ben toglierò hormai el poco necessario, che è di novo declarare lo animo mio verso di lui, et la dedicata servitù di molto tempo a su Beatitudine, alla quale, sempre vi occorre tempo, direte li baso li degni piedi, desiderosissima farlo presentialmente, etc.

Ad Vostra Signoria obligatissima,
La Marchesa de Pescara

Letter 2: Marino, 28 March 1524[5]
To Giovan Matteo Giberti

The first paragraph of this letter contains the usual healthy dose of encomiastic rhetoric, but moving beyond that it is particularly interesting for the early glimpse it offers of Colonna's desire to live a contemplative life, far from worldly concerns. Her husband Francesco Ferrante d'Avalos had recently reached the apex of his

---

più presto esser tenuto poco prudente et amorevole compiacendovi, che savio e poco amorevole non compiacendovi." For more on Castiglione see Letter 5 in this volume.

4. Pope Clement VII, who had been elected only a month earlier, in November 1523.

5. Copy: BCV, ms 810, fol. 7r: Colonna, *Carteggio*, no. VIII.

military career:[6] after the death of Prospero Colonna in December 1523, command of the imperial army had passed to Charles de Lannoy, viceroy of Naples, supported by two lieutenants, Charles III, duke of Bourbon, and Ferrante d'Avalos. In March 1524, clashes broke out with the French troops which had been in Italy since the previous autumn. One can thus easily imagine why Colonna might have been forced to think "more often of the perils and dangers of war than the tranquility of contemplation," as she says in this letter. Throughout her life she was forced to flee from the calamitous events of her day, and searched in vain for both a physical and a mental space in which to achieve the peace and silence that she sought (see Letter 18). The war between the Holy Roman Emperor Charles V and the French King Francis I in the north of Italy would not be over for a long time yet, and Ferrante d'Avalos's presence was required day and night. In fact, his wife never saw him again.

❧

From Marino,[7] 28 March 1524

Since I arrived here on Holy Monday,[8] I have not thought to bother you by sending a letter nor to appear so lacking in care, although writing to you is always a worthy act before God and the world. In fact, if visible effects allow us some perception of invisible causes,[9] what clearer and more significant effect can be seen than the many virtues resplendent in your person, bearing in mind that each of these alone would ennoble a subject, and united in one single creature they very easily allow a real sense of the Creator? I, as one who thinks more of the perils and dangers of war than the tranquility of contemplation, left off writing to you or thinking of you; but now with this letter I do so, and say to you that I am here in Marino with the usual desire and obligation to serve you, which cannot grow greater, and I dare give it no other name than the usual.

Please kiss the feet of His Holiness[10] on my behalf in thanks for the plenary indulgence that he deigned to send me, which I treasured no less than I do the health of my own soul as it came from the so-powerful hand that I long to see.

Most dutifully,
The Marchioness of Pescara

6. Colonna's husband belonged to a noble family of Spanish origin. In 1512 he led a unit of the imperial cavalry at the Battle of Ravenna, during which he was wounded and taken prisoner. As commander of the imperial infantry in Italy in 1525 he led his troops to victory in the Battle of Pavia, during which the king of France was taken prisoner.

7. A castle belonging to the Colonna family, where Vittoria Colonna was born.

8. The Monday after Easter.

9. The flavor of this phrase is distinctly Aristotelian as well as being reminiscent of a passage from Paul's epistles: Romans 1:18–20.

10. Clement VII became pope in November 1523.

❧

[Letter 2]
De Marino, a' XXVIII de marzo 1524

Arrivando qua de lunedì santo non me parse molestarlo con mia lettera, né mostrarme io de tanto poca conscientia, ancor che 'l scriver ad essa sia in ogni tempo opera meritoria appresso Dio et al mondo; che, se li effetti visibili ce danno cognitione de la causa invisibile, che più chiaro et notabile effetto si può vedere che le molte virtù resplendono in voi solo, considerando che, essendo ogniuna di esse bastante ad nobilitare un suggetto, unite insieme tutte in una creatura si viene per essa assai facilmente in cognitione del Creatore? Ma io, come quella che penso più alli periculi e fastidii de la guerra che alla tranquillità della contemplatione, lassai di scrivervi et de pensarce; follo con questa e vi dico che sto qua in Marini con el solito deseo et obligation servirve, quale, non suffrendo aumento, non oso darli altro nome che lo usato.

A Su Santità basarete per me li piedi, per la gratia dela plenaria indulgentia si è degnata mandarme, quale non meno ho prezata per venire dela mano tanto desiderata da me vederla con tal potestà che per la propria salute de l'anima, etc.

Obligatissima,
La Marchesa de Pescara

Letter 3: Marino, 15 June 1524[11]
To Giovan Matteo Giberti
The theme of this letter is Colonna's "hope for peace." War had raged in the north of Italy since the autumn of 1523, but by June 1524 there was a widespread move to agree a ceasefire. The fighting that had begun the previous March seemed to have ended by April when the French withdrew across the Alps. Pope Clement VII tried by all means possible to secure a peace. He wrote to that effect to King Henry VIII (r. 1509–1547) in England, and both announced to Charles V his intention to withdraw from the anti-French league and assured Francis I of France of his neutrality. In other words, the pope put himself forward as mediator between the rival factions, in an attempt to impose stability between the various Christian powers and then unite them against the threats of Lutheranism and of Islamic expansion.[12] In March 1524 in Bologna the first papal edict was announced requiring

---

11. Copy: BCV, ms 810, fols. 10v–11r: Colonna, *Carteggio*, no. XIII.

12. Maurizio Gattoni, "Pace universale o tregue bilaterali? Clemente VII e l'istruzione a Nicolaus Schömberg, arcivescovo di Capua, 1524," *Ricerche storiche* 30, no. 1 (2000): 174.

that all Lutheran books be turned in to the authorities,[13] even as the Christian powers fought among themselves and the Turkish Sultan Suleiman established his domination of the eastern Mediterranean.[14]

Colonna was very aware of the "unjust" war that divided Christian Europe. In her view, the "sainted union and necessary peace of all Christianity" would allow Christians to "firm up and increase our faith," so tormented by those (Lutherans and Muslims) who should long ago have been punished—not encouraged—by the Catholics.

The truce that began in June 1524 was not to last. In the same period Baldassarre Castiglione, author of the *Libro del cortegiano* (*Book of the Courtier*) and at that time Mantuan ambassador to the papal court, wrote to the Mantuan prince Federico II Gonzaga (1500–1549): "I understand that things are moving on both sides towards a truce, but a short one."[15] In fact, while Pope Clement VII was proposing to make a deal with King Francis I of France, Henry VIII of England and Emperor Charles V decided to invade France. At the end of June 1524, Colonna's husband, Ferrante d'Avalos, was given command of the imperial campaign; together with Charles III, Duke of Bourbon, he set off for Provence (southern France) and in August his troops besieged the port city of Marseille.[16]

∾

From Marino, XV June 1524

The hope for peace which I craved was as dear to me as the war within me was great, caused by the desire for something that was almost impossible, for so it seemed to me to be. Although in your letter Your Lordship shows that it lacks that basis that we hoped for, I want to base my own hope in you who write, and not in those who write to you, since it will take a strong wind to uproot it. What is more, they seem very ignorant to me, those who write a lie that will so easily be uncovered as soon as the archbishop arrives there.[17] And if it is not such a great thing that we desire, it is a great thing that those terrible events happening in England are not quite as awful as we feared.

---

13. Vittorio Frajese, *Nascita dell'Indice: La censura ecclesiastica dal Rinascimento alla Controriforma* (Brescia: Morcelliana, 2006), 43.

14. From the fifteenth century, the Ottomans had expanded their empire to include Iran and Egypt, much of the Balkans and Constantinople itself; in 1522, Suleiman had captured the strategically important island of Rhodes.

15. Castiglione, *Lettere famigliari e diplomatiche*, 2:830: "Intendo le cose essere inclinate alla tregua, dall'una e dall'altra parte, ma per poco tempo" (22 June 1524).

16. Gattoni, "Pace universale," 76.

17. The archbishop referred to is most likely Nicolaus Schömberg, archbishop of Capua, who in March 1524 was sent by Pope Clement VII to France and Spain to campaign for peace.

Given His Holiness's virtue and merit all difficulties are easily overcome. Our recent experience of these matters reassures us that, if they could convince his enemies to exalt him, and those who opposed him were impelled by force or good will to kiss his feet instead,[18] so they will be able to convince these princes, who have spent all their funds and tired themselves out in fighting, and are now frightened by the realization that their future deeds will be more unjust than those of the past, to adopt the sainted union and necessary peace of all Christianity, in order to strengthen and even increase our faith, which has been so vexed by those who should have long ago been punished by men who have instead encouraged their grave error.

I beg you, when things become clearer, do let me know, in recognition of my perfect and sincere friendship and if my request is not too audacious.

Dedicated to Your Lordship's service,
The Marchioness of Pescara

❧

[Letter 3]
Da Marino, a' XV di giugno 1524

Tanto più grata mi è stata la desiderata speranza di pace, quanto maior era la guerra che in me stessa causava el desiderar cosa quasi impossibile, che per tale fin qua la ho reputata. E benché Vostra Signoria mostri in la sua lettera non haverne quel fondamento che desideramo, io voglio fondare la mia speranza in esso che scrive, e non in quelli che li scriveno, che bisognerà sia assai grande el vento che la svella; oltra che mi pare serian bene ignoranti quelli che scrivessero una bugia che con la venuta del Signor Arcivescovo sì presto si scoprirebbe. Et quando non sia tanto quel che desideramo, assai è che quelle terribilità de Anglia non sian così extreme come ce figuravano.

Al valore et merito di Su Santità ogni difficultà è facile; del che la vicina experientia ce fa certi che, se ridussero li nimici ad exaltarlo et li contrarii soi per forza o bona voglia ad basarli li piedi, ben potran redurre questi Principi, exausti di denari, fatigati da guerre et timidi hormai de la conscientia per vedere le future imprese farse più iniuste che le passate, ad una santa unione e necessaria quiete di tutta cristianità, per firmare, anzi, ampliare questa nostra fede tanto vexata da quelli che deveriano già haver ricevuto castigo da questi che sono causa nutrirli in tanto errore.

---

18. Colonna is probably referring to those cardinals who had not supported the election of Clement VII in the papal election of October–November 1523. Such men had been forced by circumstances to "kiss his feet," that is, to accept his new status.

Ve prego, quando siano le cose più chiare, vogliate, per quanto pò meritare perfetta o sincera amicitia, avisarmelo, se la preghiera mia non è superba.

Dedita per servire Vostra Signoria,
La Marchesa de Pescara

Letter 4: Marino, 13 August 1524[19]
To Giovan Matteo Giberti

This letter opens and closes on the topic of Colonna's illness, in one of many instances when her letters allow us glimpses of her fragile health and the concern of her many correspondents. But the real reason why Colonna dictates these few lines to Giberti is to congratulate him on his recent ordination as bishop, conferred by the future Pope Paul IV, Gian Pietro Carafa (1476–1559). Colonna expresses the hope that this will be just one further step on the path to Giberti becoming pope himself one day.

The core of this letter instead concerns Colonna's husband Ferrante d'Avalos, who was in Provence engaged in besieging the city of Marseille.[20] Colonna's doctors tried to impress upon her the need to remain emotionally stable during her illness, in order to speed her recovery, but Colonna seems to imply that this is absurd advice. It would require her to pretend that her husband "were not worth all that he is, and we were not two in one flesh, and I did not owe him all that I do." She seems to be saying that the fact of being one sole flesh with her husband causes her to suffer the same mortal dangers that he is exposed to in his professional life.

From Marino, XIII August 1524

For three days joy has been fighting illness within my body. One of them, united with my reason and will, wishes me to write to you and in some way thereby to meet my great obligation; the other has not and does not allow it. In the end I have resolved to dictate this letter; in it I thank above all Our Lord God, and then His Holiness,[21] who has raised Your Lordship a further step on the ladder that I refer to,[22] and thus gives me sure hope that you will rise again after the term of years we pray Our Lord grant to him who currently occupies the highest step. I believe this is something I desire far more than you do yourself, since Your Lordship only wishes for peace, and I

19. Copy: BCV, ms 810, fols. 12v–13r: Colonna, *Carteggio*, no. XVI.

20. See Gattoni, "Pace universale," 78.

21. Pope Clement VII.

22. The papacy.

wish to deny it to you, so that the whole world will trouble you. I wish that the glory of the house of Medici[23] were such that not only they, but also their servants, would understand how to live by the grace of Our Lord God. And may it please God that this wish be a true prophecy.

About my illness, into which I have fallen many times, I can confirm that if you were to see it you could not think me anything but ill. As Master Geronimo would tell you,[24] I have never disobeyed him nor done anything wrong. As for what they accuse me of, becoming angry, it would be necessary to remove the reason for it, as if the Marquis [Avalos] were not worth all that he is, and we were not two in one flesh and I did not owe him all that I do.[25] Anyone who tells you how I feel, even if it be the Prior of Capua,[26] let him use divine power to cure me right away. I am trying to forget the meager and much delayed provisions that were sent to the Marquis, in order to avoid doing myself harm and thus obey you. As Your Lordship so greatly wishes me to be well, I will aim more truly for it myself in order to please you. In any case I am very well, and the slight lingering fever just teases me and does not bother me at all; I pass the whole day without a fever, it doesn't come on with any regularity and I can sweat it out easily enough. My stomach is fine and I hope to get up soon. I beg Your Lordship to forgive me for failing to write in the last few days, it was to obey my doctors and not because I lacked the desire, etc.

In the service of Your greatly Revered Lordship,
The Marchioness of Pescara

∽

[Letter 4]
De Marino, a' XIII de agosto 1524

Tre dì sono che in me combatte la allegria col male, che l'una insieme con la ragione et voluntà vorriano ch'io scrivesse, facendo in alcuna parte quello a che sono tanto obligata; l'altro non me l'ha consentito né consente. Al fine mi sono resoluta farli scrivere questa, in la quale rengratio prima Nostro Signore Dio et poi Su Santità che, con fare ascendere alla Signoria Vostra un scalino più alto et a dirittura de la scala ch'io dico, me dà certa speranza vederlo di qua a molti anni quali Nostro Signore conceda a chi è in la sumità di essa. Cosa, credo, molto più da me che da voi medesimo desiderata, perché la Signoria Vostra desidera la quiete, et io vorria tanto inquietarlo che 'l mondo tutto li desse molestia, et che

23. Clement VII, previously Giulio de' Medici, belonged to this celebrated Florentine family.

24. Probably Colonna's doctor.

25. Colonna is drawing here on Matthew 19:6 and Mark 10:8.

26. Brother Giuliano Ridolfi (or De Rodolfi).

fusse tale la gloria de casa de' Medici che non solo essi havessero saputo essere con gratia di Nostro Signore Dio, ma ancora li loro servitori, et piaccia a chi tutto pò che questa sia vera profetia.

De la indispositione mia, che me ha represa di tante recascate, la certifico che, se sempre l'havesse vista, mai me haveria iudicata se non inferma. Et come mastro Hieronimo potrà dirli, mai ho fatto nissuna disobedientia né disordine. Quello de che mi danno colpa, de pigliar colera, bisogneria toglier la causa, che seria che 'l Marchese non valesse quel che vale, che non fossemo doi in carne una, et ch'io non li fusse obligata come sono; sì che questi che dà relatione di me, se pure è lo Signor Priore di Capua, use de la potentia divina et potrà liberarme subito. Io ben cerco perdere la memoria delle poche et tarde provisioni che vanno al Marchese per non farme danno et obedirla. Che poi Vostra Signoria preza tanto ch'io stia sana, lo miro con maggior diligentia per servirlo. Io sto in ogni modo assai bene, et questi pochi residui di febre vanno burlando meco perché non me inquietano niente, lassanome tutto el dì netta, non servano ordine al venire, et tutti doi terminano con sudore. Tengo lo stomaco bono et spero presto levarme. Prego Vostra Signoria mi perdoni se in questi dì non li ho scritto, che è stato per obedire a' medici et non per poco deseo ch'io ne havessi, etc.

Al servitio de Vostra Signoria molto Reverenda,
La Marchesa de Pescara

Letter 5: Marino, 20 September 1524[27]
To Baldassarre Castiglione

Vittoria Colonna talks about literature in her letters on only very few occasions. Thus the "review" of Castiglione's *Libro del cortegiano* (*The Book of the Courtier*) contained in this letter is a significant historical resource.[28]

Castiglione, a writer and diplomat from Mantua, finished the third draft of his *Courtier* in May 1524: the book is a dialogue in four parts in which the speakers set out to define the perfect courtier and his lady companion. The author sent a manuscript draft to Colonna to ask her opinion, as was common practice at the time, but Colonna was very delayed in sending back the manuscript and Castiglione was eventually forced to write and ask for its return. In this reply, while still delaying in returning the work, Colonna offers her opinion of it in a highly controlled and ornate rhetorical style.

In her letter, Colonna carefully expresses her enthusiasm for Castiglione's work—she is reading it for the second time and wishes to learn it by heart. She then goes on to elucidate the book's strengths: the originality of the theme, the

27. Copy: BCV, ms 810, fols. 15r–16r: Colonna, *Carteggio*, no. XVIII.

28. Another rare example of literary discussion in Colonna's correspondence is Letter 9 addressed to Paolo Giovio.

excellence of the style, the profound concepts, the carefully chosen vocabulary, the jokes, the natural flow which disguises its careful artfulness (one of the book's central themes). Finally, Colonna highlights two aspects of the work that particularly strike her: the section dealing with the praise of women (Book III of the work), and the author's use of language (discussed in Book I). What she calls "your new vernacular," departing from the model (that of fourteenth-century Florence) proposed by Pietro Bembo, as well as from those posed by Claudio Tolomei (Tuscan) and Niccolò Machiavelli (contemporary Florentine), drew on the cultivated language used in courts across the Italian peninsula.[29] Colonna ends with witty praise for the author: it wasn't hard for him to describe the perfect courtier, as he only had to look in the mirror.[30]

The months and years that followed the composition of this letter were busy ones for both Colonna and Castiglione. From 1524, the latter served as papal envoy to the emperor. Then followed the Battle of Pavia and consequent imprisonment of King Francis I (1525); the death the same year of Colonna's husband Ferrante d'Avalos; the mounting tensions between the pope and the emperor; and the Sack of Rome (1527), when imperial armies looted the city and the pope was forced into hiding. It was not until September 1527 that Castiglione wrote again to Colonna about his book, bemoaning the fact that she had allowed it to circulate in manuscript without his permission. Angry at her treatment of him, he publicly denounced the "theft of the *Cortegiano*" in the preface to the first printed edition of the book, which was finally published in 1528.[31]

∽

From Marino, XX September 1524, to Count Baldassarre Castiglione about his book that he sent her to look at before it was printed
Excellent Signor,
I had not forgotten the promise I made you;[32] on the contrary, it pains me that it was so much to the fore in my mind that I was prevented from fully enjoying your

29. Baldassarre Castiglione, *Il libro del Cortegiano*, ed. Amedeo Quondam (Rome: Bulzoni, 2016), 1:12–15. See also Sanson, "Vittoria Colonna and Language."

30. Castiglione reprises the praise Colonna gives here in the dedicatory letter to the print edition of the *Libro del cortegiano*: "Alcuni anchor dicono ch'io ho creduto formar me stesso, persuadendomi che le conditioni ch'io al cortegiano attribuisco, tutte siano in me. A questi tali non voglio già negar di non haver tentato tutto quello ch'io vorrei che sapesse il cortegiano, e penso che chi non havesse avuto qualche notitia delle cose che nel libro si trattano, per erudito che fosse stato, mal havrebbe potuto scriverle. Ma io non son tanto privo di giudicio in conoscere me stesso che mi presuma saper tutto quello che so desiderare;" Castiglione, *Il libro del Cortegiano*, 1:19; see Maria Cristina Cabani, "Ariosto e Castiglione," *Italianistica* 45 (2016): 47.

31. See Colonna, *Carteggio*, no. XXXIV.

32. Colonna's promise was to return the manuscript of the *Cortegiano*.

delightful book, for I was constantly thinking of the fact that I must return it to you without devoting to it the time that I wished, so that at least the memory of my promise spurred me to read with great attention. Your asking for its return is very inconvenient, and since I am right now midway through my second reading, I beg Your Lordship to allow me to finish reading, and then I promise to return the manuscript to you, as soon as you inform me that you are about to depart from Rome.[33] You do not need to send anyone to collect it, because I will send it to you safely and securely.

There is no need for me to tell you what I think of it, for the same reason that you yourself give, that it is not seemly to talk of the beauty of the lady Duchess;[34] but since I promised you my opinion, I will not write an ornate letter to tell you what you know already better than me, but I will simply tell you the honest truth, confirming it with an oath whose value you will recognize, which is that I swear "on the life of the Marquis, my husband" that I have never seen, nor believe I will see again, another work in prose that is better or even equal to this one, nor worthy even to be ranked in second place to it. Apart from the wonderful new subject matter, the excellence of the style is such that, with an unprecedented smoothness it leads you to a beauteous and fertile hill, where you climb ever higher without realizing that you are far above the level at which you entered; and the path is so well tended and ornate that it is difficult to know whether it has been cultivated by nature or art. Let us leave to one side the wonderful witticisms, the deep insights, which glitter no less than gemstones mounted in only as much gold as is needed to set them off without stealing the tiniest part of their luster;[35] nor do I believe that any gems could be found to equal these, nor any finer craftsman who could improve their setting.

And what can I say of the propriety of the words, which truly demonstrate with such clarity the potential for using a language other than Tuscan?[36] It is a pity that this has come so late, for the fame of he who so strictly observed it has lived on till now. What I noticed above all is that where you use other words, departing from the Tuscan, it seems you have done this more because these words work better than

33. In July 1524 Castiglione, at the time Mantuan ambassador to the pope, was named papal ambassador to the king of Spain. He left for Spain on 7 October 1524.

34. By saying that it is not "seemly" to talk of the Duchess's beauty, Castiglione means to imply that it this beauty is both self-evident and beyond description. The Duchess he refers to is Elisabetta Gonzaga, wife of Guidobaldo I of Montefeltro, duke of Urbino. "Le ottime condizioni della quale [Duchess, Elisabetta Gonzaga] io per hora non intendo narrare, non essendo mio proposito, et per essere assai note al mondo et molto più ch'io non potrei né con lingua né con penna esprimere;" Castiglione, *Il libro del Cortegiano*, 2:16, from the preface to Book I of the *Cortegiano* added after its first draft.

35. The same imagery is found in Colonna's sonnet "L'opre divine e 'l glorioso impero" (S1:139, 8–14): "e quasi gemma cui poco lavoro / d'intorno fregia, sì ch'altra vaghezza / non può impedir la sua più viva luce, / il vostro onor, salito a tanta altezza / ch'uopo non ha di più ricco tesoro, / dentro 'l mio basso stil nudo riluce."

36. For a discussion of the "Questione della lingua" in the period, and Colonna's and Castiglione's positions, see Sanson, "Vittoria Colonna and Language."

out of any desire to reject Tuscan usage.[37] The jokes and riddles are so apt and well put that, even though many of those who spoke them are dead now,[38] I still couldn't help admiring them greatly. I am minded to keep silent about the part of your book that most pleases and compels me, which is your praise, surely well-deserved, for the chastity and virtue of women. But I will not be silent about that which aroused my greatest admiration. For it seems to me that someone who writes in Latin is different from other authors, in the same way that a craftsman who works with gold differs from someone who works with copper; for however simple the object he makes, the excellence of his base material shines through so brightly that the object is rendered beautiful; but the object made from copper, however cunningly and skillfully it is worked, still in the comparison will come off worse. Yet your new vernacular has its own rare majesty that cedes nothing to the finest Latin work.

The fact that you have modelled a perfect courtier does not surprise me,[39] for by simply holding up a mirror and observing your own inner and outer nature, you could describe him just as you have done. But since our greatest difficulty is in knowing ourselves, I judge that it was much harder for you to portray yourself than someone else. Thus on both counts you deserve the highest praise, which I am sending via the Lord Datary,[40] whom alone I consider equal to conveying this on my behalf.

∾

[Letter 5]
Da Marino, a' XX di settembre 1524 al conte Baldassar da Castiglione sopra el libro suo che li havea mandato a vedere inanzi che 'l si stampasse.

Excellente Signor,
Non haveva io perduta la memoria di observarli la promessa, anzi mi dole che la ho havuta tanto viva che continuo me ha impedita la dolceza de sì bella lettione, pensando di remandarla senza relegerla le volte ch'io vorrei, et almeno mi

---

37. In referring to "he who so strictly observed it," Colonna might be indicating Petrarch's strong influence on the poetic language and debates of the period, and his literary contributions that demonstrated the use of *trecento* Florentine. Castiglione's counterdemonstration of the effectiveness of a "lingua cortegiana" (a form of courtly vernacular) was, she implies, a useful argument in favor of a different linguistic choice.

38. The dedication to the *Cortegiano* confirms that a number of protagonists are now deceased; see Castiglione, *Il libro del Cortegiano*, 1:13.

39. See the dedicatory letter to the print edition of the *Libro del cortegiano*: "Altri dicono che essendo tanto difficile e quasi impossibile trovar un homo così perfetto come io voglio che sia il cortegiano, è stato superfluo il scriverlo, perché vana cosa è insegnar quello che imparar non si pò;" Castiglione, *Il libro del Cortegiano*, 1:13.

40. Giovan Matteo Giberti; see Letters 1–4.

servisse in retenerla in sé bene impressa. Poi me ha tanto deservita in sollicitarmi et perché son già al mezo della seconda volta ch'io la lego, prego la Signoria Vostra me la voglia lassar finire, ch'io le prometto remandarcelo come intenderò per sua lettera stia per partire da Roma. Né bisognerà mandare altri per esso, ch'io lo inviarò cautamente et securo.

Non converria ch'io li dicessi quel che me ne pare, per la medesima causa che Vostra Signoria dice non è da parlare de la belleza della Signora Duchessa. Ma perché gliel promisi, non curerò con una ornata lettera darli ad intendere quello che sa meglio di me, ma semplicemente li dirò la pura verità, affirmandola con sacramento tale che mostri la efficatia che devessi: che li dico *por vida del Marches, my Señor*, ch'io non ho visto mai né credo vedere altra opera in prosa meglio o simile né forse meritamente seconda a questa: perché, oltra el bellissimo soggetto et novo, la excellentia del stile è tale che con una suavità non mai sentita vi conduce in uno amenissimo et fruttifero colle, salendo sempre senza farve accorger mai di non esser pur nel piano dove entrasti; et è la via sì ben culta et ornata che difficilmente può discernersi chi habbi più faticato in abellirla, o la natura o l'arte. Lasciamo stare le maravigliose argutie, le profonde sententie che ci rilucono non meno che gemme legate in sì poco oro che solo li serve per necessaria compagnia senza togliere pur una minima parte de la lor luce; né credo che altre possin trovarse tali, né meno artefice megliorar l'incasto. Ma che dirò io de la proprietà de le parole, che veramente dimostrano questa chiarezza di possere usare altro che 'l toscano? È stata ventura sia venuta sì tardi, perché la fama di chi la ha sì strettamente observata sia fin qui vissa, et quel che più ho notato è che dove usa altra parola sono così da lassar le toscane che par più per seguir queste meglio che per fugir quelle l'habbi fatto. Le facetie et burle son tanto accommodate et ben dette che, anche siano morti molti di quelli che le dissero, non ho possuto lassare di non tenerli invidia grandissima. Ma di quella parte che più mi piace et obliga, che è le forsi debite laude che date alla continentia et virtù de le donne, determino tacere. Ma non tacerò già quello che più admiratione mi ha causato, che è che a me pare che chi scrive latino habbi una differentia con li altri autori simile ad uno artefice che lavora di oro a quelli che lavorano di rame, che, per semplice opera che faccia, la excellentia de la materia luce tanto che la dimostra bella; ma la opera di rame con grande ingegno et sottil modo non può farsi tale che in la comparatione non perda molto. Ma il novo vostro vulgare porta una maiestà con seco sì rara che non deve cedere a niuna opera latina.

Che habbia ben formato un perfetto cortegiano non me ne maraviglio, che con solo tenere un specchio denanzi et considerare le interne et externe parti sue posseva descriverlo qual lo ha descritto; ma essendo la maggior difficultà che habbiamo conoscer noi stessi, dico che più difficile li è stato formar sé che un altro, sì che, o per l'uno o per l'altro che sia, merita tanta laude che me ne rimetto al Signor Datario, qual solo iudico bastevole che per me la dia.

Letter 6: [Ischia], 1 May 1525[41]
To Emperor Charles V

On 24 February 1525, the imperial army, under the command of Ferrante d'Avalos, triumphed against the French at the Battle of Pavia, and King Francis I of France was taken prisoner. A month later, on 26 March, Emperor Charles V wrote personally to Vittoria Colonna to remind her of the "very significant and memorable victory against the French in Northern Italy."[42] In a seemingly spontaneous play on words, the emperor confirmed that "your name, Vittoria [Victory], will always be a good omen for us in future."[43] Colonna responded, somewhat overwhelmed by such attention from the emperor, who had written not to offer, request or order something, but simply in order to congratulate her.

Colonna's reply is divided into two parts. In the first, she heaps praise on her correspondent, drawing on the full range of epistolary rhetorical techniques to invent new and ever more ornate ways to extol him. In particular, Colonna draws a comparison, one that gradually becomes more explicit as the letter progresses, between the emperor and God himself. Charles, future leader of the Holy Roman Empire, is "the summit of all perfection," all virtue and goodness. Following this she alludes to Canto 33 of Dante's *Paradiso* [the third book of the *Divine Comedy*] as well as to the *Magnificat*,[44] and finally arrives at an explicit declaration, that Charles is "comparable to the Lord, whom you resemble more perfectly than anyone has ever done before."

In the second part of the letter, Colonna returns to the same words used by the emperor in his letter to her, but she deliberately reverses their meaning in order to make her own request—with the utmost delicacy but very clearly. Colonna has drawn on her own name, she states, only as a means to "overcome my own desires," that is, to set aside her own wishes in favor of those of the emperor. Now Charles V should furnish her with the "promised comfort" of her husband's

---

41. Copy: BNMV, Cons. Ven. 160.4.1, fols. 260r–v (C1); Copy: ASM, Archivio Gonzaga, b. 1880, anno 1525 (C2): Colonna, *Carteggio*, no. XXI. The text used here is C1, which is the more correct as well as being more closely aligned with Colonna's usual writing practices. The header, date and final signature are taken from C2, however (these elements are lacking in the Venice copy and are therefore included here in square brackets). C2 is followed also in the following cases: *culmine* [*columne* C1]; *in la propria* [*la propria* C1]; *desiderato bene* [*desiderato* C1]; *per tali che non* [*per tali che* C1]; *comodità* [*como dice* C1]; *essendomi stato* [*essendome sta* C1]; *conosco haverlo* [*conosco haver* C1]; *iminentissimi* [*inimentissimi* C1]; *sustenuti* [*illuminati* C1]. In Colonna, *Carteggio*, the editors also note a copy of this letter in a private collection in Florence, "Raccolta di lettere e notizie diverse, vol. VI, c. 79–81," but it has not been possible to identify the collection or the copy.

42. "Tam insigni, tam memorabili victoria . . . in Insubria adversos Gallos;" Colonna, *Carteggio*, no. XXI.

43. "Tuum Victoriae nomen auspicatissimum nobis semper crederemus;" Colonna, *Carteggio*, no. XXI.

44. The *Magnificat*, also referred to as the Song of Mary, is a Marian canticle forming part of the Catholic Liturgy. Its text derives from the Luke 1:46–55, which begins: "And Mary said: My soul doth magnify the Lord."

company, that is, by allowing him finally to abandon the battlefield and return to Ischia "to be at my side in peace."

∾

[Holy Emperor and Catholic Majesty],

If our Lord God, in recognition of the great merit of Your Imperial Majesty, deigned to raise you to such heights that powerful kings petition you for their freedom and are reduced to begging you for mercy, how could I find the audacity to respond to your most eloquent letter, if it were not that the letter itself endowed me with the illumination to understand it and the soul to merit it? Nor could anyone these days have the effrontery to think that, in wishing to serve you, they do not need to acquire from your favor everything they wished to give back to you, because you are the summit of all perfection, and all virtues are united resplendent in you, so that the rest of the world is left empty. We must place all our hope in your goodness, for we mortals are offered no higher model than you. And because you are happy and blessed in contemplation and understanding of yourself alone,[45] we should not ask you for more, for you can confer on us, in your splendor, the satisfaction of all our desires. May you, by your immense benevolence, consider the debt that the world owes you and cannot ever repay as already paid, for thus you will be satisfied and, making up for the universe's lack, you will render it more worthy of your noble empire.

How can I ever express my joy that Your Imperial Majesty should remember me[46] at a time when you were triumphing over so many nations, deciding the fate of royal lives,[47] dividing provinces and realms, when upon your judgment depended the peace of all Christianity and the necessary destruction of the infidels? I do not presume to believe anything else than that you wished to demonstrate how you could at the same time reduce the proud and raise up the humble.[48] There is nothing so great that in comparison to the generosity of your spirit it does not appear small, nor so small that your humanity does not endow it with greatness, wishing in this as in other things to be comparable to the Lord, whom you resemble more perfectly than anyone has ever done before.

The service, loyalty and sincerity of the Marquis my Lord and of my House I find barely worthy of Your Imperial Majesty, yet you accept them, and I desire the

45. There seems to be a Dantean echo here: "O luce etterna che sola in te sidi, / Sola t'intendi, e da te intelletta / E intendente te ami e arridi;" Dante, *Paradiso* 33:124–26.

46. Colonna is referring to the words used by Charles V in his letter to her: "per alia multa quae iucundissima nobis in mentem veniebant, fuit nominis tuis recordatio" ("Among the many other joyful things that came to mind was the remembrance of your name"); Colonna, *Carteggio*, no. XX.

47. The allusion is to the imprisonment of the king of France.

48. This is both a citation from Virgil, *Aeneid* 6.853 ("parcere subiectis et debellare superbos") and from the *Magnificat* in Luke 1:52: "dispersit superbos . . . et exaltavit humiles" ("He hath scattered the proud . . . and hath exalted the humble").

promised concession more as proof of your approval than due to my own unseemly greed, for your graciousness and generosity always reward any just request.[49] I do not know which I esteem more highly, to receive a prize from such a noble prince, or the glory of my claim to be in his debt.

I hold my name in the highest regard since Your Imperial Majesty took it as a joyful omen, nor was this unfitting since it was conferred on me because of the victory won by your forebears.[50] I myself have used it only to overcome my own desires, wishing that the Marquis my Lord should serve Your Majesty, despite the many clear and present dangers, rather than coming here to be at my side in peace.

I will continue to pray to our Lord God for the safety of Your Imperial Majesty, which is so necessary to all the world and especially to us, for by your light alone are we sustained and illuminated.

[From Ischia, the first day of May 1525.]

[From the most humble servant and vassal of Your Imperial and Catholic Majesty, Victoria Colonna de Davolos]

∽

[Letter 6]
[Sacra Cesarea et Catholica Maestà],
Se 'l nostro Signor Dio, respetando al superno merito de Vostra Cesarea Maestà, se dignò elevarla in sì excelso grado che li potenti Re ne aspettano libertà et sono constretti supplicarli mercede, che audatia teneria io de rispondere alla humanissima lettera, se da essa medesima non nascesse in me luce per capirla et animo per meritarla? Né hoggi niuno pò arrogarsi tanto che, volendo servirla, non gli bisogni col suo favore aquistare quanto ad essa vol restituire, perché ivi è il sommo culmine de ogni perfectione, et virtuti sì unite ivi refulgeno che tutto el mondo ne resta nudato: in la sua bontà convien collocare ogni speranza, che più alto segno non se concede a' mortali. Et perché in la sola consideratione et intelligentia di se stessa è felice et beata, non convien supplicarli altro se non che poi se li concede, in la propria grandeza, la fruitione d'ogni desiderato bene. Voglia qual se deve tutto el mondo et non pò darcelo tenerlo per la sua inmensa benignitade per ricevuto, che così satisfarà se stessa et, supplendo al mancamento de l'universo, lo farà più meritevole del degno Imperio suo.

49. There seems to be here another echo of Dante's prayer to the Virgin: "La tua benignità non pur soccorre / A chi domanda, ma molte fiate / Liberamente al dimandar precorre;" Dante, *Paradiso* 33:16–18.

50. It seems that Colonna was given the Christian name Vittoria precisely in order to commemorate the victories won by her forebears in service of the forebears of Charles V. Charles also refers to them in his letter.

Ma che dirò de la felicità mia, essendo stata nela memoria de Vostra Cesarea Maestà in tempo che triunfava de tante nationi, disponea dele regie vite, repartiva le provincie et regni, pendeva dal suo juditio la quiete de tutta christianità et la necessaria ruina de Infedeli? Non presumerò creder altro se non che in una medesma hora volesse mostrare che, come sapea debellare li superbi, così sapea exaltare li humeli. Né cosa così grande pò trovarse che alla magnitudine del suo animo non sia piccola, né sì minima che la humanità sua non la ricevi per grande, volendo essere conforme in questo effetto come negli altri a quel Signore che, più che mai altri facesse, rapresenta.

Li servicii, fede et sincerità del Marchese mio signore et de mia Casa tengo per tali che indegnamente sono a Vostra Cesarea Maestà accetti, et la promessa comodità desidero più per testimonio di questo che per insolita cupidità mia, benché la gratitudine et liberalità sua sempre prevene ogni iusta dimanda. Né so qual sia più da extimare: o ricevere il premio de tanto gran principe, o la gloria che dica esserne debitore.

Il nome mio tengo in grandissima stima, essendo da la Cesarea Maestà Vostra preso in augurio felice, né incongruamente, essendomi stato imposto per la vitoria de soi passati; conosco haver lo solo in vincer me stessa usato, desiderando più presto, con tanti iminentissimi et diversi pericoli, che 'l Signor mio Marchese serva Sua Maestà che vengi ad acquetarsi con me.

Pregarò sempre nostro Signor Dio per la salute de la Cesarea Maestà Vostra, tanto necessaria a tutto el mondo et precipue a noi, che da solo questo lume siamo retti et sustenuti.

[Da Ischia, a' dì primo de magio 1525.]

[De Vostra Cesarea et Catholica Maestà
humilissima serva et vassalla,
Victoria Colonna de Davolos]

Letter 7: 21 December [1525][51]
To Costanza d'Avalos del Balzo

Shortly before his death, Ferrante d'Avalos wrote to his wife asking her to organize the return of the castle of Colle San Magno to the Benedictine abbey of Montecassino, its rightful owner. In the meantime, he requested that she pay fifty

---

51. Copy: AAM, caps. LXVII, fasc. XVIII, [fol. 1r]; Copy: the same, fol. 2v; Copy: the same, fols. 76v–77r; Copy: BAV, Ferr. 433, fol. 43r: Colonna, *Carteggio*, no. XXV. The text used here that of AAM, caps. LXVII, fasc. XVIII [fol. 1r], which is closer to Colonna's writing practice and more authoritative as the only copy that includes the correct date of 21 December; the other copies record the date as 2 December. Francesco Ferrante d'Avalos died on 3 December 1525, and this letter must have been written after that date.

ducats a year to the abbey, equivalent to the yearly revenue from the castle.[52] The day before he died, the Marquis dictated a will in which he reaffirmed the request. Colonna took to heart her husband's dying wish and immediately set about petitioning her relatives for the restitution of Colle San Magno: her targets were Alfonso d'Avalos, her late husband's cousin and heir, and her aunt-by-marriage Costanza, who was an authoritative figure within the family. This, the first extant letter written by Colonna after her husband's death, therefore concerns the management of property, but it is far from being a cold, administrative document. Colonna instead uses emotive and spiritual arguments to move Costanza and persuade her to accede to Ferrante d'Avalos's dying wish.

The letter's plea proved to be in vain (see Letter 13), but Colonna did not give up and continued to send regular letters over the years to both Alfonso and Costanza petitioning for the restitution of the castle. She also faithfully continued to pay the fifty ducats a year to the abbey. Colonna's devotion to her late husband and to God were increasingly tested over time in the face of the dishonest conduct of her relatives, and her pleading began to sound almost threatening. "If I, who do not have this on my conscience, tremble at it, I do not know how Your Ladyship can be at peace," she wrote to Costanza;[53] and to Alfonso, "all this will be on the conscience of anyone who knows the truth, as does Your Lordship from me, and even more so Her Ladyship [Costanza] who received news of it."[54] The letter below is the earliest example of such fruitless appeals to the conscience of her addressee, who wrote a reply to Colonna on 9 January 1526 (*Carteggio*, no. XXVI).

∽

My Most Illustrious Lady,

That blessed soul [Avalos] set out in his will that anything in his House that belongs to others should be returned to them. Thus in this letter I confirm to Your Ladyship that he wrote to me by his own hand that I should return the Colle to the friars of Saint Benedict, and since that time I have been paying the income to the abbey while waiting for the pope to come to a decision. Since my husband stated this request unequivocally and Your Ladyship will not wish to have on your conscience your failure to comply, and these friars are content to accept all the revenues collected from the Avalos House, I beg Your Ladyship to return it to them, otherwise it will be a burden on my husband's soul and on your own. I am sure the Lord Marquis of Guasto will not object, since he would do even more for my late husband, all the more so as the friars say that they have launched a legal action and are about to win

---

52. On this incident see Veronica Copello, "Un problema di giustizia e di verità: Vittoria Colonna e la restituzione di Colle S. Magno," *Schede umanistiche* 31 (2017): 11–61.

53. Colonna, *Carteggio*, no. LXXVIII.

54. Colonna, *Carteggio*, no. CXVII.

it, and my Lord asked them to overlook it. I beg you to show the love you owe that blessed soul by not leaving him in suspense. From San Silvestro,[55] on the twenty-first day of December.

Your Illustrious Ladyship's servant,
The Marchioness

∽

[Letter 7]
Illustrissima Signora mia,
quella felice anima, la quale nel suo testamento è che quanto se trova in la Casa che sia d'altri se restituisca. Et io per questa lettera fazio fede alla Signoria Vostra che me scripse de sua mano restituisse el Colle alli fratri de San Benedetto, et da quella hora in cqua io ho facto dare la intrata al dicto loco, aspectando che 'l papa lo determinasse. Mo che dicto Signor mio resolutamente lo dice et Sua Signoria non ce vole mectere de conscentia et questi fratri se contantano benedirli tucte le intrate percepute dalla Casa, prego Vostra Signoria ce lo fazia restituire, altramente seria carrico di quella anima et de la Signoria Vostra. E 'l Signor Marchese del Guasto sono certa non ce replicarà, perché faria magior cosa per lo dicto Signor mio, tanto più che questi padri dicono feno fare processo et stanno per havere la sententia in favore, e 'l Signor li pregò sopersedessero. Supplicola monstrar lo amore che sole in non fare stare quella benedecta anima sospesa. Da San Silvestro, a' dì 21 decembro.
Servitrice de Vostra Signoria Illustrissima,
La Marchese

Letter 8: Arpino, [1529–1530][56]
To Cola Jacobacci

We know the family name of the recipient of this brief letter from the address written on the reverse: Cola [Nicola] Jacobacci, who is mentioned in the diary of an administrator of the Papal State, Marcello Alberino, as an "honored person" and "attached to the Colonna faction."[57] Jacobacci lived in Rome close to piazza Colonna, and worked in various roles for the papacy.[58] He died in 1534.

---

55. Colonna stayed in the Roman convent of San Silvestro in Capite many times after her widowhood.

56. Original, autograph signature: Copello, "Aggiornamenti: Parte I," 159.

57. Domenico Orano, "Il diario di Marcello Alberini," *Archivio della società romena di storia patria* 18 (1895): 346.

58. For more details, see Claudio De Dominicis, *La famiglia di Domenico Jacovacci* (Rome: Accademia Moroniana, 2014), <accademiamoroniana.it/monografie/Famiglia% 20Jacovacci.pdf>, 31–32.

This letter has little historical relevance, and its protagonists have left no other traces than those we find here. We know nothing of Paolo da Marino, nor of Giovan Angelo da Arpino, who stole a horse from some Spaniards and sold it to Cola. Nevertheless, these few lines cast new light on Colonna's daily concerns and activities, as she oversaw the management of lands and settlements across central Italy. The letter also reveals something about Colonna's character: we can see that in dealing with squabbles between her subordinates she behaved just as she did when voicing her opinion on the great public debates of her era, such as the restitution of Colle S. Magno (Letters 7 and 13), the defense of the Capuchin order (Letters 12 and 17) and the quarrel between her family and the pope. What is notable is a marked consistency of character: the ideals of justice, truth and peace governed her behavior regardless of the context.

∽

Magnificent Master Cola,
Previously via the mediation of Paulo de Marini I asked you to resolve that dispute you have with my servant from Arpino who took the horse from the Spanish gentlemen, but I have not seen it settled. I wish very much for this to be resolved, so that you might get what you are owed and he and his other dependents might come to work in Rome without this hanging over them. As far as I know the horse was sold for seven ducats, so to make Joan Angelo pay what he owes for his crime I will get him to pay fourteen. I beg you to settle for this, for you will have been well compensated and you would be doing me a great service. I am ready to do you every honor and service.

From Arpino.[59]

Most ready to honor you,
The Marchioness of Pescara.

On the reverse:
To the [Magnificent] Master Cola Jacobacci [. . .]

∽

[Letter 8]
Magnifico messer Cola,
Altre volte da messer Paulo de Marini ve ho facto pregare che volessemo quietar quella cosa vostra col mio de Arpino che pigliò el cavallo alli spagnoli, et non ci

59. Arpino, Cicero's birthplace, is a small town located in the hills to the east of Frosinone. It belonged to the d'Avalos family from the end of the fifteenth century.

ho visto ordine. Desideraria in gran modo che se resolvessero de manera che voi havesseno il vostro, et costui et li altri mei potesse[r]o venir et praticar in Roma senza haver fastidio di questo. Ad me consta che 'l cavallo fo ve[ndu]to septe d[uc]ati, e per dar ad Joan Angelo la penintentia che merita per lo acto [. . .]o ce ne farrò pagar quactordeci. Pregove ve ne contentati, che già così serrite ben satisfacto, et me ne farrite piacer gratissimo; offerendomi ad ogni comodo et honore vostro paratissima.

De Arpino.

Al vostro honor paratissima,
La marchesa de Pescara

A tergo
Al [Magnifico] messer Cola Jacobacci [. . .]

Letter 9: Ischia, 24 June [1530][60]
To Paolo Giovio

The historian and humanist Paolo Giovio, bishop of Nocera Inferiore, stayed at the court on Ischia in 1527–1528 in the company of Vittoria Colonna and Costanza d'Avalos, where he composed his dialogue entitled *Dialogus de viris et feminis aetate nostra florentibus* [*Notable Men and Women of Our Time*].[61] It was Giovio who in January 1530 first showed Colonna's poetry to Pietro Bembo: Bembo then wrote enthusiastically to Colonna to say how much he had appreciated her work.[62] She took the initiative from that point in establishing a poetic correspondence with Bembo, the proclaimed master of the lyric genre. In April 1530 Colonna sent him her sonnet "Ahi quanto fu al mio Sol contrario il fato!" (A1:71), in which she admonished Bembo for never having written any poems in memory of her dead husband Ferrante d'Avalos. In May, Bembo replied *per le rime* with the sonnet "Cingi le costei tempie de l'amato."[63]

In this letter to Giovio, who acted for a time as intermediary in the correspondence between the two poets, Colonna comments with great skill and acuity on Bembo's poem. The poet, she says, shows himself to be superior to all others, but not due to his careful lexical choices nor his shrewd and profound concepts—that is to say, not due to the content of his work. Colonna's attention is rather drawn to deeper stylistic questions: the naturalness of the long syntactic blocks

60. Original, autograph: BAM, Fondo H 245 inf., fols. 1r-v and 2v: Colonna, *Carteggio*, no. XLI.

61. Giovio, *Notable Men*.

62. Colonna, *Carteggio*, no. XL.

63. Pietro Bembo, *Prose e rime*, ed. Carlo Dionisotti (Turin: UTET, 1960), no. 125. On Colonna's poetic exchanges in manuscript, see Brundin, "Vittoria Colonna in manuscript."

and of the rhyming words, dictated by the sonnet's status as a response *per le rime* (a response poem that follows the rhyme scheme of the original poem); the ordering of the subject matter; the poetry as *dispositio* (meaning the arrangement of words or themes) in which each single word is valued and exalted (the art of stringing pearls). Finally, her use of the expression "raising the verse," by which she seems to mean the art of increasing the tension and gravity of each line as it proceeds, especially if read in the light of a passage from Bembo's *Prose della volgar lingua* (*Discussions of the Vernacular Language*),[64] reveals Colonna as a reader who is attentive to the phonic potency of words. What she describes in this letter could well be applied to the stylistic qualities of her own *rime amorose* (amorous verse), which belong to the same orthodox Petrarchan canon (naturalness and harmony as prized qualities, carefully ordered verses, bi- and tripartite structures, juxtapositions, sparing use of enjambment and short phrases). This letter clearly sets out Colonna's deep theoretical understanding of the genre she practiced.

∽

Revered Signor,

I will not hide from you the fact that I lack adequate means to praise the divine sonnet by my dear friend Master Pietro Bembo. So having pondered whether I could rise to such a great challenge, I judge that silence is the best and truest way to praise it. Really it seems to me that in seeking to imitate in style the most praiseworthy writer in our language,[65] he has exceeded him. If you will excuse my lowly judgment, I say that I have never read a sonnet by another poet, either living or dead, which can be compared to this. I do not mean only the vocabulary chosen with such care or the new phrases that bend subtly without ever breaking: but my wonder is primarily at seeing how by constantly raising the verse he ends the clause so far from where he began, with no effort at all. In fact the endings seem to flow so naturally from his seamless prose that their beautiful, smooth harmonies can be heard in the soul before they chime in the ears. The more one reads and ponders them, the more they elicit admiration, or even envy, such that my intellect feels itself to be so unequal to that bright light that it shrinks from it, as incapable of emulating its perfection. Thus I have resolved that I am completely in love with him, nor do I care if you become the intermediary for this love that is entirely devoid of sensual desire, for neither

64. "Ma considerando egli [Petrarca] che questa voce *Ascoltate*, per la moltitudine delle consonanti che vi sono e ancora per la qualità delle vocali e numero delle sillabe, è voce molto alta e apparente, dove *Rime*, per li contrari rispetti, è voce dimessa e poco dimostrantesi, vide che se egli diceva *Voi ch'in rime*, il verso troppo lungamente stava chinato e cadente, dove, dicendo *Voi ch'ascoltate*, egli subitamente lo inalzava, il che gli accresceva dignità;" Bembo, *Prose e rime*, 2.8.

65. The reference is to Petrarch.

Master Pietro nor I will be hurt if you tell others of it, and my Sun[66] will also rejoice. May he continue to write, and trust that God will give him many more years of life; and jealous death, resolving not to harm him, will leave him be lest he fire his bow in vain. Others may possess beautiful words in great number, but large, bright pearls are useless if one does not know how to string them together, as he does, so that one pearl sets off the next. May Our Lord God grant me the opportunity to speak with him, and grant you happiness.

From Ischia, on the 24th day of June.
Signor, at your command,
The Marchioness of Pescara

On the reverse:
To the Revered Monsignor, Signor Paolo Giovio, Bishop of Nocera

⁓

[Letter 9]
Reverendo Signor,
A voi non asconderò io che me manca ogni modo per lodar el divin sonetto del mio messer Pietro Bembo. Et poi de ben pensato se potessi elevarmi a tanta luce, concludo che 'l silentio è la propria e vera laude che li conviene. Et veramente mi par che cercando egli imitar el più lodato autor dela nostra lingua nel scrivere, lo ha superato nelo stile. Et escusandomi prima col mio poco juditio, dico che io non leggo sonetto di niun altro, tanto de' presenti como de' passati, che a lui possa aguagliarsi. Non dirò de' vocaboli elettissimi, sententie nove e sottile senza spez-zarse, ma solo la mia maraveglia consiste in veder che alzando sempre el verso va a finir la clausola così lontana senza sforzo alcuno. Anzi par che le desinentie vengano sì necessarie ala ben ordita sua prosa che la bella et suave armonia loro prima si senta ne l'anima che ne l'orecchia. Et quanto più si rileggono et più spesso si considerano, maggior admiration porgono, anzi direi invidia, se non che 'l mio intelletto si sente sì improportionato a quel lume che non lo appetisce, como cosa dela cui perfetion non è capace. Sì che io ne risolvo che son totalmente inamorata de lui, né curo che voi siate el mezzo di questo amor fora de ogni sensual appetito, perché né messer Pietro né io ce dolerà che se ne facci istoria, et se ne alegrarà molto el mio sole. Scriva pur lui e creda che Dio li darrà molti altri anni de vita, et la invida morte, già resoluta che non lo offende, lo lassarà per non tirar el suo arco in vano. Habian pur gli altri belle parole e copiose, che poco giova haver candide

---

66. The designation *sole* (sun) is a metaphor used repeatedly in Colonna's *Rime* to refer to her deceased husband.

e grosse perle senza saperle infilar di modo che l'una favorisca l'altra como fa lui.
Nostro Signor Dio me conceda che possa parlarli et voi contenti.
De Yschia, a' dì XXIIII de giugno.

Signor, al vostro comando la
Marchesa de Pescara

A tergo
Al Reverendo Monsignor, il Signor Paulo Jovio, vescovo di Nocera

Letter 10: Ischia, 31 October [1531][67]
To Eleonora Gonzaga della Rovere

Among the many letters that Colonna sent to Eleonora Gonzaga (1493–1550), duchess of Urbino and wife of Francesco Maria I della Rovere (1490–1538), this one stands out as particularly unusual.

The first part of the document is quite standard, consisting of a letter of recommendation for the Archpriest of Rocca Guglielma: it was common practice at the time to offer a guarantee of the trustworthiness of the bearer of a message to its recipient. In the second part of the letter, however, we meet a new and unexpected version of Vittoria Colonna. Although she never gave birth herself, here she offers fulsome advice to the duchess, who had had many children, on how to ensure a safe delivery. Colonna knows that Eleonora has had difficult deliveries in the past, and therefore wishes to advise her with a view to protecting Eleonora's daughter, Ippolita della Rovere (1525–1561), who is about to marry Antonio d'Aragona, Duke of Montalto.[68] The wedding took place in early February 1532, which allows us to date this letter securely to 1531.[69] In letters exchanged in the months prior to this one, Colonna and the duchess discuss the details of the marriage contract.[70]

Similarly unexpected is Colonna's reference to the new spouse's sexual desires (what she terms, politely, his "anxiety"), mentioning that he is likely to find it difficult to hold off from consummating the marriage as soon as the ceremonies are completed.

---

67. Original, autograph: ASF, Ducato di Urbino, classe I, b. 266, fols. 129r–30v: Colonna, *Carteggio*, no. LV.

68. Antonio was the brother of Maria (wife of Alfonso d'Avalos) and of Giovanna (wife of Ascanio Colonna and therefore sister-in-law of Vittoria).

69. See Copello, "Aggiornamenti: Parte I," 95.

70. See Colonna, *Carteggio*, no. XLIX.

Far from the chilly and masculine character that history has assigned her, here we find Colonna enmeshed in women's networks and wholly engaged with women's issues.

∾

My Most Illustrious and Excellent Lady,
The archpriest of Rocca Guglielma,[71] long-standing servant of the Most Illustrious Duke's mother[72] and his family, has always wished to kiss Your Lord- and Ladyship's noble hands; and he has been kind enough to convey some information on my behalf directly to you. I beg you to place all your trust in him, and believe that I could never have found a better person to send you, nor one who was more sincere and affectionate. Your Most Illustrious Ladyship will ponder my intentions with your goodness and virtue, and believe that I will be happier knowing that both God and Your Lord- and Ladyship are well served. I only beg you to express your will without reservation, and may no one else know it except your Ladyship and the Most Illustrious Lord the Duke.

Don Antonio is here now, more handsome than ever, and completely devoted to the Lady Ipolita. He longs so ardently to go to her that it makes me very happy,[73] for although the marriage has been agreed for many reasons, it is a great pleasure that he understands them all, as he really does.

I give thanks to Our Lord God for I understand Your Ladyship is pregnant: may Our Lady in her mercy bring you a healthy male child.[74] And as I understand that Your Ladyship has had some difficulties with your labors in the past, it seems wise to take precautions for the Lady Ipolita. For although I do believe that nature and constitution play a large part in these things, nonetheless one should try anything that will not cause harm, and there have been many trials of this remedy and those who have used it have had easy labors. Since the treatment must be done before she sleeps with her husband, I have given the information to the Archpriest so that the Lady Ipolita can carry out the cure before My Lord don Antonio arrives, for once he is there with her, with the anxiety he has, it will be hard to hold him off for many days.

71. This rock dominates present-day Esperia, in the province of Frosinone in Lazio.

72. Giovanna da Montefeltro (1463–1513), daughter of Federico and therefore Vittoria Colonna's aunt.

73. Antonio d'Aragona was about to depart from Ischia, where he was born and raised, in order to travel to Pesaro, where he would celebrate his marriage.

74. Renewed wishes for a male child were expressed in a letter dated 10 November (Colonna, *Carteggio*, no. LVI, datable to 1532).

I kiss Your Ladyship's hands a thousand times, as do the Lady Marchioness and my Lady Victoria.[75] My Lord don Antonio will leave within eight days at most, although he wishes to fly to her; but in order for him to be healthy when he goes, the doctors made him wait.

From Ischia, on the last day of October.

Always dedicated to the service of Your Most Illustrious Ladyship,
The Marchioness of Pescara

On the reverse:
To my Most Illustrious Lady, her Ladyship [the duchess] of Urbino, most honored sister

∾

[Letter 10]
Illustrissima et Excellentissima Signora mia,
Lo arciprete della Rocca Guglielma, antico servitor della madre de l'Illustrissimo Signor Duca et suo, ha sempre desyderato andar a basar le man delle Signorie Vostre; et ad me è stato carissimo per farli intender alcune cose che lui li exsporrà da mia parte. La suplyco voglia darli integra fede, e creda che se persona de magior prezzo havessi possuta mandar, non la haveria trovata mai, né più sincera, né più affettionata. Vostra Signoria Illustrissima con la sua bontà et virtù consyderi la intention mia, et creda che de quello che Dio serrà più servito et le Signorie Vostre restarò io più contenta. Solo la prego che senza nisciuna reserva mostri la sua voluntà, et non lo intenda altra persona che Vostra Signoria et lo Illustrissimo Signor Duca.

Qua si trova el Signor don Antonio più bello che mai, tutto dedito alla Signora donna Ipolita; et tanto desydera venirsene che me ne alegro molto; che, ancor sia con infinite ragione, è gran piacer che le cognosca tutte, come veramente fa.

Rendo molte gratie a Nostro Signor Dio che intendo Vostra Signoria esser gravida: per sua clementia, Nostra Signora li conceda con salute el figlio maschio. Et perché ho inteso che Vostra Signoria ha hauto qualche volta dificil parto, me par bene che se remedii la Signora donna Ipolita. Et benché io non credo che sia se nno natura et complessione, puro quel che non noce et se nne sono viste molte exsperientie deve farse, che a quante se è fatto hanno hauto ottimo parto. Et perché bisogna farse prima che dorma col marito, ne ho data la informatione a l'arciprete

---

75. Maria d'Aragona, wife of Alfonso d'Avalos and Marchioness of Vasto, and Vittoria Colonna junior, daughter of Ascanio, who stayed with her aunt on Ischia until January 1535.

che possa la Signora donna Ipolita farlo prima che 'l Signor don Antonio arrive, che poi de arrivato, con la ansia che v'à, serrà dificil a tenerlo troppo dì.

Baso a Vostra Signoria mille volte le mano insieme con la Signora Marchesa et donna Victoria mia. El Signor don Antonio partirà fra otto giorni al più, benché lui voria volar; ma perché vada sano, li medici lo han fatto intertener.

Da Yschia, a' dì ultimo de ottobre.

Al servitio de Vostra Signoria Illustrissima
sempre deditissima,
La Marchesa de Pescara

A tergo
Ala Illustrissima Signora mia, la Signora [Duchess]a de Urbino sorella honorandissima

Letter 11: Ischia, 9 January [1532–1534][76]
To Bernardino Rota

The recipient of this letter is the young poet and Neapolitan nobleman Bernardino Rota (1509–1574), pupil of Marcantonio Epicuro (1472–1555), whose name also appears in the letter text. Colonna is not discussing poetry or other high-flown intellectual matters in this letter, however. The subject matter is far more prosaic, concerned with the economics of luxury—prices, quality, colors, size, workmanship—and the recipients of gifts.[77] With the mediation of Rota, Colonna is concerned with commissioning a case of perfumes in the shape of a colosseum, and she insists on its completion within a very tight timeframe. The letter, which is written entirely in Colonna's hand, seems to have been dashed off rapidly, evident

76. Original, autograph: BAM, Fondo E 32 inf., fols. 89r–90v: Colonna, *Carteggio*, no. LX. The editors of Colonna's *Carteggio* dated this letter to between 1525 and 1533. In 1525, however, Bernardino was only sixteen; Colonna then left Ischia until at least the summer of 1526. The Sack of Rome followed in 1527 and the siege of Naples in April 1528, in which Bernardino participated. It seems more likely that this urgent request for a box of perfumes dates to between the end of 1528 and 1534. Colonna left Ischia for good in January 1535; see Veronica Copello, "'La signora marchesa a casa': Tre aspetti della biografia di Vittoria Colonna: con una tavola cronologica," *Testo* 73 (2017): 31–45. Tobia R. Toscano, "Due 'allievi' di Vittoria Colonna: Luigi Tansillo e Alfonso d'Avalos," *Critica letteraria* 16 (1988): 747, proposes a more restricted dating, between 1532 and 1533, based on a letter from Colonna to Tommaso Tucca, dated 14 June 1534, in which Bernardino Rota again appears as the provider of perfumes: "Dite al Signor Belardino che non fe' la meglior polvere et muschio che me ha mandato, che Antonio doman li portarà el pagamento;" cited in Ranieri, "Censimento," S. 3, 7, no. 4 (1980–1981): 278–79, corrected here based on the manuscript conserved in ASM, Archivio Gonzaga, b. 1880, anno 1534.

77. Other references to Colonna's luxurious lifestyle—almost all pertaining to the period before her widowhood—include mentions of the clothing that she designed and wore at court festivities; for more details see Copello, "'La signora marchesa a casa.'"

in the messy handwriting, the contractions and the writer's insistence on the urgency of the commission.

From these lines emerges a rich list of names, of noblemen, poets, master craftsmen and servants, which helps to reveal the web of relations that Colonna sustained far beyond her intellectual and spiritual circles, a web that is only partially visible to us today but that must have formed the scaffold of her daily life.[78]

Bound together with this letter is a note in Colonna's hand addressed to Tommaso Tucca, mentioned in the letter to Rota. It reads: "Signor Tucca, May God forgive the man who failed to give you the other letter, that is to say, who lost it after the Marquis had given it to him, so that you thought I was being tardy. The other letter is on its way. May God make it work. I send my regards to Signor Bernardino Rota, and I will send him what I owe as soon as possible."[79] The little note offers a brief reminder of the letter writer's dependency on the trustworthiness of her message bearers.

～

Most Magnificent Signor,

I am causing you a thousand annoyances, but I will reward you with all my continued efforts. I still owe you for the perfumes and will send that as soon as possible. I would like to have someone make me a case about the size of three hands[80] as quickly as possible, and I want it in the form of a colosseum, all white colonnades, with crowns and capitals all around and all gilded wherever it can be. But please do it as soon as you can, by Monday or Tuesday, because the Viceroy is going to Vico.[81] But don't tell a soul about it, not even Tucca.[82] And don't ask me for any more detail but just have

---

78. The relationship between the characters mentioned here—Bernardino Rota, his brother Ferrante, Epicuro, Alfonso d'Avalos—is confirmed by Scipione Ammirato: "Il Signor Ferrante Rota, fratello del Signor Belardino, facea il medesimo tempio, ma con queste parole: *nos aliam ex aliis*, cioè, noi acquistiamo altra fama da altre fiamme. Fu il concetto, e l'impresa del Signor Antonio Epicuro, eccellentissimo in questa sorte d'invenzioni; il lavoro della patena fu di Geronimo Santacroce . . . , di tanta bellezza, che fu donata dal Signore Alfonso Rota [altro fratello] all'Illustrissimo Signor Marchese del Vasto per una delle più belle cose di quei tempi;" Bernardino Rota, *Delle poesie del signor Berardino Rota cavaliere napoletano*, ed. Scipione Ammirato, 2 vols. (Naples: Gennaro Muzio, 1726), 1:178–79.

79. "Signor Tucca. Dio perdoni a chi non li dette l'altro, per dir meglio, a chi la perse quando el Signor Marchese ce lla dette, che me haverete tenuta per tarda. Va l'altra. Dio faccia che faccia effetto. Al Signor Belardin Rota me recomando, et li mandarò subito lo che li devo."

80. The letter does not in fact specify the precise measurement but only states, "about the size of three."

81. The Viceroy refered to here is either Pompeo Colonna (who was Viceroy from 1530 to 1532) or Pedro de Toledo (Viceroy from 1532 to 1553). Vico is probably present-day Vico Equense, south of Naples on the Sorrento peninsula.

82. This is a reference to Giovanni Tommaso Tucca, who appears elsewhere in Colonna's letters: see *Carteggio*, no. XXXIV and no. LXI. He was in service to the duke of Mantua, Federico Gonzaga, and recommended Epicuro to the duke; see Alessandro Luzio and Rodolfo Renier, "Cultura e relazioni

it made it as quickly as possible. And have it filled with the usual perfumes, all done in white. And since they are in a great hurry, make the items inside very small—that is the glass bottles and other things—maybe you can even get them ready-made. Anyway, I leave it all to you, just make sure it's beautiful, and I want to spend thirty scudos: it has to pass muster, you see, with my Lord the Marquis[83] and some other fine gentlemen. Since Master Tomas Cambio[84] gave that craftsman 15 or 20 scudos on behalf of Her Ladyship the Marchioness of Vasto[85] for a case in the form of a labyrinth, but it was never made, she is content for the outstanding sum to go towards my own case, for which I will repay Her Ladyship, and I will send the remainder along with what I owe you as soon as you let me know it is due. I hope you can get this done in time, by Thursday at the very latest. I beg you, let me know as soon as possible, and be as quick as you can. And if you think it should look like a temple instead of a colosseum that will be fine, just as long as there are lovely columns, richly wrought: you and my Epicuro can judge what should best be seen between the columns.[86] Without further reply make sure they work on it night and day, although not on holy days. I remain at your command and do just as I have instructed you, and tell me straight away if I should send the rest of the money now and I'll send it over to you immediately.

From Ischia, on the VIIII day of January.

At your command,
The Marchioness of Pescara

On the reverse:
To the Most Magnificent Signor, Signor Bernardino Rota, my dearest friend

Signor Tomas Cambio, please deliver this straight away to Signor Ferrante Rota[87]

---

letterarie di Isabella d'Este," *Giornale storico della letteratura italiana* 40 (1902): 302 and 316. He also probably worked for Alfonso d'Avalos, whom he followed to Milan; see Aron di Leone Leoni, *La nazione ebraica spagnola e portoghese di Ferrara, 1492–1559: I suoi rapporti col governo ducale e la popolazione locale ed i suoi legami con le nazioni portoghesi di Ancona, Pesaro e Venezia*, 2 vols. (Florence: Olschki, 2011), 2:677.

83. Alfonso d'Avalos, Marquis of Vasto. The "scudos" refered to are silver coins used in various Italian states in this period.

84. A Florentine merchant, he was forced to move to Naples after being accused of murder. He worked as Vittoria Colonna's agent, but Paolo Giovio also employed him; see T. C. Price Zimmermann, *Paolo Giovio: Uno storico e la crisi italiana del XVI secolo* (Cologno Monzese: Polyhistor, 2012), 156–57.

85. Maria d'Aragona, from 1523 wife of Alfonso d'Avalos, marquis of Vasto. She was born and raised on Ischia.

86. The poet Marcantonio Epicuro, a literary role model for Bernardino Rota.

87. Bernardino's brother, Ferdinando (Ferrante) Rota, was president of the Regia Camera in 1535, 1542, and 1543; he was lord of Riscioli and Marano, acquired from Fabrizio Colonna, Vittoria's father;

∾

[Letter 11]
Molto Magnifico Signor,
Io ve do milli fastidii, ma ve lli satysfarrò con ogni mia possibil forza continuo. Ancor ve devo li profumi, et subito ve lli mandarò. Vorria che me facessino far una cascetta della grandezza delle tre, ma più presto più che manco, et che fosse ad modo de coliseo, tutto a colonnati bianchissimi, et le corone, capitelli et intorno et tutto, dove se pò, molto dorato. Ma che se facessi sì presto che fosse fatta lunedì o martedì, che 'l Vyrrey va ad Vico. Ma che non lo sapessi né Tucca né persona del mondo. Et non me domandati più parere, ma fate prestissimo. Et dentro tutta piena de profumi mediocli ma lavorati bianchi. Et perché hanno grandissima prescia, fate che dentro siano minuti, dico le carafelle et altro, che forsi se trovarano fatti. Puro tutto remetto ad voi, puro che sia bellissima, et ce vorria spender trenta scuti; vedite che s'à da star al juditio del Signor Marchese et de altri boni. Et perché messer Tomas Cambio dette a questo mastro XV o XX scuti in nome della Signora Marchesa del Vasto per una cascetta ad modo de laberinto, et non se è fatto, ditta Signora se contenta che se mettano in questa cascetta mia, ch'io ly satysfarrò a Sua Signoria, et li restanti mandarò insiemi con li vostri, subito el me advisate. Che 'l se possa fare in ditto tempo, cioè per tutto giovedì. De gratia, advisatemene subito subito, et fatice dar una gran prescia. Et se nne par che sia in modo de templo, fatelo, puro che siano belle colonne, et ricca, et tra l'une et l'altre si veda quello che pare ad voi et al mio Epicuro. Senza più replica fate lavorar dì et notte, ma non le feste. Resto al comando vostro, et sya como in voi confydo, et advisateme subito se sse bisogna mandar mo lo resto, che lo mandarò volando.
Da Yschia, a' dy VIIII de gennaro.

Al comando vostro, la
Marchesa de Pescara

A tergo
Al Molto Magnifico Signor, el Signor Belardino Rota, mio amico carissimo

Signor Tomas Cambio, de gratia subito mandatela al Signor Ferrante Rota

---

see Lorenzo Giustiniani, *Dizionario geografico-ragionato del Regno di Napoli*, vol. 8 (Naples: Vincenzo Manfredi, 1804), 15–16.

Letter 12: [Genazzano, before 14 August 1535][88]
[To Ambrogio Recalcati][89]

The Capuchin Order was first established as a branch of the Franciscan Order of Friars Minor, on the initiative of two men, Matteo da Bascio and Ludovico da Fossombrone. In its early years, the Capuchin Order frequently came under attack, and Vittoria Colonna was such a fierce defender of theirs that she earned the title "mother of the Capuchins:"[90] she interceded personally on behalf of the new Order with popes and cardinals, and also wrote countless letters soliciting the support of powerful prelates and politicians.[91]

This letter is an example of Colonna's epistolary work on behalf of the Capuchin Order, and showcases four qualities that define that work. The first is the expertise with which she is able to cite details from the Order's history: with almost legalistic accuracy, she lines up all the proofs she needs in order to convince her interlocutor. The second notable quality is her sense of irony, evident in the harsh judgments she is prepared to make about even the highest ecclesiastical

88. Original, autograph: AAV, Concilio Tridentino, vol. XXXVII, fols. 182r–83r: Colonna, *Carteggio*, no. LXII. We have adopted the date proposed in Colonna's *Carteggio* as well as by D'Alençon, *Tribulationes*, rather than the one proposed, the beginning of January 1535, in Bartolomeo Fontana, "Documenti vaticani di Vittoria Colonna, marchesa di Pescara per la difesa dei Cappuccini," *Archivio della società romena di storia patria* 9 (1886): 354. Colonna was in Genazzano in that period.

89. It was previously thought that the recipient of this letter was Cardinal Gasparo Contarini, since the manuscript is kept together with a group of other letters sent to him (but among the four letters from Colonna in the collection, one is addressed to Pope Paul III); see Fontana, "Documenti vaticani," 355–56, and Cargnoni, *I frati cappuccini*. 2:193–95. As the editors of Colonna's *Carteggio* noted, however, the usual address used by Colonna for cardinals was "Illustrissimo e Reverendissimo Monsignor mio observandissimo" (with minor variations), while the address "Reverendissimo Monsignor mio" is similar to that used for Ambrogio Recalcati; see the letters edited in Tacchi-Venturi, "Vittoria Colonna, fautrice," 174–77. Pietro Tacchi-Venturi was the first to suggest that this letter was addressed to Recalcati; see "Vittoria Colonna e la riforma cappuccina," 35. We know that Contarini, nominated cardinal in May 1535, did not arrive in Rome until September of that year; see Walter Friedensburg, "Der Briefwechsel Gasparo Contarinis mit Ercole Gonzaga nebst einem Briefe Giovanni Pietro Carafas mitgeteilt," *Quellen und Forschungen aus italienischen Archiven und Bibliotheken* 2 (1899): 165. It therefore seems "non troppo naturale che da lui, lontano e appena entrato nel sacro collegio, Vittoria potesse sperare appoggio per i suoi protetti;" Colonna, *Carteggio*, 94. Ambrogio Recalcati was the powerful secretary of state to Pope Paul III from 1534 to 1537, and became apostolic protonotary in 1536; see Amadio Ronchini, "Mons. Ambrogio Recalcati," *Atti e memorie delle deputazioni di storia patria per le provincie dell'Emilia*, 2 (1877), 69–79.

90. For more information on Colonna's relations with the Cappuchins, see Tacchi-Venturi, "Vittoria Colonna e la riforma cappuccina;" Cargnoni, *I frati cappuccini*, vol. 2; Ranieri, "'Si san Francesco fu eretico;'" Veronica Copello, "Nuovi elementi;" and Liguori, "Vittoria Colonna."

91. Colonna's correspondence concerning the Capuchins is collected in Cargnoni, *I frati cappuccini*, vol. 2.

authorities.[92] The third is her insistence on truth: he "who has a greater under-standing and sees the truth more clearly, is more obliged to speak it without fear." Colonna's determination to speak truth to power is a defining characteristic of her many battles against authority: whether on behalf of the Capuchins, for the restitution of Colle S. Magno (see Letters 7 and 13), or for the rights of the house of Colonna.[93] Just as she demanded of herself all possible effort in defense of what she believed to be right, so she invited her interlocutors to offer the same: "Your Most Revered Lordship must fight for the servants of the Lord."

The fourth and final quality is Colonna's constant recourse to a higher authority in all her work: the Capuchins were born of God's will, and therefore opposition to the order "allows the devil to get his way against God," and is "a great disservice to God." The power of Colonna's eloquence is testified to by Gian Matteo Giberti, who when he was invited by Colonna to defend the Capuchins, wrote the following words to Cardinal Ercole Gonzaga: "I beg your Lordship to embrace her with words and deeds. . . . The Capuchin cause is so very close to her heart, and I will not take the time to declaim her honesty because, if it is not clear in itself, the Lady Marchioness knows how to express it so well that she could convince not only your Lordship . . . but even someone who was utterly opposed to the cause."[94]

❧

My Most Revered Monsignor,
Christ and Paul understood divine law better than Bartolo and Baldo did,[95] therefore Your Most Revered Lordship must fight for the servants of the Lord. I have learned that they mean to rule that friars may join the order *licentia obtenta*.[96] This would be

---

92. See the letter to Pope Paul III in Cargnoni, *I frati cappuccini*, 2:200–208 and Letter 17.

93. See Copello, "Vittoria Colonna a Carlo V."

94. "Prego et supplico Vostra Signoria che la voglia abbracciare con parole et opere . . . strettissima la causa de li Padri Cappuccini, non mi estendendo a dichiarare la honestà di essa perché, se non fosse da sé chiara, la Signora Marchesa la sa sì ben esprimere che non solo Vostra Signoria, . . . ma moveria uno che ne fusse alienissimo;" Verona, 12 December 1535; ASM, Archivio Gonzaga, b. 1904, fol. 266r. In the same period, Ambrogio Recalcati was also consulted by those who were supporting the reform of the Observants, as we learn from a letter from Gian Pietro Carafa, bishop of Chieti and future Pope Paul IV, to Francesco Vannucci in Rome, 15 July 1535; see Edouard D'Alençon, "Gian Pietro Carafa vescovo di Chieti e la riforma nell'Ordine dei Minori dell'Osservanza," *Miscellanea francescana* 13 (1911): 134.

95. Bartolo da Sassoferrato and Baldo degli Ubaldi, famous fourteenth-century jurists. The former wrote the *Minoricas decisiones super regulam fratrum minorum* in 1353; see D'Alençon, *Tribulationes*, 46–47.

96. On 18 May 1526 Matteo da Bascio and Ludovico da Fossombrone obtained permission to leave their monastery in order to embark on a stricter form of Franciscan life; they were allowed to wel-come other friars only by asking the permission of their superiors (termed *licentia petita*); and it

a door even more firmly closed than before, because when these poor souls faced so much hostility and opposition the license was returned to the pope,[97] which was a very bad outcome. Now how much worse will it be, as they are returned under the rule of those who wish to imprison and ruin them? If they say *petita*, as in the chapter on the rule *Licet*,[98] and as Pope Eugene's bull[99] and all the laws state, then this would be a tolerable outcome, although still damaging given the widespread ill-feeling towards them; but saying *obtenta* really allows the devil to get his way against God. Just as with their obedience and their habit, which were granted ten years ago in Pope Clement's bull,[100] why must they say "Wait until the Chapter, to produce a document,"[101] if there has never been any document on the matter? It is enough to state clearly, in order not to cast sure things into doubt, that it would be an injustice, like saying to someone: "You may possess your house only until such a time." Therefore Your Most Revered Lordship, who has a greater understanding and sees the truth more clearly, is all the more obliged to speak it without fear; for there is a real danger of doing harm to a thousand good souls, and even to all of the order. Despite our great hopes the Observants have never reformed; instead, every day they move further towards ruin. If they could only see that in truth their friars must be provided with the means to live virtuously if they want to hold on to the best of them, then they would be forced to so provision them, whereas as things now stand they destroy them, trample them underfoot, and in every way they do God a great disservice. And therefore a just conclusion would be to observe Pope Clement's bull

---

was not necessary for permission to be granted (termed *licentia obtenta*) in order for new friars to join the Order; see Michael Wickart, ed., *Bullarium Ordinis FF. Minorum s.p. Francisci Capucinorum, seu Collectio bullarum, brevium, decretorum, rescriptorum oraculorum, &c. quae à Sede apostolica pro Ordine capucino emanarunt*, vol. 1 (Rome: Typis Joannis Zempel austriaci prope Montem Jordanum, 1740), XV Kal. Junii Clem. p.p. VII pont. a. 3, 18 May 1526. In 1534 the newly elected Pope Paul III abolished the privilege granted by his predecessor and forbade the Capuchins from admitting any new friars to the Order until the general Chapter, which was due to be held at Pentecost in 1535. This prohibition was moderated in early 1535 and in August 1535 all Franciscans were permitted to join the order, although Observants still required special permission; see Tacchi-Venturi, "Vittoria Colonna e la riforma cappuccina," 34.

97. See the papal briefs of Clement VII dated 9 April 1534 and of Paul III dated 14 August 1535.

98. *Caput* 18 of the *Decretali di Gregorio IX*, libro III, tit. 31; see Tacchi-Venturi, "Vittoria Colonna e la riforma cappuccina," 36.

99. Pope Eugene IV issued a bull on 11 January 1445 which allowed the Observants to receive Conventuals into the Order as long as they had requested permission from their superiors.

100. This is the papal bull of 3 July 1528, which refers to the friar's habit: "habitu vestro semper retentor."

101. With his brief of 18 December 1534, Pope Paul III forbade the Capuchins from accepting Observants into the order without his special authorization until the time of the Chapter (council), referred to here. The Chapter was due to take place at Pentecost 1535 (the seventh Sunday after Easter), and aimed to undertake the reform of the Observants.

in other matters, and in this matter of entry [to the Capuchin order] to use *licentia petita*, as the Chapter on *Licet* requires, even if this is somewhat risky.

Servant of Your Most Revered Lordship,
The Marchioness of Pescara

Your Most Revered Lordship knows that saying *licentia ottenta* is equivalent to excommunicating all virtuous souls from this time forward. Your Lordship should think about how it will play out to excommunicate all those who wish to do good, and it will seem thus, above all in God's hearing. Ruling *petita* is already excessive, since they will immediately imprison any who request it, but *ottenta* is another matter entirely. To date the worst thing that has been written against them was ruling that they could not join till Pentecost,[102] when they would be reformed, and now that much more clarity has been achieved about them, they are treated worse than ever. Think, Your Lordship, what a mistake this is! May Our Lord God allow you to state all that I know you wish to, yet God's immense bounty did not grant them a papal audience that day because they thought better of it, and they knew that there would be no end to the bull, and *licentia ottenta* has never been ruled. And if the chapter *Licet* could be produced against them, they would have closed their mouths a thousand years ago. Why must they say *ottenta* to some when we know it can never be obtained?

∾

[Letter 12]
Reverendissimo Monsignor mio,
Della legge divina s'intese più Christo e Paulo che Bartolo et Baldo, però Vostra Signoria Reverendissima bisogna pugni per li servi del Signore. Intendo pensano dire che possan venire i frati *licentia obtenta*. Questo seria una porta più chiusa che fusse mai perché, quando questi poverini hebbero tutti i desfavori et le desgratie se remetteva la licentia al Papa, et hera malissimo. Hor quanto peximo seria remetterla a chi l'incarcera e li ruina? Se dicesse *petita* come el capitulo *Licet*, la bolla eugeniana et ogni legge vole, serria comportabile, benché puro dannoso per l'odio che li mostrano; ma *obtenta* è far proprio ottener al demonio contra Dio quel che vole. Similmente de l'obedientia e de l'abito, che ne sono in possessione X anni con la bolla de Clemente, che bisogna dir "sin a conciglio, per scrittura," se mai scrittura in ciò s'è fatta? Basta dirlo a parole, per non metter le cose certe in dubio, che seria una iniustitia, como se sse dicesse a uno: "Possedi la tua casa sin al tal tempo." Sì che Vostra Signoria Reverendissima, che ha più consientia et vede più la verità, è più obligato dirla senza respetti: che è un periculo de far danno a mille anime bone, immo danno a tutta la religione; che con queste provate speranze

---

102. Colonna is referring here to the pope's brief of 18 December 1534. See note 96 to this translation.

mai quelli se emendano, anzi ogni dì se ruinano; che, se vedessero che in verità li bisogna proveder de comodità de ben vivere a' frati loro per detener i boni, serrian forzati a farlo, che così li abbatteno, li conculcano, et se fa da ogni banda summo deservitio a Dio. Et però serria assai iusta conclusione che nelle altre cose se observasse la bolla de Clemente et nel venire *licentia petita*, come vole el capitulo *Licet*, benché sia pur con periculo.

Serva de Vostra Signoria Reverendissima,
La Marchesa de Pescara

La Signoria Vostra Reverendissima sa che tanto è a dir *licentia ottenta* quanto scomunicar da mo tutt'i boni. Pensi Vostra Signoria como sonaria bene che scomunicassero quelli voglion far bene, et così è questo, maxime a l'orecchia divina. È troppo dir *petita*, che subito l'incarcerano, ma *ottenta* non se è ditto mai. Immo la peggio scrittura contra questi fu che quelli non venissero sin al Spirito Santo, sin che se reformavano, et che addesso, poi de dato tanto lume de loro, se lli facesse peggio che mai. Pensi Vostra Signoria che errore! Nostro Signor Dio li faccia dir quel che so che vorria, che però la immensa bontà de Dio non li fece haver audientia quel dì perché ce pensassero meglio, et sapessero che mai se prefisse tempo alla bolla, né se disse *licentia ottenta*; et se 'l capitulo *Licet* se potesse allegar contra questi, milli anni sono che li haverian chiuso la bocca. Che bisogna dir *ottenta* a quello che se sa non se pò ottenere?

Letter 13: Rome, 10 June [1536][103]
To Costanza d'Avalos del Balzo

As seen in Letter 7, Colonna had taken to heart the cause of the restitution of the castle at Colle S. Magno to the Abbey of Montecassino, and since 1525 she had been petitioning Costanza and Alfonso d'Avalos to submit to the final will of her husband. Her letters on this topic are repetitive, both linguistically and in terms of content. Yet the repetition, which continues over a period of fifteen years from 1525 to 1540, is really a form of fervent insistence ("I have written many times to your Ladyship and to the Marquis;" "Often have I written to your Ladyship;" "Many times have I written to the Princess and to your Ladyship").[104] Each time she writes, Colonna patiently retraces the various stages of the legal battle.

103. Original, autograph: AAM, caps. LXVII, fasc. XVIII; Copy: the same, fol. 7r–v; Copy: the same, fol. 80r–v; Copy: BAV, Ferr. 433, fols. 47v–48r: Colonna, *Carteggio*, no. LXIX. The year 1537, which is written on the *verso* of this letter, cannot be correct as Colonna was in Ferrara by May 1537. Müller and Ferrero hypothesized that this letter must date from 1536, as Colonna was definitely in Rome in the month of June; see Colonna, *Carteggio*, 106.

104. "Io ne ho scritto molte volte a Vostra Signoria et al Signor Marchese;" "molte volte ho scritto a Vostra Signoria;" Colonna, *Carteggio*, no. LXXII; "molte volte ho scritto alla Signora Principessa et a

For many years, Alfonso and Costanza passed the responsibility from one to the other, or blamed a third party—Giacomo Nomicisio,[105] or the vassals at the castle who did not want to come under the control of the monks. Colonna was caught in the middle, trying to instill reason in all parties, and above all appealing to their consciences. Thus in this letter she invites her powerful relations to shoulder their own responsibilities and points out their dissembling behavior: their ostentatious concern for the vassals is just an excuse not to give up the Colle. Its restitution, on the other hand, would fulfil two fundamental obligations: dignity and justice. Renouncing the second of these would require "accounting to God." She also succeeds in raising the stakes: this is not just an administrative or political matter: it concerns a question of justice. To prove this, Colonna never tires of repeating to her correspondents the truth of the matter as she sees it.

Colonna was quite right in saying that in this matter she "did all she could." Along with her dogged correspondence she also paid fifty ducats a year from her own pocket for more than ten years, as well as offering herself as guarantor, intermediary and temporary proprietor of the Colle. Her obstinacy got her nowhere: the matter was not finally resolved until the end of the nineteenth century.[106]

◆

My Most Illustrious Lady,

Even though so much has been done, in the days when my late lamented husband was alive and ever since, to resolve things at the Colle, they have continued to savage each other like dogs. And now that their souls are so burdened with the wrongs that have been done to them by the bad management of those in charge, so many more have died that I suffer greatly for it. I fear that it has certainly never pleased God that it was under our control. I have written about this many times to Your Ladyship and to the Marquis.[107] I have done what I can, and the agreement to pay them fifty ducats a year was all my work.[108] Now, for the love of God, for such a miserable sum! As God gives so generously to the Marquis, may you not seek to draw out these troubles, but end them. You know well that the Marquis of Pescara took the cause to heart, so too the Marquis of Vasto; and Your Ladyship has always spoken the right words, but the deed has not followed because you bow to the will of the vassals, who would never say that the castle must be returned, and in truth it is not in their power to say so. It is up to Your Lordships to do your duty to God, above all now that the pity you

---

Vostra Signoria;" Colonna, *Carteggio*, no. CXVII.

105. "Se Vostra Signoria se recorda, ne lli ho parlato doi volte, et se è remesso alla Signora e Iacobo;" Colonna, *Carteggio*, no. LXXXII.

106. See Copello, "Un problema."

107. Alfonso d'Avalos, marquis of Vasto.

108. This is the document edited in Colonna, *Carteggio*, no. XXXIX.

had for the vassals is no longer relevant as most of those who were opposed are no longer among us. I wanted once again to make this final attempt to tell you the truth. I beg you to send this letter to the Marquis. Nor can you say: "You only say this now that you are going abroad."[109] I have always said the same thing, in fact I have already paid out far more than the castle is worth. May Our Lord God keep Your Ladyship.

From Rome, on the tenth day of June.

Always in service to Your Most Illustrious Ladyship,
The Marchioness of Pescara.

The widespread belief that our estates are being abandoned has caused everyone to lose all trace of obedience, so I have sent Signor Juan Batista Conte there: I hope he will be able to calm things down, although the rest is very calm. Still it would be good if these things could quickly be resolved in Naples.

On the reverse:
To my Most Illustrious Lady, my Lady the Princess of Francavilla

❧

[Letter 13]
Illustrissima Signora mia,
Per molto che in tempo della felice memoria del Signor mio et poi continuo se sia fatto per quietar el Colle, sempre se sono amazzati como cani; et hora, per haver trovati gravidi li animi loro per li error fatti col mal governo delli uffitiali, se ne sono morti tanti che ne ho un dolor excessivo. Temo certo sia che mai ha piaciuto a Dio sia in poter nostro. Io ne ho scritto molte volte a Vostra Signoria et al Signor Marchese; ce feci quanto posseva, et la convention de darli cinquanta ducati l'anno, fui io. Hor, per amor de Dio, per una miseria! Poi che Dio usa sì larga la sua mano col Signor Marchese, non vogliate stare in questo affanno, ma fornitela. Sa che 'l Marchese de Pescara se ne fe' consientia, questo del Vasto pur così; et Vostra Signoria sempre ha parlato bene, ma non segue lo effetto, perché se remetteno a' servitori, quali mai dirriano che un castello se restituisse, e in vero non è uffitio loro. Tocca alle Signorie Vostre determinarse al servitio de Dio, maxime che la piatà che haveva de' vaxalli non ce è più, che quasi tutty quelli che non volevano non ce sono. Io ho voluto de novo far questo ultimo uffitio de dirli el vero. La suplico mandi questa proprio al Signor Marchese. Né si pò dir: "Tu lo

109. Colonna was probably already planning her pilgrimage to Jerusalem, which would begin in May 1537 and end in Ferrara much too soon, in June of the same year.

dici mo che lassi lo stato." Io lo ho ditto sempre, immo ho pagato più che 'l castello non vale. Et Nostro Signor Dio guardi Vostra Signoria. Da Roma, a' dì X de giugno.

Al servitio de Vostra Signoria Illustrissima sempre,
La Marchesa de Pescara

Questo intender che 'l Stato se lassa ha fatto perder in tutto la obedientia. Ce ho mandato el Signor Juan Batista Conte: spero quietarà ogni cosa, benché el resto sta quietissimo. Puro serria bene che presto se resolvessero in Napoli.

A tergo
Ala Illustrissima Signora mia, la Signora Principessa de Francavilla

Letter 14: Monte San Giovanni Campano, 22 April 1537[110]
To Ercole Gonzaga

Ercole Gonzaga (1505–1563), son of the rulers of Mantua, Francesco II and Isabella d'Este, was a highly educated humanist who corresponded with some of the leading writers and thinkers of the age. He became a cardinal in 1527 and lived in and around Rome until 1537 when he returned to Mantua. There he began to study theology, grew passionate about the reform of the diocese, and was in close contact with the group of so-called Spirituals.[111]

This letter is entirely concerned with the friar Bernardino Ochino, a highly talented preacher, closely associated with the Spirituals, who became a Capuchin in 1534.[112] The year after this letter was written, in 1538, Ochino was elected Vicar General of the Capuchins, an office to which he was re-elected in 1541. But in 1542 he fled to Geneva in fear of the Inquisition, after refusing to obey a command from the pope to present himself in Rome.

Colonna first met Ochino in March 1535, and from that time she admired him as a model for the Christian life and followed him around central Italy in order to hear him preach till 1538. She described Ochino as the man in whom "the potent spirit of Christ is most alive." Significantly, she used the same expression to

---

110. Original, autograph postscript and signature: ASM, Archivio Gonzaga, b. 1906, fols. 706r–707v: Colonna, *Carteggio*, no. LXXXIII.

111. See in particular the letter from Ercole Gonzaga to Gasparo Contarini dated 6 June 1537: "Aspetto anco con grandissimo desiderio di intendere qualche cosa della vera riformatione; però V. S. me ne darà sempre aviso che haverà qualche cosa da poterlo fare, et non si scorderà di mandarmi quelli suoi opuscoli ultimamente composti, sicome mi promise di volere far al partir mio;" in Friedensburg, "Der Briefwechsel Gasparo Contarinis," 167.

112. On Ochino, see Camaioni, *Il Vangelo e l'anticristo*; Campi, "Vittoria Colonna and Bernardino Ochino."

describe Reginald Pole, who later replaced Ochino as Colonna's spiritual mentor (see Letter 35).

In this letter Colonna is seen operating at the center of a network of correspondence arriving from all over Italy to request a visit from Ochino to preach in particular Italian cities. The friar was widely admired, although already in 1536 accusations of heresy—inspired, according to Colonna, by "false jealousy"—were circulating. This early defense of Ochino's integrity, penned by Colonna some five years before his flight from Italy, is heartfelt: she describes the friar as a humble man, obedient to the Church and the pope, a brilliant preacher with the capacity to provide much "fruit" to save "so many souls" (see also Letter 15).

∾

My Most Illustrious, Revered, and Esteemed Monsignor,
Having now tried out Your Lordship's mule, I wish to thank you again for it is excellent and serves me very well.[113]

While I was in Arpino, Father Bernardino passed that way, where the letters (which I am attaching) from Don Ferrante reached him.[114] Since the Prince of Salerno[115] had a letter from Cardinal Sanseverino,[116] saying that His Holiness was content to allow Ochino to travel to Salerno at the Prince's request, he replied that he would be delighted to go to Sicily, but that His Holiness might do as he wants, as he must go where he has been instructed. The Marquis of Vasto also wishes very much to have him there, and it makes one appreciate the goodness of Your Lordships, since you and Don Ferrando are all content with this.

I must not forget to mention that I had a letter from a Spanish gentleman saying that, in the house of your friend the cardinal,[117] they had been glossing his

113. While the image of the refined Colonna riding a mule seems very odd, the reference here seems to be, literally, to the receipt of such an animal from Gonzaga.

114. Don Ferrante is Ferrante Gonzaga (1507–1557), son of Isabella d'Este and Francesco II Gonzaga, therefore brother of Cardinal Ercole, and viceroy of Sicily from 1535. The reference here is to his desire to have Ochino preach in Palermo, a desire which is also expressed in a letter from Nino Sernini to Ercole Gonzaga dated 1 June 1537 (edited in Luzio, "Vittoria Colonna," 33), and in a letter from Carlo Gualteruzzi to Colonna (Colonna, *Carteggio*, no. LXXXIV). Ochino preached in Palermo in 1540.

115. Ferrante Sanseverino (1507–1568), Prince of Salerno, was a soldier in the imperial army who took part in the siege of Tunis in 1535. His secretary was Bernardo Tasso, father of Torquato. In 1552 he opposed the introduction of the Spanish Inquisition into the Kingdom of Naples, and as a result, he was forced into exile in France.

116. Antonio Sanseverino, from Naples. He was one of six cardinals appointed to a commission by Pope Paul III to settle the dispute between the Capuchins and the Observant Franciscans and he took the side of the Capuchins with some vigor. In 1538 he was nominated papal legate to Rome on the occasion of Paul III's journey to Nice.

117. Colonna deliberately obscures the identity of this cardinal, almost as if adopting a coded language.

[Ochino's] holy words with falsehoods provoked by jealousy. I certainly believe this was not done at the behest of the cardinal, for I know that the Neros to whom God's light is hateful have not returned,[118] and that things can be misunderstood even where there are thousands of sincere witnesses. All the more so as so many of his sermons in Perugia and in Naples[119] have been written down by good men[120] and are so highly esteemed that in its arrant presumption envy consumes itself. As there is no other remedy than for him to remain silent,[121] the envy against him grows daily. Now that I am departing,[122] I ask Your Lordship to take over his defense against these accusations, not for his sake but for the benefit of so many souls, for, although there are others who preach, they do not move people's souls, so their sermons are not as effective as his (as we have seen). I think he will make for Rome now, although he is uncertain: for if he stays there, they will say that he seeks or desires greatness; but if in humility he goes out to preach, they will say that he is fleeing from Rome. He offers no excuses and says nothing, in order not to suggest that he thinks others are concerned with him, and his silence could be interpreted as presumption. They see that their repeated attacks have only served to make the powerful Spirit of Christ yet stronger, so now they seek to defame this light that we have; and thus the heretics scratch our eyes out, for as soon as Christ appears, like the Pharisees people revert to calumnies, to perverting words, and sowing hidden thorns.[123] I wanted to warn Your Lordship of this so that, where necessary, you can do your duty, as your virtue and goodness require of you. Thus if they cannot love him and honor him, as they have done in all the cities where he has preached, may they at least leave him to do his hard work of saving souls. You can see that he does this work most marvelously,

118. The reference is to the Roman emperor Nero, who persecuted Christians (because to him "God's light was hateful"); he and those like him, the other Neros, are long dead and no longer a threat.

119. Ochino had preached in Perugia and Naples the previous year (1536).

120. This is a glimpse of the manuscript circulation of Ochino's sermons, which had not yet been printed by this date.

121. Colonna means that the only cure for the envy of others would be for Ochino to cease preaching altogether.

122. Colonna intended to set out on her pilgrimage to the Holy Land (see Letter 15), but only got as far as Ferrara.

123. See Genesis 3:17–18, in which Adam and Eve are cast out of the Garden of Eden and thorns and thistles grow up as a result of their sin. Colonna wrote in a similarly strong vein to Pope Paul III and to the commission of cardinals who were asked to mediate in the dispute between the Capuchins and the Observants: "Ma me dole de quelli che in tanta *luce* son cechi, et che tante volte habiano hauta *invidia* a quelli che servirono Cristo in terra; et ogni dì diciamo: 'Fortunati pastori, beati Magi, felice ab Arimathia, gloriossa Magdalena e Marta!,' e poy habiamo le cose de Cristo in terra chiare e vive, e la observantia dela sua evangelica vita, e le perseguitamo;" to Pope Paul III, Jan–Feb 1536; see Copello, "Aggiornamenti: Parte II," 115.

although I, sadly, have had no other consolation than to hear so many others tell me this.[124]

I am sending the attached letter to his Reverence, [the Cardinal] Santa Croce,[125] because God knows I have sometimes been critical of the outcomes of his actions, but never of his Reverence's person. I beg Your Most Revered Lordship to command that it be given to him.

From Monte San Joanni, on the twelfth day of April 1537.

Most dutiful servant of Your Most Illustrious and Revered Lordship,
the Marchioness of Pescara

On the reverse:
To my Most Illustrious, Revered, and Esteemed Monsignor, the Cardinal of Mantua
In another hand:
From the Marchioness of Pescara from Monte Joanne on the 22nd April, received on the 25th
From reserved letters received in Rome early in 1537

∽

[Letter 14]
Illustrissimo et Reverendissimo Monsignor mio observandissimo,
Poi de provata la mula de Vostra Signoria, me par ringratiarla de novo, che è bonissima et serve molto bene.

Essendo in Arpino, passò de llì il padre fra Bernardino et lì vennero le alligate del Signor don Ferrante. Et perché el Principe de Salerno hebe lettera dal Cardinal Sanseverino che se contentava Su Santità che a preghere de decto Principe andasse a Salerno, lui ha risposto che li seria molto caro andare in Sicilia, ma che Su Santità faccia lei, perché bisogna vadi dove li è comandato. Il Marchese del Vasto ancor molto lo desidera, sì che se vede sempre la bontà de le Signorie Vostre, che a lei como al Signor Don Ferrando piace.

Ma non lassarò dirli che un spagnolo me scripse che in casa del vostro Cardinale amico se andavano glosando de falsa invidia le sue sancte parole. Credo, certo, non con voluntà del decto Cardinale, perché so non son tornati li Neroni che 'l lume de Dio li sia odioso et che le cose ove son migliara de sinceri testimonii

---

124. By this date Colonna had only heard Ochino preach twice, once in San Lorenzo in Damaso in Rome during Lent 1535, and once in San Pio in Genazzano in June of the same year. In 1537 she would get the opportunity to hear him preach in Ferrara, and in 1538 in Pisa, Florence and Lucca.

125. Franciscos de los Ángeles Quiñones (1475–1540), cardinal of Santa Croce, protector of the Franciscan order.

se possano extorcere, tanto più che le sue prediche et in Perusa et in Napoli son state tanto scripte da boni et tanto estimate che è gran ardir che l'invidia confonda sé stessa, a la quale non c'è altro remedio che mancar de esser bono, però ogni dì crescerà in lui. Il quale mo che parto ricomando ad Vostra Signoria che da tante insidie lo difenda, non per sé, ma per il fructo de tante anime, che se ben altri predica, non moveno, non fanno la utilità de le sue (como se vede). Credo che andarà però verso Roma, benché stia perplexo: che, se sta, li dicono che cerca o desidera grandeze, se va humilmente predicando, dicono fuge Roma. Lui non se excusa né parla, per non mostrar credere che de lui se facci conto, et tanto tacere potria attribuirse a presumptione: vedeno che a le passate diverse insidie el potente Spirito de Christo se fa più vivo, cercano hor caluniar questo lume che havemo et de cqua nasce che li heretici ce cavan li occhi, perché, como Christo compare, a modo de Pharisei andamo a le calunnie, a pervertir le parole, a seminar occulte spine. Io ho voluto advisarne Vostra Signoria perché, ove bisogna, facci l'offitio che la sua virtù et bontà conviene: che almeno, se non lo amano et honorano, como ne le città ove non è passione han facto, almeno lo lasseno ne la sua fatigha salvar le anime. Il che se vede fa maravigliosamente, benché io per mia tristitia non ne habia hauta altra consolatione che de udirlo dire da infinite persone.

Scrivo la alligata al Reverendissimo Santa Croce, perché, como Dio sa, li effetti – et non Sua Santità – ho alcuna volta deslodati. Suplico Vostra Signoria Reverendissima ordini li sia data.

Dal Monte San Joanni, il dì XXII de aprile 1537.

Serva obligatissima de Vostra Illustrissima et Reverendissima Signoria,
La Marchesa de Pescara

A tergo
A l'Illustrissimo et Reverendissimo Monsignor mio observandissimo, il Cardinal di Mantua

Di altra mano
De la Marchesa di Pescara da Monte Ioanne di 22 aprile, ricevuto il 25

Di lettere reservate, principio del 1537, ricevute in Roma

Letter 15: Ferrara, 12 June [1537][126]
To Ercole Gonzaga

In the spring of 1537, Vittoria Colonna embarked on a pilgrimage to the Holy Land, which she recounts in the sonnet "Già si rinverde la gioiosa speme."[127] On March 13, she received permission from Pope Paul III to depart.[128] En route for the port of Venice, she stopped in Ferrara: "On the eighth day of May, the Marchioness of Pescara arrived in Ferrara dressed in humble clothing, and she said that she is heading for Jerusalem with only a small retinue, that is four or five modest women."[129] In Ferrara, Colonna met two of the companions of Ignatius of Loyola, Claudio Jay and Simón Rodríguez, who were themselves planning a journey to Jerusalem, and who received their own permission from the pope on 27 April. In Venice, Colonna was warmly awaited by Pietro Bembo, who wrote joyfully about her arrival (which never took place) to Carlo Gualteruzzi.[130] We learn from this letter that by 12 June the pilgrimage had already been postponed. The project ultimately failed, as Colonna wrote to the emperor on 6 December 1538: "For two years I was on the point of leaving for Jerusalem, more to get away from the confusion in Rome than for any other reason, but since I could not go I retired to Lucca, which seemed to me a place where one can serve Christ."[131]

Colonna's stay in Ferrara was a long and happy one, which is mentioned many times in subsequent letters.[132] There she enjoyed the "longed-for freedom to attend only to true charity," devoting her time—finally "mine alone," as she says—

---

126. Original, autograph: ASM, Archivio Gonzaga, b. 1906, fols. 661–62: Colonna, *Carteggio*, no. LXXXV.

127. S1:67; Colonna, *Sonnets*, 77.

128. See Colonna, *Carteggio*, no. LXXIX.

129. "A dì 8 di maggio è venuta a Ferrara la S[ignora] Marchesa di Pescara in abito rimesso, qual si dice nel andare in Gerusale con poco gente, cioè in 4 o 5 donne rimesse;" *Cronica Estense di Fr. Paolo da Lignago*, in Cargnoni, *I frati cappuccini*, 2:426. Colonna was presumably clothed in the penitent's rags suitable for a pilgrim.

130. "Della S.ra Marchesa di Pescara io non arei potuto intender cosa più casa che questa: che S.S. venisse qui. Et è cosa sì a me piacevole, che subito non abbia ad avere effetto, con ciò sia cosa che non mi soglion venir fatte le cose che io sommamente desidero. Faccia NO.S. Dio in ciò tutto quello che egli estima lo migliore. Io di nuovo l'aspetterò con sommissimo disiderio," 7 March 1537, in Bembo, *Lettere*, 4:27; and again, "Ho un'altra vostra del venerdì Santo. Alla quale non aviene che io risponda altrimenti, se non che io non veggo l'ora che la S.ra Marchesa sia qua; la quale mi dà l'animo di ritrovare. E venga per secreta e celata, se sa. Disidero grandemente che NO.S. rissolva dintorno alla bisogna. Se potete con quel modo spronar S.S. a ciò fare, a me fia molto caro;" 4 April 1537, in Bembo, *Lettere*, 4:30.

131. "Yo soi estada dos años por yrme en Jerusalem, más por quitarme d'esta confusion de Rome que por otra cosa, y no podiendo passar me firmé en Luca, paresciéndome lugar donde Cristo se puede servir;" in Copello, "Vittoria Colonna a Carlo V," 98–99.

132. See Targoff, *Renaissance Woman*, 132–43.

exclusively to the service of Christ. We know that the "true charity" to which Colonna refers focused on support for the foundation of a Capuchin convent,[133] and that she did not neglect her habit of dispensing donations among the poor of Ferrara.[134] She also came to know the Duchess Renée de France, sister-in-law of the king of France and known supporter of the reformer John Calvin (1509–1564), an association that deepened her understanding of reform. The final part of this letter is devoted to a defense of Bernardino Ochino. Ochino, the best preacher in all of Italy, is the victim of envy, as expressed also in the previous letter. The proof is the demand for his sermons all over Italy. Once again, Colonna is the facilitator of multiple requests for Ochino's presence. She hopes that he will travel to Mantua to preach, and knowing her own power, she suggests that she will "try to obstruct the others," that is, all those other cities that requested a visit from the preacher. Indeed, Ochino traveled to Mantua in 1539 and again in 1541.

When Letter 15 was written in 1537, Ochino was already a controversial figure. The postscript to Ercole Gonzaga's reply to this letter makes clear that he no longer wishes to discuss the friar in writing: "I did not make any reply in relation to our Brother Bernardino, about whom I have never had any doubts despite the bad things they say about him in Rome, as they do about everyone: but as to his circumstances I would not know what to do without speaking first with Your Illustrious Ladyship. Since to achieve this either I would have to come to you or you would need to make your way here, I will only say what seems to me true, which is that God will act here and elsewhere using him as his instrument."[135]

❧

My Most Illustrious, Revered, and Esteemed Monsignor,
My intention, as Your Most Revered Lordship knows, for I wrote to you about repaying the money, was to stop in Mantua since I could not for the time being continue to Jerusalem. However, I feared that many people would gather there for the Council,[136] so then I thought to stay in Venice while I could. But then it pleased God that I should find myself at peace and blessed in Ferrara, thanks be to God, where His Excellency

133. See Copello, "Nuovi elementi," 314–15.

134. See Colonna, *Carteggio*, no. XCVIII, and Letter 16.

135. "Non le ho risposto cosa alcuna intorno al nostro frate Bernardino, del quale non ho mai dubitato anchora che in Rome si dicessero di molte cianze, come si sole di ogni uno; ma quanto alli casi suoi non mi saprei risolvere, se non parlassi prima con V. Ill.ma S.; però dovendo essere questo o ch'io venga così o ch'ella si trasferischi qua, mi riserbo di dirle quanto mi parerà che Dio potrà operare qua et altrove per instrumento di lui;" Colonna, *Carteggio*, 146; Gonzaga's response to Colonna's letter was never sent.

136. The Council of Trent was originally convened in Mantua on 2 June 1536. Pope Paul III tried once again to establish Mantua as the location for the Council on 23 May 1537, with support from Cardinal Ercole, but he was once again unsuccessful.

the Duke[137] and everyone else allow me that longed-for freedom to attend only to true acts of charity and not to the polluted ones that are brought about by worldly interaction. May it please God that these hours that are mine alone may be spent such that none of them are mine, but all are Christ's.

My Lady the Duchess of Urbino[138] told me that Your Lordship is due to come here: I was delighted to hear it, to learn something about your good soul that has been so badly treated.

I wrote already to Your Lordship about the webs spun out of envy against Brother Bernardino, and since Your Lordship left immediately, I did not want there to remain any shadow in your mind concerning the light he has from God. I can tell you that from letters from many sources I understand he has been in Rome, and the pope and all good men showered him with praise for the honor he does the Church; now he departs with all possible blessings, but one could see envy sprouting from that marvelous fruit, etc. Today I have received the attached letter: so many people ask for him, and I want him there in Mantua, which seems to me to be a place where Your Lordship could help him to bring forth fruit. I pray you to let me know if you think you will do this work in the service of God, because if so I'll try in some way to obstruct the others.[139] No need to say any more: just let me know your opinion, and then God will send him wherever he can best serve Him. Do me the favor of telling the Duke and Madame that I kiss their hands, and may God who has opened your mind and softened your heart make it burn with the heat of his fire and be perfected by his grace.

From Ferrara, on the twelfth day of June.

Most dutiful servant of Your Most Illustrious and Revered Lordship,
The Marchioness of Pescara

On the reverse:
To my Most Illustrious, Revered, and Esteemed Monsignor, the Cardinal of Mantua etc.

In another hand:
From the Marchioness of Pescara, from Ferrara on 12 June, received on 15 June

❧

137. Ercole II d'Este (1508–1559).

138. Eleonora Gonzaga, daughter of Isabella d'Este and Francesco II Gonzaga, and thus niece of Cardinal Ercole to whom this letter is addressed.

139. The other individuals who were petitioning for Ochino to travel to their cities.

[Letter 15]

Illustrissimo et Reverendissimo Monsignor mio observandissimo,

La mia intentione, como Vostra Signoria Reverendissima sa, che li scrisse de quel remetter de denari, hera firmarme in Mantua non possendo per hora passar in Ierusalem. Poi, per timor che lì se congregasse molta gente per el Concilio, pensai stare in Venetia, finché posseva passare. Poi a Dio ha piaciuto che sia qui in Ferrara molto quieta e consolata, Dio gratia, perché la Excellentia del Duca e tutti me satysfanno della mia desiderata libertà de solo attender alle vere carità et non tanto misturate como quelle che se causano dalla conversatione. Piaccia alla bontà divina che queste hore tutte mie le spenda in modo che non ne sia nisciuna mia, ma tutte de Christo.

La mia Signora Duchessa de Urbino me disse che Vostra Signoria verria qui: l'ebbi molto caro per imparar dal suo bono et da lui maltrattato spirito alcuna cosa.

Scrissi a Vostra Signoria de quelle tele ordite dalla invidia contra el padre fra Belardino, e perché Vostra Signoria partì subito, non vorria rimanesse con qualche ombra contra la luce che lui ha da Dio. Li dico che per lettere de molti intendo che fu in Roma, e il papa e tutti i boni li ferno grandissime carezze, et che honora la Chiesia, che vada con tutta la beneditione possibile, che se vedeva dalli mirabil frutti nascer l'invidia, etc. Ogi me scrivono l'alligata, sì che molti el dimandano et io lo vorria lì in Mantua, che me pareria ove è Vostra Signoria l'aiutassi a far frutto. La prego me faccia intender se crede serria per farce opera in servitio de Dio, perché in qualche modo vederia de impedir l'altri. Ma non bisogna dirne altro: li basta me advisi el suo parere, et Dio lo mandarà ove più lo servirà. Facciame gratia dire al Signor Duca e Madama che li baso le mano, e quel Signor che li ha aperta la mente e molificato el core se degni farcelo arder del suo fuoco e perficer nella sua gratia.

Da Ferrara, a' dì XII de giugno.

Serva obligatissima de Vostra Signoria Illustrissima et Reverendissima,
La Marchesa de Pescara

A tergo
A l'Illustrissimo et Reverendissimo Monsignor mio observandissimo, el Signor Cardinal de Mantua etc.

Di altra mano
Della Marchesa di Pescara da Ferrara di 12 di giugno, ricevuta il 15

Letter 16: Ferrara, 6 November 1537[140]
To Pietro Aretino

There is a note of irony in the expression of haste with which Colonna writes to
Pietro Aretino in this letter ("I don't have time to reply now"). Only the day before,
the Tuscan poet and dramatist, famous for satirical and licentious literary works,
had sent Colonna a long letter full of praise for the Marchioness's "saintly fame,"
her dedication to the "study of Christ," and her ability to "transform poetic books
into prophetic volumes."[141] Refusing to be seduced by Aretino's rhetoric, Colonna
bluntly invited him to follow her in her chosen path, that is, in the composition
of spiritual literature. In his defense, Aretino cited economic necessity as well as
the expectations of his readership: "I do confess that I am less useful to the world
and less gracious to Christ in spending my time on deceptive tittle-tattle instead of
true works: but the cause is the pleasure of others as well as my own survival. If the
prices were as pious as I am needy, I would write nothing but *miserere*."[142] Only a
few years later, Colonna would issue similar invitations to Pietro Bembo, who had
just been made a cardinal (see the sonnet "Bembo mio chiaro, or ch'è venuto il
giorno"),[143] and to Luigi Alamanni. The latter wrote in Autumn 1539 to Benedetto
Varchi: "I am spending a lot of time with Cardinal Bembo . . . , and any remaining
hours I pass with the Marchioness of Pescara, who wishes to draw me onto her
own path. But for now I only think of remaining on the trail of my lady Beatrice."[144]

The second paragraph in this letter is concerned with the repayment of
sixty scudos that were owed to Aretino by Colonna's husband, Ferrante d'Avalos.
Giovan Battista Castaldo, faithful servant to d'Avalos, had written about the
matter to Aretino as early as 1534: "I don't neglect to assure you that the Lady
Marchioness of Pescara will do as she has promised you."[145] Seemingly actions did
not follow words, however. Thus in November 1536, Benedetto Varchi wrote to
his friend Francesco Maria Molza: "Finding myself at Pietro [Aretino]'s house, the
same, in the presence of various gentlemen . . . , after talk of other things, began to
speak of the Marchioness of Pescara, and to cut a long story short the upshot was

---

140. Original, autograph signature (?): ISGM, n. 34; Copy: BAV, Ferr. 886, fol. 144r; LSA 1551, II, p.
18: Colonna, *Carteggio*, no. LXXXVIII.

141. Colonna, *Carteggio*, no. LXXXVII. For Aretino see Raymond B. Waddington, *Pietro Aretino:
Subverting the System in Renaissance Italy* (Farnham, Surrey, UK– Burlington, VT: Ashgate, 2013).

142. Colonna, *Carteggio*, no. LXXXIX.

143. "Bembo mio chiaro, or ch'è venuto il giorno / Ch'avete solo a Dio rivolto il core, / Deh rivolgete
ancor la musa al vero!" S1:137; Colonna, *Sonnets*, 168–69.

144. Luigi Alamanni, "Lettere," in *Lettere di L. Alamanni, B. Varchi, V. Borghini, L. Salviati e d'altri
autori citati dagli Accademici della Crusca per la più parte fin qui inedite*, ed. Francesco Zambrini
(Lucca: Tip. Franchi e Maionchi, 1853): 31. In 1539-41 Alamanni wrote a number of love poems for
Beatrice Pio, a lady from Ferrara.

145. "Non voglio lassar di dirvi che la signora Marchesana di Pescara attenderà quanto v'ha promes-
so;" Pietro Aretino, *Lettere scritte a Pietro Aretino*, Part. 1, no. 126.

that he had in mind to deprive her of the sanctity of her body (although he did not say 'of her body') if she failed to pay back some money that her husband owed him and that she had been promising to pay for some time (or so he said) but had never actually done. And so he showed his bad feeling towards her and he claimed to have written some sonnets maligning her."[146]

After receiving thirty scudos together with this letter, Aretino was soon back on the attack in order to obtain the rest of the money: "May Jesus inspire you to instruct Master Sebastiano da Pesaro, who paid me the thirty scudos, to pay the rest of the debt." [147]

∾

Most Magnificent Signor,

I don't know whether to praise or blame you for the book you have sent me: praise you because you truly merit it for this composition,[148] or blame you because you waste such talent on things that are not godly, thus revealing that you are less appreciated by Him and less useful to the world. The man who brought me your book did not come back, and so I was delayed in replying to your letter while I waited for him.

I have written warmly to the Marquis of Vasto[149] about your business: but since you are content to accept sixty scudos to release me from the debt, I am sending you thirty now, and I have written to ask Sebastiano Buonaventura[150] to pay them over to you as I don't have sufficient here now and I am on my way to Bologna to a place where I go for the air as here it is so bad for me. I'll send you the remainder as soon as I am able.

May Our Lord God inspire you to speak and think of him. I don't have time to reply now to the young man of yours who sent me the book, forgive me.

From Ferrara, the sixth day of November, 1537.

Ready in every way to honor you,
The Marchioness of Pescara

On the reverse:
To my Magnificent and Esteemed Signor, Signor Pietro Aretino

146. Benedetto Varchi, *Lettere, 1535–1565,* ed. Vanni Bramanti (Rome: Edizioni di Storia e letteratura, 2008), 42.

147. Colonna, *Carteggio,* no. LXXXIX.

148. Aretino probably sent Colonna a copy of the *Marfisa*; see Colonna, *Carteggio,* no. LXXXVIII.

149. Alfonso d'Avalos, marquis of Vasto.

150. A gentleman who worked for the House of Urbino; see Colonna, *Rime e lettere,* 456. He was also lieutenant of the troops belonging to Francesco Maria della Rovere.

⤳

[Letter 16]

Molto Magnifico Signor,

Non so s'io debba più lodarvi che dislodarvi del libro che m'havete mandato: lodarvi perché veramente il meritate in questa compositione, o dislodarvi perché così buono ingegno habiate a occupare in altre chose che in quelle de Dio, mostrandove a lui men grato et meno utile al mondo. Colui che mi diede il ditto libro non è mai più chomparso, però aspettandolo ho tardato a rispondervi.

Ho scritto caldamente al Marchese del Guasto circa il negotio vostro; ma poiché sete chontento quetarmi per sessanta schudi, ve ne mando adesso trenta, et ho scritto a messer Sebastiano Buonaventura che ve li paghi, che in verità io non ho qui tanto che mi basti andar in bolognese a un certo loghetto dove vo per l'aere, che questo mi è dannoso al possibile. Il resto vi manderò più tosto che potrò.

Nostro Signor Dio v'inspiri a parlar et pensar di lui. A quel vostro giovane che mi mandò il libro non ho tempo risponder adesso, eschusatemi.

Da Ferrara, a' dì VI di novembre MDXXXVII.

Al vostro honor paratissima,

La Marchesa de Pescara

A tergo

Al Magnifico Signor mio observandissimo, Signor Pietro Aretino

Letter 17: Lucca, 16 September 1538[151]
To Pope Paul III

In 1538, after two years of peace, Colonna was once again obliged to take up her pen in defense of the Capuchins. In response to the behavior of Pope Paul III, she wrote in the strongest possible terms to point out what seemed to her to be a self-evident truth: "Is this the reform that Your Holiness wishes to bring about, to spoil the best that there is?" The Capuchin Order is the "best that there is," and if the pope has been told otherwise he has been lied to, Colonna claims: she is certain that it will be enough to point out this truth to the pope, so that he can behave according to justice and not ignorance. As in her other letters in defense of the Order, the defense of truth is a key theme (see also Letter 12). Colonna refers repeatedly to the Capuchins' obedience and devotion to papal authority, and also

---

151. Original, autograph: ASN, Carte Farnesiane, fasc. 252, fols. 36r–37v: Tacchi-Venturi, "Vittoria Colonna e la riforma cappuccina," 32–33.

advises the pope on how he should deal with their detractors: "Your Holiness should impose silence" upon them.

This letter was followed very quickly by another on the same subject that Colonna sent to Cardinal Agostino Trivulzio. Since Cardinal Girolamo Ghinucci and Pope Paul III, despite their fine words on church reform, "send out contrary rulings every day" to the Capuchins, Colonna tells Trivulzio about all the injustices suffered by Observant friars who wished to become Capuchins, and who were obliged to remain Franciscans and undergo reform in a very hostile context.[152]

❧

Most blessed father,

I was hoping to have the great consolation of kissing your holy feet, and after eight or ten days in Prato,[153] to come to Rome. That consolation has been mixed with great bitterness, so that I do not think any longer of coming to Rome, for they wrote to me that Your Holiness allows new attacks to be made on the Capuchins, those poor, modest and obedient servants of Your Holiness, who do not defend themselves, nor do they conspire, and I have not written about them to anyone for two years now. The general of the Observants,[154] *dilato capitulo*,[155] left for Nice[156] and there he plotted and caused others to speak ill of them and to gossip to Your Holiness, and in all ways he took the side of wordly prudence which is the enemy of God. But if Your Holiness wishes to understand the wondrous fruit that the Capuchins harvest and the obedience and honor they pay to Your Holiness, send two honest representatives through all the cities of Italy and you will see their spirit, their value, their fight against heresy, their obedience to all of Your Holiness's commands, and how popular they are everywhere, and how they bitterly scolded a preacher of their order for one single word that he spoke in Genoa, as everyone does, which seemed to menace possible future harm; anyway they are most zealous about not straying into any kind of error that would displease Your Holiness. Alas, my Most Holy Father, is this the reform that Your Holiness wishes to bring about, to spoil the best that there is? Alas, do we not

152. "Ogni giorno emanano ordini contrarii;" Colonna, *Carteggio*, XCVII; Copello, "Aggiornamenti: Parte I," 169–73.

153. Prato is a small town just north of Florence.

154. The Observants, a branch of the Franciscans that gained autonomy in 1517; see Letter 12. In 1538 their general was Vincenzo Lunel.

155. "The chapter deferred." The general of the Observants had obtained from the Pope a postponement to the convocation of the council.

156. The encounter between Emperor Charles V and Francis I of France took place in Nice; the pope also attended to mediate a truce.

know that they were unable to reform themselves?[157] You will understand better from the letters I sent that yesterday evening by some miracle the two friars arrived here! Alas, do we not know that Your Holiness does nothing out of ignorance? If you wish to ruin them, do it by your own hand and not by means of others; for then I will be obliged to go about crying that they help me to ensure that all good souls will leave Italy, since they cannot remain here where Your Holiness's goodness does not act to control the wicked. I have firm hope in Your Holiness's prudence, which is the only thing that keeps me here, for the lies that you and other princes have been told will quickly expire as soon as someone arrives to tell you the truth. What a fine prize is awarded to poor Brother Bernardino,[158] that he is sought in every city,[159] and he never moves a foot without asking to know Your Holiness's will, and he expressly ordered the friars to consider Your Holiness as the light of all their thoughts. Your Holiness should impose silence on those who are trying to close the door against them,[160] since every day new accusations are levelled against them to bring them down, and witnessing the fact that they remain perfect is not enough. May God forgive them, and may he grant Your Holiness ever more clarity in serving him.

From Lucca, on the sixteenth day of September. Only the Capuchin's habit . . . is in direct opposition to him.[161]

Your Holiness's servant,
The [Marchioness of Pescara]

On the reverse
Most Holy and Most Blessed Lord, our Lord the Pope

Further down, in another hand
1538 from Lucca

---

157. In a letter to Trivulzio, Colonna confirms that the internal reform of the Franciscan Order "goes backwards everyday;" Colonna, *Carteggio*, no. XCVII.

158. Bernardino Ochino, elected Vicar General of the Capuchins only a few days previously; see Letter 14.

159. Many Italian cities competed for Ochino, who was one of the most famous preachers of his day.

160. Since April 1534 Pope Clement VII had forbidden the Capuchins from receiving new friars from the Observants. Pope Paul III would subsequently take the same approach, first ordering them not to receive new converts, and subsequently not to allow friars to transfer from the Observants; see the brief *Regimini universalis Ecclesiae*, 4 January 1537. In the letter to Trivulzio we read: "they closed the door against the entry of new friars;" Colonna, *Carteggio*, no. XCVII.

161. Some words here are indecipherable in the Italian text.

The Marchioness of Pescara / on the sixteenth of September / received on the twenty-fourth / reply sent the twenty-seventh[162]

                              ∽

[Letter 17]

Beatissimo padre,

Stava con somma consolation sperando presto basarli i piedi e starme otto o X giorni in Prata, poi venirmene [là]. Han mista questa dolcezza in tanta amaritudine che non penso più a Roma scrivendome che Vostra Santità condexende a dar nove molestie a' capucini, poveri minimi obedientissimi servi de Vostra Santità, quali non se defendono, non tramano, et son doi anni che io mai ne ho scritto in loco alcuno. E il general de l'Observ[antia], *dilato capitulo*, andò a Nizza, tramò, per tutto induce[ndo] a dirne male, a informar Vostra Santità, et fa proprio [la parte] della prudentia carnale inimica de Dio. Ma se Vostra Santità vol saper el frutto mirabil che fanno ' capucini et la obedienti[a] et lo honore che fanno a Vostra Santità, mande doi commissarii sincer[i] per tutte le città de Italia, et vederà che spirito, che cre[dito], che inimicitia con li eretici, che obedientia a ogni c[o]m[ando de] Vostra Santità, et como son domandati, et como aspramente ripresero una sola parola che disse un loro predicato[re] in Genova che mostrava minacciar de futuro danno, c[he] è cosa che ogniun lo fa; *tamen* stanno lor[o] zelantissimi de non errare in cosa che despiacessi a Vostr[a] [Santi]tà. Maxime, oimè, patre santyssimo mio, questo è il reformar che Vostra Santità disse voler fare, ruinar lo meglio che ce è? Oimè, non se sa le reforme loro fra loro tutte guaste? Et intenda[rà] meglio dalle lettere mando che iersera per miraculo arrivaro qui i doi frati! Oimè, non se sa che Vostra Santità non fa cosa per ignorantia? Se vol ruinarli, facialo de sua mano, et non per altri, che in tal caso serrò constretta andar gridando che me aiutino a procurar che li boni vadano for de Italia, poi che qui non ponno stare perché la bontà de Vostra Santità non opera per l'impedimento de' tristi. Io ho ferma speranza nella prudentia della Santità Vostra, la qual sola me tien qui, perché le buscie ditte a Vostra Santità o ad altro principe haveran corte gambe quando se andarà a dirli el vero. Bel premio se dà al pover fra Belardino de l'esser ricercato da tutte le città et mai mover passo senza desiderar saper li cenni de Vostra Santità, et così ha exspressamente ordinato a' frati [che] Vostra Santità sia sempre come lume de ogni pensier loro. [A . . .]i che han l'intento loro de haver fatto chiuder la porta, dovria Vostra Santità imponerli silentio, che così movono ogni dì novi litigii per ruinarli, et tanta exsperientia vista del preservarsi più perfetti non basta. Dio li perdoni et dia a Vostra Santità ognor più lume del suo serviti[o].

---

162. The pope's reply, sent on 27 September 1538, has not survived.

Da Lucca, a' dì XVI de settembre. Solo l'abito l[. . .] vita de' capucini è un roverso a ponto de lu[i].

Serva de Vostra Santità,
La [Marchesa de Pescara]

A tergo
Santissimo ac Beatissimo Domino, Domino nostro pape
Più sotto, di altra mano
1538 da Lucca
La Marchesa di Pescara
di 16 di settembre
ricevuta a 24
responsa 27

Letter 18: Rome, 3 December 1538[163]
To Pietro Bembo

This letter to the great humanist and poet Pietro Bembo deals with three themes: the recently published first edition of Colonna's *Rime*; the preacher Bernardino Ochino; and Colonna's stay at the convent of San Silvestro in Capite during a bitter dispute between her brother Ascanio and Isabella Colonna (1513–1570) together with Philippe de Lannoy (1514–1553).

The letter from Bembo that elicited this reply has been lost, but a number of letters written between November and December 1538 by Bembo, Colonna, and Carlo Gualteruzzi discuss the printing of Colonna's verses in Parma a few weeks earlier. We can assume that Bembo wrote to Colonna in similar tones to those he used in a letter to Gualteruzzi on 8 November 1538, where he expressed disdain for the unknown editor and printer of the volume and proposed a new, corrected edition. The letter from an unidentified individual from Parma that Colonna refers to here might be the dedicatory letter to that pirated edition of her *Rime*, or perhaps the adjective *parmigiano* (meaning "the man from Parma") is intended as a reference to the volume as a whole or its anonymous editor. We might hypothesize, alternatively, that the editor or the printer of the Parma edition wrote directly to her about his volume. Either way, Colonna here asks Bembo to desist from his "corrective" editorial project, as she wishes her works to pass from memory with the passage of time or else to live on as a form of authorial penitence, as she is guilty of becoming too involved in worldly pursuits. Bembo referred to this letter from Colonna when he wrote to Gualteruzzi the following

---

163. Copy: BAV, Chigi L III 58, fol. 10r–v: Copello, "Aggiornamenti: Parte I," 176–77.

week: "I had a lovely letter from the Illustrious Marchioness of Pescara. But I will not allow Her Ladyship on any account to resist giving me a draft of her *Rime* to print there. And I beg you to do everything possible to have them printed, corrected and cleaned up."[164]

From the subject of her poems, Colonna moves on to speak briefly of Bernardino Ochino, who was going to preach in Venice. In fact, Bembo had been campaigning since the previous April to get Colonna to intercede with Ochino and convince him to preach the Lenten sermons in that city.[165]

The final paragraph of the letter describes the poet's frustration. She had arrived in the Roman convent of San Silvestro in Capite two months previously, and was still measuring the distance between the solitude she truly desired, "peaceful and sweet" and made up of "conversation with my books and my thoughts," and the "restless" solitude that is made up of "worldly conversation." The reason for the continued disturbance of her peace was a dispute that had arisen between Vittoria and her brother Ascanio and Isabella, wife of Philippe de Lannoy, prince of Sulmona. The dispute concerned a number of feudal territories, but it threatened to take on unexpected proportions due to the involvement of Pope Paul III, who was trying to turn the argument in his favor. By taking sides with Isabella and Philippe, the pope wished to provoke Ascanio into a rash response, thus giving the pope an excuse to invade the Colonna territories around Rome. The Colonna, for their part, were quick to turn to the emperor to ask for his support.[166] Colonna's time was thus occupied constantly with politics: she was engaged daily in letter writing, meetings and debates with people who did not understand "the offices of charity," all of which she managed with a steady hand in her role as mediator. Much as she longed to retreat into spiritual conversation, her life was engulfed by the worldly conversations that left her only with a feeling of complete estrangement: "in their company I am completely alone."

⌘

Most Magnificent Signor,

I remain most obliged to you for the kindness demonstrated in your letter, so different from that of the man from Parma. To tell you the truth, I think that blaming others, even if I had really wanted this outcome, would be a good way to lessen the pain. But I am fearful that this would be even worse, because it would mean I am in pain without anyone to blame[167] and repenting without any remedy, so I pray you

164. Bembo, *Lettere*, 4:159.

165. Colonna, *Carteggio*, no. XCIII.

166. On this series of events see Copello, "Vittoria Colonna a Carlo V."

167. Colonna's complaint is legitimate because she was not responsible for the printing of her works and never desired it.

please let it drop, since my poems will either be extinguished by time, or else it will please God to let this abomination live on as a justified penance for my sin.

I am delighted by what you write about Brother Bernardino.[168] May God allow him to harvest those fruits there[169] that I understand he gathers in other cities, and even more given the excellence of your city and its illustrious rulers.

I am here in San Silvestro,[170] where I had hoped to spend time in that solitude that I think of as peaceful and in sweet conversation with my books and my thoughts. Instead I find myself embroiled in worldly conversation which is truly a restless solitude, because I have to spend the whole day talking to people who are like trees or stones when it comes to their understanding of works of charity, so that in their company I am completely alone, since I see they do not respond to the demands of the spirit and I lose all my cherished solitude, which should be spent in spiritual conversation. Yet I hope that this dispute will end soon, and I will write more fully about it to Carlo.[171] May Our Lord God preserve your most excellent person.

From Rome, on the third day of December 1538.

At Your Lordship's command,
The Marchioness of Pescara

꙳

[Letter 18]
Molto Magnifico Signor,
Gli rimango obbligatissima della carità mostra nella sua lettera, molto contraria a quella del Parmigiano; ma – gli dirò il vero – io ho pensato che il possermi doler d'altri, quando pur questa cosa la sentissi, saria un giusto mitigar l'affanno; ma io temendo che sarà forse peggiore, vedo che causerà poi un dolermi senza giusta querela e un pentirmi senza rimedio, di che di gratia la prego che li lassano stare, perché o si estingueranno, o piacerà a Dio che viva questo obbrobrio per degna penitenza del mio errore.

---

168. Bernardino Ochino; see Letters 14 and 19.

169. In Venice, where Ochino was due to preach the following Lent.

170. This is a reference to the Clarissan convent of S. Silvestro in Capite, in Rome, where Colonna took refuge after her husband's death in December 1525. She remained there until April 1526, and returned in March 1535, and from October 1538 to June 1539 (or perhaps to March 1541). The Colonna family had been closely linked to the convent for centuries, as the relics of the blessed Clarissan nun Margherita Colonna (d. 1284) had been conserved there since 1285.

171. Carlo Gualteruzzi, faithful friend and correspondent of Bembo.

Ho carissimo quello che scrive del Padre fra' Bernardino. Dio faccia, produca quei frutti lì ch'intendo produca nelle altre città, e tanto maggiori quanto all'eccellenza della città et alla dignità delle Signorie Vostre conviene.

Io me ne sto qui in San Silvestro, ove pensai di star in una solitudine che la soglio chiamare pacifica e dolce conversazione coi libri e coi pensieri; ma mi trovo in una conversazione mondana ch'è veramente una inquieta solitudine, perché mi bisogna parlare tutto il dì con persone che quanto al far con loro gli offizi della carità sono come arbori e sassi, sì che sto con loro in solitudine, poiché non odo rispondere a cose di spirito, e perdo la mia cara solitudine, che saria spirituale conversatione. Pure spero che questi litigi forniranno presto, come più a pieno scriverò a Carlo; e Nostro Signore Dio sua molto eccellente persona guardi.
Di Roma, a' dì III di decembre 1538.

Al commando di Vostra Signoria,
La Marchesa di Pescara

Letter 19: Rome, 10 April [1539][172]
To Pietro Bembo

Here Colonna replies to a letter from Bembo dated 4 April,[173] expressing her joy at the official announcement of his election as cardinal a few weeks earlier.[174] It is likely that Colonna's influence on the pope played no small part in this outcome.[175] Colonna's frank advice to Bembo is to beware the false atmosphere in the College of Cardinals. She maintains that this will not be difficult for Bembo if he holds fast to his "usual virtue" and "usual sincerity."

The style of this letter is very elegant, as befits its addressee; witty wordplay is extended across long clauses. Metaphors and similes also come into play with marked lightness of touch: among them the thousand vice-tipped spears that will menace Bembo in the Cardinal's College; and the chameleon which changes its colors.

---

172. Copy: BAV, Chigi L III 58, fol. 13r–v; see Concetta Ranieri, "Ancora sul carteggio tra Pietro Bembo e Vittoria Colonna," *Giornale italiano di filologia* 14 (1983): 149.

173. Colonna, *Carteggio*, no. CIV.

174. The College of Cardinals is the highest group of Catholic bishops who assist the pope in the governance of the church. They are appointed for life and have responsibility, among other things, for the election of new popes.

175. See the letter from Bembo to Colonna dated 4 April: "Vostra Illustre Signoria ha più da rallegrarsi della nuova dignità et grado datomi da Nostro Signore, per ciò ch'ella ne è stata in buona parte cagione, che per alcun mio merito;" Colonna, *Carteggio*, no. CIV.

My Most Illustrious and Esteemed Monsignor,

I beg Your Lordship not to go to the trouble of replying, I only wish to thank you for your very sweet letter and beg you to arm yourself with your habitual virtue, so that your new dignity[176] in no way diminishes your old dignity, which is noble, and true. Instead, let that dignity be so strong and firm that it can resist the sharp prongs of a thousand vice-tipped spears that will surround you, and can disarm them all and take them prisoner, so that you enrich that dignity with honorable ensigns in the service of that Lord who chose you to be his knight in this battle, which is much greater than the battle to vanquish kingdoms or oneself, and less difficult; because here all you need do is avoid imitating the chameleon, which dresses in another's colors. Live in the solitude of your usual sincerity which has already made the grade, and do not let the grade make you.

I give you infinite thanks for what you write about your father Ochino, and indeed I have always believed him to be of the kind that would greatly please Your Most Illustrious Lordship, and it pleases me greatly that he was such a good omen for you since, when he preached for you, you became a cardinal. I pray send him the enclosed, for I think he is now in Padua. May our Lord God preserve Your Most Illustrious Lordship, as both Carlo[177] and I desire.

From Rome, on the tenth of April.

Most devoted servant to Your Most Illustrious Lordship,
The Marchioness of Pescara

~

[Letter 19]
A Pietro Bembo
Illustrissimo Monsignor mio osservandissimo,
Supplico Vostra Signoria non pigli fatica di rispondermi, basta solamente ch'io la ringrazi della sua dolcissima lettera, e la supplichi si armi delle sue solite virtù, sì che la nuova dignità non sminuisca punto della sua antica, nobil e vera dignità, anzi si mostri sì forte e salda che non solo resista alle acute punte di mille lance di vizi che li saranno d'intorno, ma li disarmi tutti e li faccia suoi prigioni in modo che la doni delle sue onorate insegne in servizio di quel Signore che lo elesse per suo cavaliere in questa pugna, maggior assai di vincer i regni e se stesso, e con minore difficoltà, perché qui non ha da fare altro se non fuggire di somigliarsi al

---

176. The reference is to Bembo's election as cardinal. Colonna repeats back the same words used by her correspondent, who in a letter of 4 April had written to her of his "new dignity;" see Colonna, *Carteggio*, no. CIV.

177. Carlo Gualteruzzi.

camaleonte, che si veste de gli altri colori. Viva solo nella solita sua sincerità, quale ha tirato a sé il grado, e non faccia ora che il grado tiri lei.

Le rendo infinite grazie di quello che scrive del suo padre, e certo io l'ho giudicato sempre per tale che satisfacesse a Vostra Signoria Illustrissima, e mi piace molto le habbia havuto sì buon augurio che, nel suo predicarvi, siate cardinale. La prego gli mandi l'alligata, che credo sarà in Padoa. E nostro Signor Dio guardi Vostra Signoria Illustrissima come desidera messer Carlo e io.

Di Roma, a' 10 d'aprile.

Deditissima serva di Vostra Signoria Illustrissima,
La Marchesa di Pescara

Letter 20: Rome, 15 February 1540[178]
To Marguerite d'Angoulême, queen of Navarre

There are five extant letters between Colonna and Marguerite d'Angoulême, Queen of Navarre: three from Colonna and two from Marguerite.[179] This letter was written in reply to one from Marguerite dating from the end of January or early February 1540 (*Carteggio*, no. CXX).

The friendship between the two women was founded in their shared spiritual interests, and thus overcame any potential political obstacles, although these were considerable. The Colonna family, with its strong Spanish ties, was historically opposed to the French. Marguerite was the French king's sister, the same king who had been taken prisoner by Colonna's husband, Ferrante d'Avalos, during the battle of Pavia in 1525, where Marguerite's first husband was also fighting on the French side.[180] Marguerite was tasked with writing to the Emperor Charles V after the battle to plead for the king's release.[181]

---

178. Copy: BQB, E VII 16, fasc. 2, fols. 5r–6v; Copy: BAV, Ferr. 433, fol. 63r–v: Ve 42, fol. 126v; Ve 56, pp. 609–12; Ve 65, p. 577: Colonna, *Carteggio*, no. CXII. The text cited here is the copy in Brescia, which is closest to Colonna's normal linguistic and writing practices, as well as being more correct and the only text to include the date.

179. For English translations of the complete set of letters between the two women, as well as a useful contextualizing introduction, see Barry Collett, *A Long and Troubled Pilgrimage: The Correspondence of Marguerite d'Angoulême and Vittoria Colonna, 1540–1545* (Princeton, NJ: Princeton Theological Seminary, 2000).

180. Marguerite de Navarre's first husband was Duke Charles IV d'Alençon. In 1527 she married Henri d'Albret, king of Navarre.

181. On the relationship between Colonna and Marguerite de Navarre, see Domenico Tordi, *Il codice delle* Rime *di Vittoria Colonna, marchesa di Pescara, appartenuto a Margherita d'Angoulême, regina di Navarra* (Pistoia: Flori, 1900); Verdun-Louis Saulnier, "Marguerite de Navarre, Vittoria Colonna et quelques autres italiens de 1540," in *Mélanges à la mémoire de Franco Simone: France et Italie dans la culture européenne*, vol. 1, *Moyen Age et Renaissance* (Geneva: Slatkine, 1980), 281–95; Itala T. C.

The French queen's support for evangelical movements in France was notable: she was a correspondent of the high-profile reformers John Calvin and Philip Melanchthon (1497–1560). Colonna probably first came into contact with Marguerite during Calvin's stay in Ferrara in the years 1537–1538, at the court of the evangelical sympathizer Renée de France, duchess of Ferrara, and sister of Queen Claude, wife of King Francis I. In 1540, the correspondence between Colonna and Marguerite was greatly enhanced when two of Colonna's Italian correspondents, Luigi Alamanni (1495–1556) and Pier Paolo Vergerio, traveled to the French court in the retinue of Cardinal Ippolito d'Este (1509–1572). The women never had an opportunity to meet in person, although they often expressed a strong desire to do so.[182] Marguerite, herself a talented writer of works in poetry and prose, was also in possession of poems by Colonna, obtained at her express request at some time during 1540.[183]

In this beautifully crafted letter Colonna underlines the need for a spiritual guide on the difficult path through life. "Examples from one's own sex" are preferable, she suggests, and there are many possibilities including Marguerite herself, alongside Saint Catherine of Alexandria, Mary Magdalene, and the Virgin Mary (see Letter 26). Marguerite is even compared to a divinity: in receipt of the queen's "lofty and religious words," Colonna feels obliged to observe "that sacred silence which one offers to divine things in place of praise." Colonna expresses a shy reverence for Marguerite, similar to the one felt by the Hebrews when confronted by "the fire and glory of God on the summit of the mountain." The poet also compares herself to John the Baptist, who had hailed the coming of Jesus, one greater than he, announcing "in the desert of our misery . . . the longed-for arrival of Your Majesty."

Rutter, "La scrittura di Vittoria Colonna e Margherita di Navarra: Resistenza e misticismo," *Romance Languages Annual* 3 (1991): 303–8; Abigail Brundin, "Vittoria Colonna and the Virgin Mary," *Modern Language Review*, 96 (2001): 61–81; Collett, *A Long and Troubled Pilgrimage*; Franco Pignatti, "Margherita d'Angoulême, Vittoria Colonna, Francesco Della Torre," *Filologia e critica* 38 (2013): 122–48; as well as the monograph on Marguerite by Jonathan A. Reid, *King's Sister—Queen of Dissent: Marguerite of Navarre (1492–1549) and her Evangelical Network* (Leiden–Boston: Brill, 2009).

182. See the letter from Paolo Giovio to Cosimo de' Medici dated 3 March 1540: "c'è venuto nova da Rome come la Regina di Navarra desidera conoscersi et abboccarsi con la nostra Divina Marchesa di Pescara in Milan;" Tordi, "Vittoria Colonna in Orvieto," 519.

183. On the debates around precisely which poems, in which manuscripts, were owned by Marguerite de Navarre, see Brundin, "Vittoria Colonna in Manuscript;" Tordi, *Il codice delle Rime*; Brundin, "Vittoria Colonna and the Virgin Mary;" Brundin, *Vittoria Colonna and the Spiritual Poetics*, 101–31; Dionisotti, *Appunti sul Bembo*, 1:284–85; Colonna, *Sonetti: in morte*, 25; Antonio Corsaro, "Manuscript Collections of Spiritual Poetry in Sixteenth-Century Italy," In *Forms of Faith in Sixteenth-Century Italy*, edited by Abigail Brundin and Matthew Treherne, (Aldershot, UK–Burlington, VT: Ashgate, 2009), 35. On Marguerite de Navarre and her literary works, see Gary Ferguson and Mary B. McKinley, ed., *A Companion to Marguerite de Navarre* (Leiden-Boston: Brill, 2013).

∼

Most serene Queen,

The lofty and religious words contained in Your Majesty's most eloquent letter ought to teach me that sacred silence which one offers to divinity in place of praise. Yet I fear that my reverence might be interpreted as ingratitude, therefore I dare, if not quite to reply, then equally not to remain entirely silent, if only to raise up the counterweights of your celestial clock so that in your goodness you will make it toll, and thus will delineate and organize the hours of my confused life until God allows me to hear Your Majesty talking in person of holy things, as you are kind enough to let me hope. And if you will accord me so much grace and infinite bounty, then my dearest wish will be fulfilled, which has for a long time been this: since on this long and difficult path through life we have dire need of a guide to show us the way with sound doctrine and good works, and invite us to overcome our fatigue; and since I believe that examples from one's own sex are more fitting and it is more appropriate for one to follow the other, so I turned to the great women of Italy in order to learn from them and imitate them.[184] But although I found many virtuous women, I did not consider that any one of them could serve as a model, but in one woman alone outside Italy could be found united the perfections of the will together with those of the intellect. Yet since she was so noble and so far away, I was overcome by the same sadness and fear that afflicted the Hebrews when they witnessed the fire and glory of God on the summit of the Mountain,[185] where they did not dare to climb, still being imperfect; and silently in their hearts they asked God if his divinity, in the incarnate Word, might deign to draw near to them.[186] Just as God's holy hand comforted them in their spiritual thirst first with water miraculously drawn from a rock,[187] then with manna from heaven;[188] in the same way, Your Majesty was moved to console me with your most sweet letter. And if for the Hebrews the grace they received far surpassed their expectations, so I too believe that the benefit of seeing Your Majesty would exceed all my desires. And the journey will certainly not be difficult for me if the end is to illumine my mind and quieten my conscience. I hope it is not displeasing to Your Majesty either, the idea of having before you the subject on whom you can exercise your two best virtues, that is your humility (because you will have to stoop so low

---

184. On the need for a spiritual guide to lead one to God, see Letter 36.

185. Exodus 19:18: "Totus autem mons Sinai fumabat, eo quod descendisset Dominus super eum in igne : et ascenderet fumus ex eo quasi de fornace, eratque omnis mons terribilis" ("And all mount Sinai was on a smoke: because the Lord was come down upon it in fire, and the smoke arose from it as out of a furnace: and all the mount was terrible"). See also Exodus 19:16: "timuit populus" ("And the people that was in the camp, feared").

186. John 1:14.

187. Exodus 16:1–6.

188. Exodus 16.

in order to teach me) and your charity (because you will find in me so much resistance to receiving your gifts). Yet since it is commonly known that the most difficult labors produce the most beloved children, I hope that Your Majesty will delight in giving birth to me in spirit with such great pain as to make me God's and your own new creation.[189] I could not imagine how Your Majesty could see me before you,[190] only I know that your most noble nature moved you to turn back to call me, and you needed to take me from far off and see me close up; or perhaps in the same way that the servant John[191] walked ahead of the Lord, so may I too serve at least as that voice which in the desert of our misery summons all of Italy to prepare the way for the longed-for arrival of Your Majesty.[192] But since I am estranged from your lofty and royal consideration I will content myself with speaking of you to the Most Revered Cardinal from Ferrara,[193] who shows his good judgment in every matter and particularly in honoring Your Majesty. I am pleased to find in this gentleman virtue equal in excellence to the ancients, but very new to our eyes that have grown used to sin. I often talk of these matters with the Most Revered Pole, whose conversation always resides in heaven and who only attends to worldly matters on behalf of other people. And frequently, too, with the most Revered Bembo, who is so enthused with the desire to work in this vineyard of the Lord,[194] that although he was chosen late, every great reward belongs to him, despite other people's negative talk.[195] And I try to ensure that all these conversations have their beginning and end in so worthy a subject, in order to derive some small part of that light which, in the fullness of its rays, so clearly reveals and so greatly exalts Your Majesty. May you add luster day by day to this most precious pearl,[196] since you know how to spread and disperse its splendor, and by accumulating such treasure for yourself, you will enrich us all. I kiss your royal hand, and humbly recommend myself to your most longed for grace.

From Rome, on the fifteenth day of February 1540.

Most dutiful servant of Your Most Serene Majesty,
the Marchioness of Pescara

189. "New creation" is a citation from Galatians 6:15.

190. John 1:30.

191. John the Baptist who announced the coming of Christ.

192. "Hic est enim, qui dictus est per Isaiam prophetam dicentem [Isiah 40:3]: Vox clamantis in deserto: Parate viam Domini: rectas facite semitas ejus;" Matthew 3:3; see also Mark 1:3; Luke 3:4; John 1:23.

193. Cardinal Ippolito d'Este (1509–1572), who was in France from 1536 to 1539. On 26 October 1539 he arrived in Rome, and left again in early 1540.

194. For the parable of the vineyard see Matthew 21:33–44; Mark 12:1–11; Luke 20:9–18.

195. Many others in the Church spoke against Bembo's cardinalate.

196. Colonna is making a play on words here with Marguerite's Christian name, which derives from the Latin word for pearl, *margarita*.

༄

[Letter 20]

Serenissima Regina,

Le alte et religiose parole dell'humanissima lettera di Vostra Maestà mi devriano insegnare quel sacro silentio che in vece di lode s'offerisce alle cose divine. Ma temendo che lla mia riverentia non si puotesse riputare ingratitudine, ardirò non già di rispondere, ma di non tacere in tutto, et sol quasi per alzare i contrapesi del suo celeste horologgio, acciò che, piacendole per sua bontà di risonare, a me distingua et ordini l'hore di questa mia confusa vita, in tanto che Dio mi concederà udire Vostra Maestà raggionare dell'altra con la sua voce viva, come se degna darmi speranza. Et se tanta gratia l'infinita buontà mi concederà, sarà compìto il mio intenso desiderio, il quale è stato gran tempo questo: che havendo noi bisogno in questa lunga et difficile via della vita di guida che mostri il camino con la dottrina et con l'opre insieme n'envìti a superare la fatica, et parendomi che gli essempi del suo sesso a ciascuno sieno più proportionati e il seguire l'uno l'altro più lecito, mi rivoltavo alle donne grandi dell'Italia per imparare da lloro et imitarle. Et benché ne vedessi molte virtuose, non però giudicavo che giustamente l'altre tutte quasi per norma se le proponessino, in una sola fuor d'Italia s'intendeva essere congionte le perfettioni della volontà insieme con quelle dell'intelletto. Ma per essere in sì alto grado et sì lontano, si generava in me quella tristezza e timore c'hebbero gli Hebrei vedendo il fuoco e la gloria di Dio sulla cima del Monte, ove essi ancora imperfetti salire non ardivano, et tacitamente nel cuore loro domandavano al Signore che lla sua divinità, nel Verbo humanando, se degnasse approssimarsi a essi; et con quella spirituale sete la man pia del Signore li andò intertenendo hor con l'acqua miracolosa della pietra, hor con la celeste manna. Così Vostra Maestà s'è mossa a consolarmi con la sua dolcissima lettera; et se a quelli l'effetto della gratia superò di gran lunga ogni loro espettatione, a me similmente l'utilità di vedere Vostra Maestà credo che avanzerà d'assai ogni mio desiderio. Et certo non mi sarà difficile il viaggio per illuminare il mio intelletto e pacificare la mia conscientia. Et a Vostra Maestà spero che non sia discaro, per havere dinanzi il suggetto ove possa essercitare le sue due più care virtù, cioè l'humiltà, perché s'abbasserà molto ad insegnarmi, la carità, perché in me troverà resistentia assai a ricevere le sue gratie. Ma essendo usanza che 'l più delle volte de' parti più faticosi sono i figlioli più amati, spero che poi Vostra Maestà debbia rallegrarsi di havermi sì difficilmente partorita con lo spirito et fattami di Dio et sua nova creatura. Non saprei mai imaginarmi come mi vedea la Maestà Vostra avanti a sé, se non fosse che, essendosi per sua nobilissima natura rivolta indietro a chiamarmi, è stato necessario che di lontano et dinanzi a sé mi vegga; o forse nel modo che 'l servo Giovanni precedeva il Signore, a similitudine del quale potessi io almen servire per quella voce che nel diserto delle miserie nostre esclamasse a tutta Italia il preparare la strada alla desiderata venuta di Vostra Maestà. Ma mentre sono dalle sue alte et regali cure differita, attenderò a raggionare di llei col Reverendissimo di Ferrara, il cui bel giuditio si dimostra in ogni cosa et particolarmente in riverire Vostra Maestà. Et mi godo di vedere in questo Signore le virtù in grado tale che paiono di quelle antiche nell'eccellentia, ma molto nove a gli occhi nostri troppo hormai al male usati. Ne raggiono assai col Reverendissimo Polo, la cui conversatione è sempre in cielo, et solo per l'altrui utilità riguarda et cura la terra, et spesso col Reverendissimo Bembo, tanto acceso di desiderio a lavorare in questa vigna del Signore ch'ogni gran pagamento, senza mormoratione de gli altri, se ben tardi fu condotto, gli conviene. Et tutti i miei raggionamenti m'ingegno c'habbino principio et fine da sì degna materia, per havere un poco di quella luce che nell'ampiezza de' suoi raggi Vostra Maestà sì chiaramente discerne et sì altamente honora; la quale se degni illustrare ogni giorno più sì pretiosa margherita, poi che sa sì bene dispendere et compartire i suoi splendori che, thesaurizzando a sé, fa ricchi noi altri. Baccio la sua regale mano, et nella sua desideratissima gratia humilmente mi raccommando.

Di Roma, alli XV di febraro del MDXL.

De Vostra Serenissima Maestà obligatissima serva,
La Marchesa di Pescara

Letter 21: [Rome, early March 1541][197]
To Ascanio Colonna

In 1540 Pope Paul III imposed a new tax on salt and the city of Perugia, which refused to pay the tax, was invaded by papal troops. Despite the harsh response to resistance in Perugia, Ascanio Colonna still declined to buy salt from the papal contractor at the newly elevated price. As a result a number of his vassals were imprisoned, and in retaliation he raided the contractor's lands, stealing thirty cows. On 25 February 1541 the pope ordered Ascanio to attend a meeting. Ascanio once again refused and began amassing his troops, confident of imperial support against the pope. In this he was mistaken. Charles V was anxious not to upset his friendly relations with Paul III—their families had recently intermarried—and offered no support to Ascanio. At last the pope had a concrete reason for invading the Colonna lands around Rome, something he had wished to do for some years. In the so-called Salt Wars that followed, the Colonna family lost all its property in papal territories and was sent into exile.[198]

197. Original, autograph: BSSS, Archivio Colonna, Corrispondenza di Ascanio Colonna, Sottoserie 2: Colonna, *Carteggio*, no. CXXIX.

198. On the Salt Wars see Tordi, "Vittoria Colonna in Orvieto;" Diana Robin, "Rome: The Salt War Letters of Vittoria Colonna," in Diana Robin, *Publishing Women: Salons, the Presses, and the*

In the months preceding the outbreak of hostilities Vittoria Colonna was in Rome, trying with all her might to broker a peace between the two factions. As she said, "there was no need for so much war over thirty cows." This letter makes clear that she was under no illusions about the hidden reasons for the pope's campaign against Ascanio, a long-standing vassal of the emperor. As she could see, his aim was to reduce Spanish influence in the south of Italy:[199] "I think that the motives for this armed response go far beyond just yourself."[200] Despite Ascanio's intemperance, Colonna sided with her blood relative, for "the House of Colonna always comes first," and she gave permission for her own men to join her brother's army.[201]

The many letters written in the first days of March 1541 allow glimpses of Colonna's apprehension over the outcome of this dispute.[202] Her sentences are short and perfunctory, which is unusual in Colonna's letter-writing style; the epistolary formalities are more rushed than usual; there is no date, but just the hour of writing; in Letter 22, there is even—uniquely in Colonna's correspondence—a complete absence of signature.

Most Illustrious Lord,

From Conciano[203] you will learn what Your Lordship had guessed, that these shenanigans have only been undertaken to make a pretence of good will.[204] I think that the motives for this armed response go far beyond just yourself. But the House of Colonna always comes first. All this has been written to His Majesty. Your Lordship must watch out, since for everything that you do once His Majesty's order has come you will be honored. May God in his mercy keep you and remove from you all ills. All these serious acts such as the murder of captains, governors, and cardinals have been put right, thus there was no need for so much war over thirty cows.

Counter-Reformation in Sixteenth-Century Italy (Chicago: University of Chicago Press, 2007), 79–101; and Targoff, *Renaissance Woman*, 208–26.

199. Tordi, "Vittoria Colonna in Orvieto," 486.

200. "Io credo che presto si scopriranno cose di Francia, per donde se vederà che il motivo di Sua Santità non è per voi solo;" Colonna, *Carteggio*, no. CXXVIII.

201. "'L Marchese del Vasto e la Marchesa di Pescara hanno permesso e dato licenza a' lor sudditi di andare a servire il predetto signore [Ascanio];" letter from Giovanni Guidiccioni to Pope Paul III dated 24 March 1541, in Giovanni Guidiccioni, *Opere di monsignor Giovanni Guidiccioni*, ed. Carlo Minutoli (Florence: Barbera, 1867), 2:374.

202. Colonna, *Carteggio*, nos. CXXVIII–XXXVII.

203. Secretary to Juan Fernández Manrique de Lara (ca. 1490–1553), marquis of Aguilar and imperial ambassador to Rome.

204. This is an allusion to the steps that were being taken to avoid a war. Ascanio must soon have understood that they were not well motivated.

Your Lordship never offers a defense of your motives, but you should tell the truth, that is that they used this as a pretext for going to war and you didn't wish to be caught sleeping,[205] since each day you heard fine words but saw spiteful deeds, so you defend yourself. And may God in his mercy help you, as I hope. The Marquis[206] conducts himself well, spreads the word in all corners, and the men will be ready to respond to the pope's movements and the orders of His Majesty. In the meantime it is all down to you, since here they place too much faith in fine words.

The marriage with France is confirmed,[207] as I have written to His Majesty; and they advise us not to seek to understand everything at the moment, since I cannot write more clearly now,[208] until God grants that they see that these things are not down to us alone.

At your service,
The Marchioness

On the reverse
The Most Illustrious Lord Ascanio

∾

[Letter 21]
Illustrissimo Signor,
Da Conciano intenderà che Vostra Signoria ha indovinato che per altro non se son fatti questi maneggi che per mostrar bona vuluntà. Penso li motivi de tanta armata siano per altro che per voi solo. Ma Casa Colonna sempre è la prima. Tutto se è scritto a Sua Maestà. Vostra Signoria attenda a guardarsi, che per ogni cosa che farà poi de venuto l'ordine de Sua Maestà serrà honorato. Dio per sua bontà ve guardi etc. A tante cose grandi de amazar baricelli, governatori, cardinali se è preso remedio, però non bisognava tanta guerra per trenta vacche.

Vostra Signoria non difenda mai il suo motivo, ma dica la verità: che hanno voluto armar con questo colore et che voi non volevate essere preso in letto, poi

---

205. The reference to Ascanio being "caught sleeping" implies that he needed to prepare his military defenses.

206. The marquis of Aguilar.

207. Colonna is referring to the marriage that was arranged between Vittoria Farnese (1521–1602), the pope's niece, and Claude de Lorraine, duke of Aumale, which, however, did not end well. See Emilio Re, "Una missione di Latino Giovenale: Un disegno di matrimonio fra Vittoria Farnese e Francesco, duca d'Aumale," *Archivio della società romena di storia patria* 34 (1911): 5–33.

208. Colonna is expressing her fear that her letters on this matter might be intercepted. In another letter to Ascanio (Colonna, *Carteggio*, no. CXXXV) she even resorts to code in two instances. See also the letter to Ercole II d'Este, duke of Ferrara, of 9 April 1538: "Non ho cifra, però non posso dir più" ("In the absence of a coded alphabet I can write no more"); Colonna, *Carteggio*, no. XCIV.

che ogni dì vedevi bone parole et tristi fatti, però ve defendete. Et Dio ve aiuti, come spero, nella sua bontà.

El Signor Marches se governa bene, advisa in tutti i lochi, et starran preparati secondo i motivi del Papa et l'ordin de Sua Maestà. Interim a voi tocca solo, poi che se crede troppo alle bone parole, qui.

Il matrimonio con Francia è concluso, et così ho scritto a Sua Maestà; et questi dicono de non mirare bene a tutto, che ormai non potrò scriver chiaro troppo, finché Dio volrà che vedano che non tocca a noi soli.

A suo servitio,
La Marchesa

A tergo
A lo Illustrissimo Signor Ascanio

Letter 22: [Rome, 8 March 1541][209]
To Ascanio Colonna

As stated earlier (see Letter 21), there is only one example of a letter where Colonna fails to include her signature, and it is this one to her brother, written in a great hurry as is evident in the short sentences and the note of the hour of writing. The correspondence between the siblings in this period must have been extremely frequent. Having lost patience with Ascanio's bullish stance, the Marquis of Aguilar, imperial ambassador to the pope, turned to Vittoria Colonna to ask for her help in bringing her brother back to a reasonable position.[210] On 7 March 1541 a settlement was proposed: Ascanio, as head of the House of Colonna, would temporarily hand over Rocca di Papa (positioned strategically in the Castelli Romani) to Pier Luigi Farnese, duke of Castro and the pope's son; the duke in turn would cede Castro or Nepi to the Marquis of Aguilar.

Vittoria offered this settlement to her brother alongside another of her own devising. She invited him to respond calmly and courteously, and ended with a plea for peace. But still Ascanio refused any kind of agreement and would listen to none of his sister's advice. Instead he asked her to cease from meddling in these matters: "I beg Your Ladyship to refrain from further involvement in these

---

209. Original, autograph: BSSS, Archivio Colonna, Corrispondenza di Ascanio Colonna, Sottoserie 2: Colonna, *Carteggio*, no. CXXXIII.

210. See the letter from Reginald Pole to Gasparo Contarini of 31 March 1541: "Quod ad Illustrissima Marchionissam Piscarie attinet . . . , ad fratris pertinaciam vincendam illa quidem . . . nihil intentatum reliquit ut fratrem a furore belli ad obedientiam revocaret" ("As for the most illustrious Marchioness of Pescara, she herself . . . in order to overcome her brother's obstinacy has left nothing untested to lead her brother back from the fury of war to obedience"); BAV, Vat. lat. 5826, fols. 74r–75v.

affairs. . . . Whatever may arise from the will of His Majesty, it is better that his ministers attend to it than Your Ladyship. So calm yourself."[211]

As Charles V wrote to Colonna, "the terms Ascanio has employed in these negotiations . . . have exceeded the limits of reason and honesty."[212] Thus, on the morning of 15 March, papal troops set out for Marino. The war was disastrous for the Colonna who lost all their territories around Rome, forcing Ascanio into exile in the Kingdom of Naples. The Colonna lands were recovered only in 1550, thanks to the intervention of Pope Julius III.

∾

Most Illustrious Signor,

After every possibility had been ruled out, the Marquis[213] came to speak with me in some anger, stating that he cannot do any more. He showed me a letter from His Majesty, very recent, telling him to do all he can to make the pope happy, and it's clear to him that, as the emperor has just given up his daughter[214] to the pope, the Marquis can't be seen to be acting in any way against the pope unless the emperor commands it. He has undertaken that the soldiers will not be paid until tomorrow morning, and finally he writes to Your Lordship that in his opinion—and it will be ordered in writing by His Majesty—you should hand over Rocca di Papa to the Duke of Castro with a promise to tell the emperor to give it back to you. And he responded in kind that he would hand over either Nepe or Castro, whichever you prefer of the two, to the Marquis until Rocca di Papa was returned to Your Lordship. Attend to it well: they would give Nepe or Castro to the Marquis, and we would give Rocca di Papa to the Duke of Castro without any of our men nor of theirs. And if we don't want this, then no more will be said of it etc. Now, Signor, I beg you for the love of God, don't be roused to anger, but behave well with the Marquis, above all because he is advising His Majesty. If you don't want to do it, then reply courteously that they can give Nepe or Castro to the Marquis and you can hand over Rocca di Papa to the same man. Or if they want it to be in the Duke's name, that the Marquis provide the men, for they won't do it and you will be better off. And if they do it, it is neither a bad thing nor dishonorable to hand over everything to the Marquis in the name of His Majesty. For the love of God, think hard because this is the last possible solution. Consider how

211. "Supplico Vostra Signoria non se voglia intromettere più a questi partiti. . . . Di quello che pò nascere de la voluntà de Sua Maestà, meglio lo sanno li suoi ministri che Vostra Signoria, però quietise;" Colonna, *Carteggio*, no. CXXXIV.

212. "Los terminos que Ascanio ha usado en le negocio presente . . . ayan salido de los limites de razon y honestad;" Colonna, *Carteggio*, no. CXXXVI.

213. Juan Fernández Manrique de Lara, marquis of Aguilar, imperial ambassador to Rome: see Letter 21.

214. Margaret of Austria (1522–1586), natural daughter of Charles V and widow of Alessandro de' Medici, married Ottavio Farnese (1524–1586), the pope's nephew.

much suffering and danger are at stake, and may God in his goodness inspire you. You must reply immediately and write to His Majesty, because it would look bad for me to send a post without our letter: and I will send a copy of your final decision to the emperor. From Rome, today Tuesday.

The Marquis believes more in the Duke's good faith than that of God himself. Such are the times we live in. For my own part I responded as was appropriate. He told me: "I command you on behalf of His Majesty to write this, because I have struggled like a dog and cannot do any more, and when all the men are paid, there will be no further way out." So, Signor, I beg you, write sweetly and in good part, for he believes he offers a good deal by taking Castro or Nepe, etc. Let me know when the posts are leaving for Naples, and where I should send your letters if not to Marino.[215] Please, treat the Marquis with respect when you write and show him that you trust him.

From Rome, today, Tuesday, at twenty hours. Send your reply this evening.

On the reverse
To Signor Ascanio

&

[Letter 22]
Illustrissimo Signor,
Havendo già esscluso ogni cosa, è venuto el Signor Marchese a parlarme con colera, escusandose che non pò più; et me ha mostrata lettera de Sua Maestà, freschissima, che li dice faccia ogni opera per tener il Papa contento, et che lui vede che li ha data sua figlia et che non pò mostrarse in conto alcuno contra loro finché l'Imperator non comanda altro, che lui ha intertenuta la gente che non sia pagata sin in domatina, che per ultimo scriva a Vostra Signoria che suo parer è – et che cel comandarà *in scriptis* da parte de Sua Maestà – che dia Rocca de Papa al Duca de Castro con fede che dica lui a l'Imperator tornarvela. Et che lui replicò et recluse che desser o Nepe o Castro, a vostra election de queste due, al Signor Marchese, sinché entregassen Rocca de Papa a Vostra Signoria. Intendite bene: loro dar Nepe o Castro al Marchese, noi Rocca de Papa al Duca senza homini nostri né loro. Et che non volendo noi questo, non se ne parli più, etc. Or, Signor, ve prego per amor de Dio, non ve ne movati a furia, conservative el Signor Marchese, maxime per lo advisar a Sua Maestà. Se non lo voleti far, respondete cortessemente che diano Nepe o Castro al Signor Marchese et voi Rocca de Papa al ditto Signor Marchese; o, se vogliono che in nome sian del Duca, che metta li homini el Signor Marchese, che loro non lo farranno et voi restareti bene; et s'el fanno, non è né male né

215. Ascanio was probably leaving Marino en route for his castle in Genazzano, in order to be farther from Rome.

desonore dare ogni cosa al Signor Marchese in nome de Sua Maestà. Per amor de Dio, considerate bene che mo è l'ultima resolutione. Vedete quanti affanni et periculi sono, et Dio per sua bontà ve inspiri. Respondeti subito et scriveti a Sua Maestà, che è mal mandar io una posta senza nostra lettera: et la copia de l'ultima vostra resolution mandarò allo Imperatore. Da Roma, ogi martedì.

El Marchese crede più alla fede del Duca che se fosse quella de Dio. Li tempi sono così. Da me li fu resposto come conviene. Me disse: "Ve comando da parte de Sua Maestà che scrivate così, per che ho stentato come un cane et non se pò più, et, come la gente è tutta pagata, non ce è remedio." Sì che, Signor, de gratia, scriva dolcemente et in bono modo, che a lui par offerir assai pigliando Castro o Nepe, etc. Advisateme quando vanno le poste a Napoli, dove più in là de Marini se haveria a indirizar la vostre. De gratia, honori molto il Marchese nello scriver et in mostrarli fede.

Da Roma, ogi martedì a XX hore. Venga la resposta stasera.

A tergo
Al Signor Ascanio

Letter 23: Orvieto, 28 May [1541][216]

To Ercole II d'Este

After the outbreak of the Salt Wars Vittoria Colonna was forced to leave Rome very suddenly: she arrived in Orvieto on 17 March 1541 and took up residence in the Dominican convent of San Paolo.[217]

In this letter, Colonna reaffirms her affection for Ferrara, where she had spent some of the most peaceful and enjoyable months of her life in 1537 and 1538, in the company of Ercole II d'Este and his wife Renée de France (see Letter 14). In contrast to the dramatic events that have now overtaken her family, here Colonna proclaims herself to be tranquil, "most consoled," even though in the midst of "current difficulties." For some years she had kept her distance from courtly society, and now she realizes that the loss of material riches has endowed her with spiritual ones. The spiritual riches Colonna refers to are meant in an evangelical vein, the *thesaurum non deficientem in caelis* ("treasure in heaven that faileth not;" Luke 12:33), to which she refers frequently in her poetry.[218] To the

216. Original, autograph: ASMo, Cancelleria ducale, Carteggio principi esteri, b. 1248/4: Colonna, *Carteggio*, no. CXXXVIII.

217. On Colonna's stay in Orvieto, see Tordi, "Vittoria Colonna in Orvieto."

218. See for example "Anima, il Signor viene, omai disgombra" (S1:19; Colonna, *Sonnets*, 78) and "Vedremmo, se piovesse argento ed oro" (S1:33; Colonna, *Sonnets*, 128).

governor of Orvieto Colonna expressed it succinctly: "Let possessions come and go, as long as people are saved."[219]

☙

Most Illustrious and Excellent Signor,

If I could complain of the person whom I have praised most highly, I would complain of Your Excellency, for they tell me that you believed that in Lombardy I was headed somewhere else than to my most beloved Ferrara to find shelter under the religious and loving protection of Your Lordship. This would certainly be ample evidence of my ingratitude!

Your Excellency should know that even in my current difficulties I am most consoled, and I thank God that in losing all the riches of fortune he offers me the opportunity to gain those of the spirit. I am in a holy place, and most blessed since it belongs to His Holiness.[220] If I ever decide to leave the papal territories, Your Excellency will hear from Prudentia from Rome[221] at the church of Saint Paul, as last time. And I kiss your hand with all due humility and servitude, and also that of Her Excellency your wife.[222]

From Orvieto, in San Paulo, on the twenty-eighth of May.

Most dutiful servant of Your Most Excellent and Illustrious Lordship,
The Marchioness of Pescara

On the reverse:
To my Most Illustrious, Excellent and Esteemed Signor, the Duke of Ferrara

☙

[Letter 23]

Illustrissimo et Excellentissimo Signor,

Se io potessi dolerme della persona che più me ne sono lodata, me dolerei de Vostra Excellentia, che me dicono ha creso che io in Lombardia andasse altrove che alla mia desideratissima Ferrare et a star sotto la religiosa et amorevol protiption de Vostra Signoria. Certo gran testimonio serria questo della mia ingratitudine!

219. "La robba va e viene, purché sian salve le persone;" letter from Brunamonte de' Rossi, Governor of Orvieto, to Cardinal Alessandro Farnese, 15 May 1541; Tordi, "Vittoria Colonna in Orvieto," 528.

220. Orvieto was part of the Papal States.

221. Prudenza de Palma di Arpino was one of Colonna's servants.

222. Renée de France, duchess of Ferrara.

La Excellentia Vostra sappia che sto in questi travagli consolatissima, et ren-gratio Dio che con perder li beni della fortuna me dia occasion de acquistar quelli de l'animo, et sono in un santo loco et, per esser de Sua Santità, gratissimo. Et se mai determinasse partir da terra de Sua Beatitudine, Vostra Excellentia senteria Prudentia romana alla chiesia de San Paulo, come l'altra volta. Et con la debita humilità et servitù li baso le mano, et così alla Excellentia de Madama.
Da Orvieto, in San Paulo, a' dì XXVIII de maggio.

Serva obligatissima de Vostra Excellentissima et Illustrissima Signoria,
La Marchesa de Pescara

A tergo
Alo Illustrissimo et Excellentissimo Signor mio observandissimo, il Signor Duca de Ferra[ra]

Letter 24: Viterbo, 8 December [1541][223]
To Giulia Gonzaga

After her brief stay in Orvieto (see Letter 23), Colonna arrived in Viterbo in September 1541 in pursuit of the English Cardinal Reginald Pole,[224] who had recently been nominated as papal legate to that city. It was in Viterbo that the so-called *Ecclesia viterbiensis* (Church of Viterbo) was established in Pole's household, and its principal actors are named in this letter: Marcantonio Flaminio, Alvise [Luigi] Priuli, and Pietro Carnesecchi. These individuals, prominent members of the group known as the *Spirituali* or Spirituals, while they remained members of the Catholic Church, were in this period very open to dialogue with Protestant reformers, especially in relation to the key Lutheran doctrine of justification by faith. Vittoria Colonna was a discreet presence in this circle, but always actively there and able to establish solid and deep bonds with other members of the group. Without them "I would really be feeling low," as she writes to Giulia Gonzaga (see also Letter 36).

Giulia Gonzaga herself participated in the group of *Spirituali*, although from a distance in this period. Daughter of the Marquis of Sabbioneta, Gonzaga had been married aged only thirteen to Vespasiano Colonna, count of Fondi (ca. 1485–1528). In a complete break with tradition, on his death in 1528 her husband's will named Giulia Gonzaga as sole inheritor of his estate, as well as tutor to Isabella, his daughter from a previous marriage. From this extraordinary will

223. Original, autograph: ACDF, Stanza Storica, R 5–a, I.5, fols. 188v–89r; Copy: the same, R 5–c, fols. 659v–61r; Copy: the same, R 5–b, fol. 74r–v; Copy: the same, R 5–b, II.5, fols. 281v–82r: Colonna, *Carteggio*, no. CXLII.

224. See Letters 28 and 29.

resulted a dispute with the Colonna family that lasted for decades, and which eventually involved Giulia directly, brought in to negotiate with Isabella.[225] From 1535, Giulia Gonzaga resided in the convent of S. Francesco alle Monache in Naples. In Naples she met Juan de Valdés, a humanist and reformer who had come under suspicion of heresy in his home country of Spain and had fled to Rome and then to Naples; there he brought together a group of reformers which provided the foundation for the later Viterbo group. Gonzaga became devoted to Valdés, and featured as the interlocutor in his dialogue, the *Alfabeto cristiano* (*Christian Alphabet*), as well as inheriting all his manuscripts on his death in 1541. Gonzaga's very close relations with Valdés, as well as with Bernardino Ochino and Pietro Carnesecchi, brought her to the attention of the Inquisition, so that she is cited multiple times in the Inquisition trials of Carnesecchi and Cardinal Giovanni Morone.

A full transcription of this very letter from Colonna to Gonzaga is found within the records of the Inquisition trial of Pietro Carnesecchi. During his trial, Carnesecchi was asked to comment on the letter's contents, in particular on the phrase "for the health of my soul and for that of my body." The accused replied that "the lady Marchioness, before she came to know the cardinal [Pole], used to torment herself so much with fasting, hair shirts, and other kinds of mortification of the flesh that she had brought herself to a state of skin and bones. And she did this probably because she placed too much hope in these kinds of works, believing that they constituted true piety and religion, and thus the salvation of her very soul. But the cardinal admonished her, explaining to her that in practicing such austerity and rigor against her own body she actually offended God rather than pleasing him . . . and the lady began then to cease to practice such austerities, increasingly retreating to a far more reasonable and decent middle way."[226]

This letter testifies to the coldness with which Pole was treating Colonna by this date, and her frustration at being unable to demonstrate her affection openly to him. This frustration is a recurring theme in later years (see Letters 28, 29, 36 and 39).

225. Copello, "Vittoria Colonna a Carlo V." On Giulia Gonzaga see Camilla Russell, *Giulia Gonzaga and the Religious Controversies of Sixteenth-Century Italy* (Turnhout: Brepols, 2006); and Susanna Peyronel Rambaldi, *Una gentildonna irrequieta: Giulia Gonzaga fra reti familiari e relazioni eterodosse* (Rome: Viella, 2012).

226. "La signora Marchesa avanti che pigliasse l'amicitia del cardinale si affliggeva talmente con degiuni, cilicii et altre sorte di mortificationi della carne che si era redotta ad havere quasi la pelle in su l'osso: et ciò faceva forse con ponere troppa confidentia in simili opere, imaginandosi che in esse consistesse la vera pietà et religione, et per consequente la salute dell'anima sua. Ma poi che fu admonita dal Cardinale ch'ella piuttosto offendeva Dio che altrimenti con usare tanta austerità et rigore contra il suo corpo . . . la sudetta signora commincò a retirarsi da quella vita così austera, reducendose a poco a poco a una mediocrità ragionevole et honesta;" in Firpo and Marcatto, ed., *I processi inquisitoriali di Pietro Carnesecchi*, 2.1:1034. See Copello, "La signora marchesa," 25–28.

૮ᴗ

My Most Illustrious Lady,

Your Ladyship has always been so gracious to me: since that first time that I met you in Fondi[227] you must know that I have found nothing but courtesy in you, and now you have afforded me great consolation by sending so many good things to the Cardinal [Pole] and to these other gentlemen. For not only was I able to partake of them myself, thanks to the humanity of the Most Reverend Monsignor, but I have another great satisfaction, which is that Your Ladyship is causing him to begin to lose a certain strange habit he has of accepting any gift with terrible unwillingness. For just this morning Master Luigi Priuli[228] told me that he [Pole] received Your Ladyship's gifts with the greatest pleasure, seeing in them so much affection and charity, and he never considered that anything had prompted them other than his continuous desire to honor her and please her. Thus, My Lady, I who am so indebted to His Most Revered Lordship [Pole] for the health of my soul and for that of my body, for the first was endangered by superstition and the second by bad management,[229] imagine how much I wish to serve him, yet I have never been permitted to until now. But now I hope that he will be a little more flexible about such a reasonable wish. And if Your Ladyship, though absent, can achieve so much through Christian kindness, what might be achieved if, God willing, you could be here? Above all since, if I could have the consolation of conferring with you or rather learning truly what God through such excellent means has communicated to you,[230] I would have less need of these

227. The date of this meeting is unknown. Giulia inherited Fondi from her husband.

228. Alvise [Luigi] Priuli (?–1560) became Pole's closest friend and companion in 1536, and followed him on his various missions in Italy and overseas. Priuli was with Pole in Viterbo, at the Council of Trent, in England and at the Roman conclave. He paid a visit to Colonna on the very last day of her life; see Fabrizio Colonna, *Sulla tomba di Vittoria Colonna* (Rome: Stabilimento tipografico dell'opinione, 1887), 16.

229. Colonna's lack of consideration for her physical condition is made clear in a letter from the most famous doctor of the period, Girolamo Fracastoro, addressed to Carlo Gualteruzzi on 12 August 1543; Girolamo Fracastoro, *Hieronymi Fracastorii Veronensis, Adami Fumani canonici Veronensis, et Nicolai Archii comitis Carminum . . .* 2nd ed., 2 vols. (Pavia: Giovanni Antonio Volpi et Gaetano Volpi, 1739), 1:74–75: "Ma quello, ch'importa il tutto per l'opinion mia, è, che voi sapete, che sì come il corpo, quando si fa tiranno dell'animo, corrompe, e guasta tutta la sanità di quello, così anco l'animo quando si fa tiranno e non vero signor del corpo, strugge e corrompe la sanità di lui prima. . . . Questo poco discorso signor mio ho premesso, perché io dubito, che tutta l'origine delli suoi mali habbia principio da questo capo. . . . Per il signor M. Carlo vorrei che si trovasse il suo medico all'animo, che minutissimamente calculasse tutte le sue operationi, et fatto giusto equilibrio, desse al signor [= l'animo] quel che è suo, et al servo [= il corpo] quel che è suo, et tal medico bisogna sia et saggio, et di tanta auttorità, a cui sua signoria creda et obedisca, come l'Illustriss. et Reverendiss. Inghilterra. Et rassettato questo principio, io non dubio che tutto che è seguito non si rassetti."

230. Carnesecchi, during his trial, said: "In quella parte dove dice 'Quello che Dio per ottimi mezzi li ha communicato,' dico non sapermi imaginare che detta signora volesse intendere altro che la dottrina

gentlemen for I tend to long too much for their company, not only that of the Monsignor, who is very busy and thus I forgive him, but also of our excellent soul Master Flaminio,[231] whom I have seen but twice since he arrived, so that if it weren't for Master Luigi Priuli and Signor Carnesecchi, I would truly be distressed.

Certainly it will be good for Your Ladyship to return for a while to your homelands in Lombardy,[232] since you are already so well informed about the true celestial homeland, because you would greatly benefit from it; and passing through here, Viterbo, you could stop for a couple of months to give the Monsignor the opportunity to act on his desire to satisfy you, and me the chance to be blessed by you and serve you. On the assumption that everyone else writes to Your Ladyship of the Monsignor's good will towards you, I will not dare to prolong this letter further, for the pleasure of writing to you has taken me too much time; and I kiss your hands.

From Viterbo, in Santa Catharina, on the eighth of December.

Most devoted to serving Your Illustrious Ladyship,
The Marchioness of Pescara

I understand Your Ladyship has sent the commentary on Saint Paul,[233] which was much desired, above all by me for I have most need of it, thus I will thank you further and properly when I see you, God willing.

On the reverse:
To my Most Illustrious Lady, Lady Giulia Gonzaga de Colonna

Autograph by Giulia Gonzaga:
Peschara. 8 of December. Viterbo

In the hand of an inquisitorial official:
Among the writings of Lady Iulia

---

et instituzione che la signora donna Giulia haveva havuta per mezzo del Valdés;" Firpo and Marcatto, *I processi inquisitoriali di Pietro Carnesecchi*, 2.1:1034.

231. Marcantonio Flaminio was a humanist and Latin poet. He associated with Gian Matteo Giberti, knew Valdés in Naples, and was responsible for revising and publishing the *Beneficio di Cristo* by Benedetto da Mantova. He also accompanied Pole to the Council of Trent.

232. Giulia Gonzaga was born and raised in Gazzuolo, near Mantua.

233. The manuscript of Valdés's *Commentario o declaracion breve*, edited in Venice, 1556.

[Letter 24]

Illustrissima Signora mia,

Sempre Vostra Signoria me fece gratie, che la prima volta che la viddi in Fundi sa che non trovai cortesia se non in lei, et hor me ha dato molta consolatione a mandare tante et sì bone cose al Signor Cardinale et a questi altri Signori perché, ultra che io ne habia participato per humanità di Monsignor Reverendissimo, ne ho un'altra magior satisfatione, cioè che Vostra Signoria sia causa che comenzi a perdere una certa strana consuetudine che tiene di aceptar di malissima voglia ogni presente, perché questa matina messer Luisi Priuli me ha ditto che ha prese le cose della Signoria Vostra con grandissimo piacere, vedendo tanta affettione et charità, senza parer a Sua Signoria di haverneli dato causa con altro che col continuo desiderio de honorarla et compiacerli. Sì che, Signora mia, io che sono a Sua Signoria Reverendissima della salute de l'anima et di quella del corpo obligata, che l'una per superstitioni, l'altra per mal governo era in periculo, pensi Vostra Signoria si desidero posserlo servire, et non me è stato mai concesso sin qui; et hor spero che serrà un poco più flexibile a così ragionevol cose. Et se lla Signoria Vostra absente pò tanto con la sua christiana cortesia, hor che serrà se per gratia de Dio potessi esser qui? Masime che, havendo io la mia consolation di conferire con lei, anzi di imparar veramente quel che Dio per ottimi mezzi li ha comunicato, non haveria sì gran necessità di loro, che me bisogna desiderarli troppo. Non dico solo Monsignor, che è occupatissimo et lo ho per scusato, ma il nostro ottimo spirito messer Flaminio non lo ho visto se non doi volte poi che venne, sì che, se non fusse messer Luisi Priuli et il Signor Carnesechi, io starrei male. Et certo serria conveniente che la Signoria Vostra revedessi un poco la sua patria di Lombardia, hor che della vera celeste patria è sì ben informata, che li potria giovar pur assai; et passando de qui se potria firmar un par di mesi, dando a Monsignor occasion de mostrarli in effetto il desiderio che ha di satisfarla, et ad me di recever gratie da lei et di servirla. Et pensando che tutti scrivano a Vostra Signoria la ottima volontà de Monsignor verso lei, non ardirò di far questa lettera più longa, che 'l piacer di scriverli me ha trasportato pur troppo. Et ly baso le mano.

Da Viterbo in Santa Chatarina, a' dì VIII di decembre.

Deditissima servir Vostra Signoria Illustrissima,

La Marchesa di Pescara

Ho inteso che Vostra Signoria ha mandato la exposition sopra San Paulo che era molto desiderata, et più da me che ne ho più bisogno, però più ne lla rengratio et più quando la vederò, piacendo a Dio.

A tergo, autografo

Ala Illustrissima Signora mia, la Signora donna Iulia Gonzaga de Colonna

Autografo di Giulia Gonzaga
Peschara. De 8 de decembre. Viterbo

Di mano di un funzionario inquisitoriale
tra le scritture di donna Iulia

Letter 25: [before 1544][234]
To Costanza d'Avalos Piccolomini, Duchess of Amalfi

In 1544, a small book was published with the ponderous title *Litere della divina Vetoria Colonna Marchesana di Pescara alla Duchessa di Amalfi sopra la vita contemplativa di santa Caterina e sopra de la activa di santa Madalena non più viste in luce* (*Letters from the divine Vittoria Colonna Marchioness of Pescara to the Duchess of Amalfi on the contemplative life of Saint Catherine and the active life of Saint Magdalene never before brought to light*).[235] The work is significant as the first published collection of letters by a woman, as well as being the first book of spiritual letters, and it emerged at the beginning of the outpouring of epistolary works from the Italian presses.[236] Although no concrete evidence exists to prove the connection, it is hard to believe that such a work would have been printed without the author's consent.

The three letters contained in this slim volume are all addressed to the same person, Costanza d'Avalos Piccolomini, sister of Alfonso, cousin of Colonna's husband Ferrante and niece of the other Costanza d'Avalos. Costanza was raised on Ischia and remained there after her marriage in 1517 to Alfonso II Piccolomini, Duke of Amalfi (1499–1559). She was herself the author of spiritual poetry. She seems to have hosted Bernardino Ochino at her home,[237] and he sent her a letter of consolation after the death of her son. When her husband died in 1559, Costanza retired to the convent of Santa Chiara in Naples.

In the guise of personal letters, Colonna's missives to Costanza are really literary works, "characterized by singular expressive force and tonal complexity through ample recourse to metaphors drawing on biblical language, signaling deep theological and spiritual reflection."[238]

"The first letter in the triptych, constituting the necessary introduction as well as the connective theme, exhorts the reader to undertake direct spiritual

234. Colonna 1544, fols. A2r–3r; Ve 45, fols. 33v–34v: Colonna, *Carteggio*, no. CLXVIII.

235. On these letters see Doglio, "L''occhio interiore;'" Ranieri, "Vittoria Colonna e Costanza d'Avalos Piccolomini;" Camaioni, "'Per sfiammeggiar;'" Chemello, "Vittoria Colonna's Epistolary Works."

236. Doglio, "L''occhio interiore,'" 1001.

237. Firpo and Marcatto, *I processi inquisitoriali di Pietro Carnesecchi*, 2.3:1027.

238. "Caratterizzate da singolare forza espressiva, complessità di toni per l'ampio uso di metafore tratte dalla tradizione del linguaggio biblico, segno di una grande riflessione teologica e spirituale;" Ranieri, "Vittoria Colonna e Costanza d'Avalos," 488.

reading, *lectio divina*, privately in the peace and intimacy of the home."[239] Using the metaphor of the banquet, Colonna invites Costanza to read the Scriptures as the soul's only nourishment. In the second letter, dedicated to the Madonna, she goes on to outline the method with which one should approach sacred reading, confirming that "my dearest thought saw our Lady with its inner eye."[240] As she reaffirms in a later letter to Antonio Bernardi (Letter 35), in order to understand the Scriptures you must approach them with an inner vision, the vision provided by faith. The third letter to Costanza considers two saintly role models, Catherine of Alexandria and Mary Magdalene (Letter 25), both named in the book's title. All the letters have a "pedagogical structure," counterbalanced, however, by a "continuous and growing impulse towards the divine."[241]

The first part of this letter, which opens the collection, is located firmly in heaven and recounts the passage of the author's mind to contemplation of God the Trinity and the hierarchy of angels. In the second part it returns to earth, where the author insists on the importance of preparing the "thirsty soul" to receive divine grace. The soul must distance itself, cancel itself (see Letter 39), in order to become perfect, a process which bears close comparison to that outlined by Bartolomeo Cordoni (1471–1535) in the *Dyalogo della unione spiritual de Dio con l'anima* (the second edition of this work was published in 1539 by a close collaborator of Bernardino Ochino).[242] Once the contemplative journey is concluded, Colonna goes on, the soul can continue on its path towards God through the study of the Scriptures (Saint Paul), or the Church fathers (Saint Augustine), or else by meditating on exemplary figures (Mary Magdalene). Meditation on the life of Mary is particularly significant, and through this the discussion returns from its focus on the earthly back to the heavenly, as well as laying the ground for the second letter which will deal with Mary more fully.

~

239. "La prima lettera del trittico, che ne costituisce la premessa necessaria e insieme il principio connettivo, esorta alla lettura diretta, privata, nella quiete e nell'intimo della casa, della *lectio divina*;" Doglio, "L'occhio interiore,'" 1005.

240. "Il mio più caro pensiero vedeva con l'occhio interno la Donna nostra."

241. Doglio, "L'occhio interiore,'" 1004.

242. Bartolomeo Cordoni, *Dyalogo della unione spirituale de Dio con l'anima dove sono interlocutori l'amor divino, la sposa anima, et la ragione umana* (Milan: Francesco Cantalupo e Cicognara Innocenzo, 1539), in particular fols. 53r–57v; see also Michele Camaioni, "Libero spirito e genesi cappuccino: Nuove ipotesi e studi sul *Dyalogo di unione spirituale di Dio con l'anima* di Bartolomeo Cordoni e sul misterioso trattato dell'Amore evangelico," *Archivio italiano per la storia della pietà* 25 (2012): 303–72.

Most elevated spirit,

If during a domestic dinner[243] you imagined yourself, as I believe, to be that beloved young man[244] who understood the divine secrets in Christ's sacred and holy breast,[245] through that wondrous delight which joins us warmly in a single desire, I beg you on your awaited return to let me share, as you usually do, in the blessings received, so that, carried on his wings, I may be brought by your merit where I do not dare to hope to go. For I know that, by God's mercy, it will be clear to your mind how the high invisible light makes itself visible to his elect, how on the marvelous throne without sitting that light is quieted[246] and how generous it is of its own accord with itself, and how that great Father generates his Son, and how this supreme principle is equal to him in everything,[247] just as the burning flame proceeding from these two is not in any way inferior.[248] You will see how the unity of their divinity is mere substance, without any accident.[249] You will see how wisdom incarnate,[250] without adding a fourth name to the three persons, has so sublimated our humanity that it has become one being with God. You will see the first order of the first hierarchy all burning, as it is fed and satisfied by a single flame;[251] and the second order, like bright intellects that live ever sated by pure understanding;[252] and the third order,[253] that are like thrones made ready that embrace the highest good, and like wise judges stand by, blessed and sincere. And because I know that the living spirit will pause the

243. See Doglio, "L'occhio interiore,'" 1006.

244. St. John the Evangelist; see in John 13:22–23. Colonna's sonnet "Quando quell'empio tradimento aperse" (S1:17; Colonna, *Sonnets*, 88) draws on the same passage.

245. In both the Latin and vernacular traditions, John's act of resting on Christ's breast was interpreted as a moment of revelation, related to the vision recounted in the Apocalypse.

246. This is a reference to Aristotelian philosophy, in which God is defined as "unmoved mover."

247. This is a paraphrase of the Nicene Creed according to which Christ is "genitum, non factum, consubstantialem Patris" ("Begotten, not made, being of one substance with the Father").

248. Another paraphrase of the Nicene Creed: "qui ex Patre Filioque procedit." The phrase was added to the Creed to clarify the natures of Christ and the Holy Spirit, which were in no way inferior to God the father (as Colonna makes clear). The clarification distinguishes the Catholic Creed from the Orthodox one.

249. This is the mystery of the Trinity expressed in Platonic language deriving especially from Saint Augustine's *De trinitate* (*On the Trinity*).

250. Christ was defined as "wisdom incarnate" in the medieval Trinitarian tradition, again drawing on Saint Augustine; see his *De utilitate credendi*, XV: "Sapientia Dei incarnata, via ad religionem commodissima." Dante was also influenced by the tradition; see, for example, *Inferno* 3.6; *Paradiso* 23.37.

251. A reference to the Seraphim. Pseudo-Dionysius the Areopagite, in his work *De coelesti hierarchia* (*On the Celestial Hierarchy*), constructed a scheme of three angelic hierarchies, each of which contains three choirs. The first hierarchy contains the Seraphim, the Cherubim, and the Thrones; the second contains Dominions, Virtues, and Powers; and the third Principalities, Archangels, and Angels.

252. A reference to the Cherubim.

253. The Thrones.

glorious inner vision at this height, here I will pause my mind, leaving contemplation of the highest hierarchies to a day which is not devoted to our Holy Counselor.[254]

And if you have time to hear how from that great banquet blessings were sent down to us mortals, then learn, I pray you, how to prepare your thirsty soul to receive them.[255] But since I know that in your annihilation you will shine so brightly in that divine light, so aflame in that beautiful fire and so perfect in the highest supreme perfection that you will think only of nourishing yourself, it seems to me that when your Spirit draws away, and you start to feel the earthly heaviness calling you down, you will pause with my most observant father, the apostle Paul, and my great wise Augustine, or else with my most fervent servant Magdalene, and from them you will learn all that which I asked of you. And above all I pray you to try to see how our most singular patron and queen Mary has incarnated within herself the miraculous mystery of the highest Word,[256] and how she melts with divine passion to see her own flesh made a living eternal sun,[257] and how she lives blessed in the refreshing and secure peace of heaven, and how she rejoices to see that from her living light are born the rays that make Paradise beautiful, and through her kindness they pass through the elect to make them one and at peace in the holy eternal light of God, towards which in her goodness may she guide us.

༄

254. The Day of Pentecost.

255. The metaphor of the banquet at which the soul is fed returns in Colonna's sonnet "S'io, mossa con Zacheo da intenso affetto:" "Sperar potrei che questo indegno petto / Gli fosse albergo . . . / Tal che lieta ed umil nel gran convito / Gli apparecchiassi una candida fede / Per mensa, e poi per cibo l'alma e 'l core" (S1:57; Colonna, *Sonnets*, 66): "I could then hope that my unworthy breast / might give him shelter . . . ; and then joyfully, humbly, at the eternal banquet I would lay down for him my sincere faith as the table and my soul and heart as his food." Divine thirst—a recurring metaphor in Colonna's poetry—has scriptural origins in Psalms 41:2, as well as in the gospel of the Samaritan woman in John 4:13–14. See also Dante, *Purgatorio* 21:1–4: "La sete natural che mai non sazia / Se non con l'acqua onde la femminetta / Samaritana domandò la grazia, / mi travagliava."

256. Colonna seems to be paraphrasing the expression "O magnum mysterium et admirabile sacramentum" from the responsorial chant from the Matins of Christmas.

257. The image of Mary melting with divine passion returns in Colonna's sonnet "Donna, dal ciel gradita a tanto onore:" "Or non si sciolse l'alma, e dentro e fore / Ciascun tuo spirto ed ogni parte viva / Col latte insieme a un punto non s'univa / Per gir tosto a nudrir l'alto Signore?" (S1:103; Colonna, *Sonnets*, 96): "Did your soul not melt away, / and within and without your spirits and all / living parts not flow out in your milk / and speed to nurture your holy Lord?" It derives from the devotional tradition, as found for example in the poetic collection *Thesauro de la sapientia euangelica* (Milan: Gottardo da Ponte, 1525), fol. D2r: "Liquefar sentivi el core / sì somersa in tal dolcezza."

[Letter 25]

Ellevatissimo spirito,

Se in questa tua domestica cena ti figurarai, come io credo, esser tu quel amato giovene che nel sacro santo petto intese i divini segreti, per quella cara dilectione che caldamente ci lega in un desio ti prego al tuo aspettato ritorno voglii farmi, come suoli, participe delle gratie recevute, acciò che, dalle ale sue sospinta, sia dal tuo merito portata ove dal mio sperar non lice. Perché so che, mercé del Signor Nostro, sarà chiaro alla tua mente come l'alta invisibil luce si fa visibile a' soi elletti; come sopra il mirabel trono senza seder si quieta et di se stessa con sé medesma si rende facile; et come quel gran Padre genera il suo Figliolo; et come questo summo principio gli è simile in ogni cosa; come l'ardente fiamma, procedendo da questi dui, non è lor ponto inferiore. Vederai l'unità della divinità loro esser solo una sostantia senza poterci esser accidente alchuno. Vederai come l'incarnata sapientia, senza aggionger nome de quattro alle tre persone, ha sublimato tanto questa nostra humanità che l'ha fatta una medema cosa con Dio. Vedrai il primo ordine della prima gerarchia tutto ardente come di sola fiamma si pasce e si contenta; il secondo, quali lucidi inteletti che di puro intendimento si vivono sempre sacii; il terzo, che come preparate sedie abbraciano il sommo bene e a modo de saggi giudici assisteno beati et sinceri. Et perché so che 'l vivace spirito in questo alto fermerà l'alma interna vista, qua fermerò la mente, lasciando la speculatione de l'alte gerarchie per giorno non dedicato al Santo Consolator nostro.

Et se pur hai tempo de intender come da quella larga mensa si mandano le gratie alli mortali, sappi, ti prego, come se ha da preparar la sitiente anima per riceverla. Ma perché so che nel tuo alienarti starai sì lucida in quel divin lume, sì accesa nel bellissimo fuoco et sì perfetta ne l'alta somma perfectione che attenderai sol a cibarti, mi par che a l'allentar dello Spirito, quando già senti che la gravezza terrena vol richiamarti, ti fermi col mio osservandissimo padre Paulo, o col mio gran lume Agostino, overo con la ferventissima serva mia Madalena, et da essi t'informa di quel che te ho supplicato. Et sopra tutto ti prego ti sforzi veder come la singularissima patrona et regina nostra Maria il mirabil mistero de l'altissimo Verbo ha incarnato in lei, e come se liquefa di divino ardore di veder la sua istessa carne fatta un vivo eterno sole, et come vive beata nella riposata et sicura pace del cielo, et quanto gode di vedere che dal suo vivo lume nascono i raggi che fanno bello il Paradiso e che della sua benignità passino ne i beati per unirli e aquetarli ne l'alta eterna luce di Dio, alla qual per sua bontà ci conduchi.

Letter 26: [before 1544][258]
To Costanza d'Avalos Piccolomini

Although the title of the work suggests the opposite, in her collection of spiritual letters Colonna presents Catherine of Alexandria as the model for an active life and Mary Magdalene as the model for a contemplative life. In fact the letters at no point deal in any depth with either concept.[259] Nor is Colonna interested in entering into the contemporary debates about the identity of Mary Magdalene:[260] she simply continues the ancient tradition of amalgamating into the one persona a number of evangelical women (Mary of Magdala, Mary of Bethany and the prostitute). She does draw more heavily on medieval hagiographic sources in writing of the Magdalene's thirty years in the wilderness in Provence[261]—the region where, in the town of St. Maximin-la-Sainte-Baume, stood the great basilica of Mary Magdalene, to which Colonna had planned a pilgrimage (never undertaken).[262]

This letter is divided into three parts. The first serves as an introduction, in which the author sets out the main focus of her discourse, that is the "grades and graces" that Christ bestowed upon the two female saints. In the second part of the letter, the two women are examined in parallel and compared: the emphasis on vision and interpretation is clear: *vedo, credo, considero, penso*.[263] The verbs that Colonna cites in Latin draw out the key quality of each saint: Mary Magdalene *dilexit* (loved) Christ; while Catherine *agnosce* (knows), with the sublime intelligence of faith. The final part of the letter is a prayer for intercession with God by these two female saints.

In the 1546 Valgrisi edition of Colonna's *Rime spirituali* the paralleling of Mary Magdalene and Catherine of Alexandria is repeated: the sonnets dedicated to the two saints are printed side by side, reinforcing Colonna's implication that together they represent the highest model of female sanctity, uniting a burning love for Christ with an unusual intellectual capacity used in the service of faith.[264] It is interesting to see her examining and clarifying the roles of these holy women, in light of her confirmation to Marguerite de Navarre that the spiritual examplars provided by members of one's own sex are the most useful (see Letter 24).

༄

258. Colonna 1544, fols. B1v–3r; Ve 45, fols. 37–38r: Colonna, *Carteggio*, no. CLXX.

259. Camaioni, "'Per sfiammeggiar,'" 136; see also 133–34.

260. Camaioni, "'Per sfiammeggiar,'" 138.

261. Sources such as the scriptural commentaries of Rabanus Maurus and Jacopo da Varagine's collected hagiographies, the *Legenda aurea* (*Golden Legend*).

262. Colonna, *Carteggio*, no. LXXIX.

263. Doglio, "L''occhio interiore,'" 1011.

264. The sonnets in question are "Donna accesa, animosa, e da l'errante" (S1:121; Colonna, *Sonnets*, 77) and "Ne l'alta eterna rota il pie' fermasti" (S1:122; Colonna, *Sonnets*, 123).

Most beloved sister, I wish to speak with you of two glorious women: our advocate and most faithful escort Magdalene; and the one whose painful death is celebrated today, or indeed her joyful life, Catherine. And even though the great king told his disciples, "Whosoever will be great among you, let him be your minister; and whosoever will be chief among you, let him be your servant,"[265] so that any kind of comparison is a grave error, nonetheless because I will speak of the glory of heaven, of which this incarnate truth [i.e., Christ] said "In my Father's house are many mansions,"[266] trusting in my humble and loving, longstanding and renewed obedience to them, I will dare to distinguish a little the grades and graces which our great and true husband and Lord granted to them.[267] And then we will pray to the true judge who predestined them to such glory that, just as he sees them on high with his compassionate judgment, so he should depict them in our low minds, not with the same rays which decorate them on high, but in such a way that we here below may understand and sustain the image.

I see the most fervent Magdalene listening at the feet of the Lord, "Dilexit multum,"[268] and Catherine, imprisoned, "Agnosce, filia, creatorem tuum."[269] The first seems to fly on wings of love to the high rank of the seraphim, the other on those of intellect to take her place among the seraphim. I see that to one is given the name "contemplative," and to the other the beautiful and rare name of beloved virginity. I see the tears of the first reviving her brother on the fourth day,[270] and the prayers of the second summoning the Angel from heaven to break the cruel wheel, turning it instead on four thousand gentiles, not to bring death to them, but to bring life to infinite others. I see both of them, with their passionate, wise and sweet words, converting queens and all their kingdoms and great numbers of people. She [the Magdalene], that beloved disciple, I believe deserved above all others to see him glorious and immortal;[271] and the grateful Lord made clear how her passion, perseverance and faithful and cherished love were pleasing to him. And to confirm her as his apostle, he commanded her to be the first to bring word of the long-awaited news and the wondrous mystery of his resurrection.[272] I imagine that he said to the

---

265. Matthew 20:26–27.

266. John 14:2.

267. The "grades and graces" to which Colonna refers here are probably the steps taken by these two women towards heaven and holiness, and the blessings each received from God.

268. This is a citation from Luke 7:47, "she loved much:" in the gospel passage Christ pardons a sinful woman whom Colonna—in line with a long-standing hagiographic tradition—identifies as Mary Magdalene.

269. The citation is from the *Legenda aurea* by Jacopo da Varagine: "know, daughter, your creator."

270. The reference is to Lazarus, brother of Mary and Martha, who had been dead for four days before he was revived by Christ; see John 11:1–44.

271. As reported in John's gospel, Mary Magdalene was the first to see the risen Christ; John 20:1–18.

272. See John 20:17: "Vade autem ad fratres meos, et dic eis: Ascendo ad Patrem meum, et Patrem vestrum, Deum meum, et Deum vestrum" ("But go to my brethren, and say to them: I ascend to my

other woman [Catherine]: "Do not fear anything, for I will always be with you,"[273] and he openly proclaimed how much he appreciated her intrepid spirit, her most learned and passionate disputations, the true and constant faith that she had shown in him. I see that the first of these women underwent thirty-three years of continuous martyrdom and once she had purified her gold, she wished so ardently to test it that she transformed into a most pure virgin and her lamp shone brightly for her most beloved husband.[274] To the other woman, a true, immaculate virgin, he conveyed the light of his wisdom through his martyrdom and the shedding of his blood. I see the convert, from the time when each day she loved him more, following him to the cross with attitudes of ever greater humility, and when his death caused the faith of other people to grow weaker, her love grew only stronger as she followed and served the holy mother, and received with her, Queen of Heaven, the Holy Spirit; and when she became a passionate and wise preacher of the divine word, on the high mountain of her penitence, she was visited frequently by the radiant sun of his exquisite love. The other, a brave and intrepid virgin, I see submitting with firm and sure faith to every kind of torment, longing to give her life for her redeemer out of her pure and deep love, and through her sufferings securing the faith of those she had converted with inexpressible joy and exceptional steadfastness. I think about how amazing it was that her virginal and sacred body was carried by angels over such a distance to that noble mountain where ancient law was passed down to the chosen people.[275] I think that it was a wondrous thing that the living body of the beloved Apostle was carried seven times a day by angels to listen to the harmony of the heavens.[276] In this way, Catherine in a brief space of time with her death and martyrdom showed how she would always serve him, and Magdalene through her long suffering testified that she would have willingly embraced any bitter torment or brutal martyrdom. So now I see them both, standing ecstatic and joyous before the true sun that looks upon them with a loving gaze, and it seems to me that with abundant light from its brightest rays it adorns and caresses them always, and with a generous hand it rewards and bestows upon them its deepest and most cherished blessings.

Father and to your Father, to my God and your God").

273. The *Legenda aurea* states: "Agnosce, filia, creatorem tuum pro cuius nomine laboriosum subiisti conflictum, constans esto, quia ego tecum sum."

274. As stated earlier, Colonna believed that Mary Magdalene and the prostitute described in Luke 7:36–50 were one and the same person, now transformed into a Bride of Christ awaiting the arrival of the Bridegroom with a burning lamp, as in the Parable of the Wise Virgins from Matthew 25:1–13.

275. According to the legend, angels carried Catherine's body to Mount Sinai, that is, to the same place where Moses had received the stone tablets on which the Ten Commandments were inscribed.

276. Colonna follows a long-standing tradition in defining Mary Magdalene here as an Apostle, as the first to witness Christ's resurrection and carry the news to the other disciples. Mary Magdalene was deemed to be the "apostle to the apostles" ("apostolorum apostola") in texts by both Rabanus Maurus (*De vita beatae Mariae Magdalenae*, XXVII) and Thomas Aquinas (*In Ioannem Evangelistam Expositio*, c. XX, L. III, 6).

Thus may these women permit us to ask him whether, without the intervention of darkness, by their saintly intercessions we may approach that ultimate truth and light,[277] as though mirroring the works of their beautiful bodies and imitating the thoughts of their pious and noble minds, that we may pay the true homage that we owe to our Lord, at whose divine feet, I believe, one of these women rests eternally in immense joy and true peace, and the other lives jubilantly at the right hand of the Queen of Heaven as bride to her son.[278] So she who was chosen before all other women [Magdalene] and she who was the first among virgins [Catherine] together give thanks with incessant praises to the glorious Queen for the first principle, God.[279]

∽

[Letter 26]

De due gloriose donne, sorella amantissima, vorrei ragionar teco: della nostra advocata et fedelissima scorta Maddalena et di quella che hoggi si celebra la penosa morte, ançi felice vita, Catherina. Et benché il sommo Re nostro dicesse a' suoi discepoli "Qui voluerit inter vos maior fieri, sit vester minister, et qui voluerit inter vos primus esse, erit vester servus," per donde ogni comparatione è massimo errore, pur, perché io vo considerando la gloria del Cielo, della quale questa incarnata verità parlando disse "In domo patris mei mansiones multe sunt," confidando ne l'humil et amorosa mia verso loro antica et rinovata servitù, ardirò distinguere un poco i gradi et le gratie, che 'l grande et vero sposo et Signor nostro ha loro concesse. Et poi supplicaremo esso vero giudice che le ha degnate a tanto bene che, quali col suo piatoso giudicio ne l'alte sedi le discerne, nei bassi pensieri nostri le dipinga, non già con quei raggi con quai là su viveno ornate, ma come qua giù et capir et sostener le possiamo.

Vedo la ferventissima Maddalena udir, a' piedi del Signore, "Dilexit multum," et Caterina, nella carcere, "Agnosce, filia, creatorem tuum." L'una pare che per amore sen voli a l'alto grado de' seraphini, l'altra che per intelligentia nei seraphini se collochi. Vedo a quella esser dato il titolo della contemplativa et a questa il bello et raro nome de l'amata virginità. Vedo alle lagrime de l'una resuscitare il quatriduano fratello, et alle preghiere de l'altra scender l'Angel dal cielo et rompendo la cruda rota rivoltarla a danno de quattro milia gentili, non per causar morte a quelli, ma per dar vita ad altri infiniti. Ad ambedue con le ignite, saggie et

---

277. This phrase, which makes explicit reference to the orthodox belief in the intercession of the saints, does not appear in Ve 45.

278. Catherine is often represented as the mystical bride of Christ.

279. The final words of this letter recall the fourth-century hymn of thanks, the *Te Deum*: "Tibi omnes angeli, / tibi caeli et universae potestates, / tibi cherubim et seraphim / incessabili voce proclamant: / "Sanctus, sanctus, sanctus" ("To thee all Angels cry aloud, the Heavens, and all the Powers therein, to thee Cherubim and Seraphim continually do cry: Holy, Holy, Holy").

dolci parole convertir vedo regine con li regni et numero grandissimo di persone. Considero che quella amata discepola meritò prima de tutti vederlo glorioso e immortale, dando chiaro testimonio il Signor grato quanto il suo ardore, la sua perseveranza et il suo fido et accetto amore gli fosse piacciuto; et per certificarla che era sua apostola, le comandò che fosse la prima annunciatrice de la aspettata novella et del mirabil mistero della sua resurrettione. Considero che a quest'altra disse: "Non temere cosa alcuna, ch'io sarò sempre teco," onde apertamente dichiarò quanto l'intrepido animo, la dottissima et calda disputatione, la sincera et costante fede che haveva per lui mostrata gli era stata accetta. Vedo che l'una con trentatré anni di continuo martirio, poi di già esser purgato il suo oro, volse talmente cimentarlo che purissima vergine et luminosa aparesse la sua lampa nel conspetto de l'amantissimo sposo; a l'altra, sincerissima vergine immaculata, col martirio et col proprio sangue egli mostrò nel lume suo la sua prudentia. Vedo la convertita donna, da l'hora che ardentemente lo amò ogni giorno più accesa, con nuovi et humili affetti fino alla croce seguirlo, et quando agli altri per la sua morte s'intepidì la fede, accendersi a lei l'amore, accompagnare et servir sempre la santa madre, haver con lei, Regina del cielo, lo Spirito Santo; fatta poi ferventissima et dotta pronunciatrice del verbo divino, et ne l'alto monte della sua penitentia, spessissimo dal suo fulgente sole esser con somma carità visitata. Vedo l'audace et intrepida vergine con saldissima et sagace fede esporsi ad ogni tormento, desiderar con puro et forte affetto dare al suo redentore la propria vita, con letitia innarrabile et fermezza inusitata confermar nella passione li convertiti da lei. Penso quanto gran cosa fu quel virgineo et sacro corpo fosse per man de gli angeli portato per sì longo spatio al prezzato monte, ove l'antica legge si diede al popol caro. Et penso che mirabil cosa fu che sette volte il giorno da l'Apostola diletta per gli angeli fosse portato il corpo vivo ad ascoltar l'armonia del cielo; sì che l'una nel breve tempo con la morte et al martìre dimostri quanto haveria sempre servito, et l'altra con la longa fatica fece fede che ogni grave tormento et ogni grave martìre gli sarebbe stato caro. Sì che ambe due felicissime dinanzi al vero sole, che con piatoso occhio le riguarda, lietissime le discerno, et parmi che con abbondanti luci delli suoi più vivi raggi le adorna et ablandisse continuo, et con larga mano le sue più interne et gratie care l'impartisce et dona.

Così ne concedino elle impetrare da lui che, senza interposition di tenebre, per lor santo mezo ad esso vero luminoso fine condur ci possiamo, et quali specchi le opre dei bellissimi lor corpi e i pensieri delle sante et chiare menti imitando, rendiamo il vero culto conveniente al nostro Signore, ai divini piedi del quale l'una credo con immenso gaudio in tranquilla et vera pace eternamente si riposa, et l'altra alla destra della donna del Paradiso, come sposa del suo figlio, felicissima vive. Onde poi alla gloriosa Regina quella come eletta sopra ogni altra donna et questa come prima vergine rendono con incessabil lode gratie del principio vero.

Letter 27: [1535–1542][280]
[To Bernardino Ochino]

We know this letter only via a printed edition of 1545 in which the recipient is not recorded. The hypothesis that it was written to Bernardino Ochino[281] is based above all on the form of address, "My Revered and most Esteemed Father," very suitable for a friar.[282] The decision to omit the recipient's identity from a letter published in 1545 also points to the likelihood that the missing name was Ochino's: he had fled to Switzerland in 1542, so that just three years later the inclusion of his name would have been extremely risky. A further letter to an unnamed recipient, probably again Ochino, included in the same printed edition is a kind of postscript to this one on the same theme.[283] It has also been suggested that Colonna's prose work, the *Pianto sopra la Passione di Cristo*, was originally written in the form of a letter addressed to Ochino.[284]

In the 1545 edition, the two letters to Ochino follow the three addressed to Costanza d'Avalos (see Letters 25 and 26), and share many thematic and stylistic qualities. Adriana Chemello suggests that "they constitute a small 'appendix,' a related reflection on the sermons of the friar."[285] The two sets of correspondence certainly share a tendency to cite and paraphrase liberally from the gospels, just as Ochino did in his famous sermons.[286] They also offer us further insight into the manner in which Colonna mined those gospels in order to excavate the experiences of the female protagonists that so fascinated her.

This letter is born out of a "simple meditation" on the gospels, specifically the story of the adulteress from John 8. This same meditative practice led Colonna to compose her prose works including the *Pianto sopra la Passione di Cristo*, the *Oratione sull'Ave Maria* and the letters to Costanza d'Avalos (Letters 25 and 26), as well as a number of her sonnets. In one of her sonnets, "Doi modi abbiam da veder l'alte e care," she details the two instruments needed in order to grow ones

---

280. Ve 45, fol. 38v: Colonna, *Carteggio*, no. CXLIV. If this letter was in fact addressed to Ochino, it cannot have been written after he fled Italy in summer 1542. Colonna met Ochino in March 1535, but it seems more likely that this letter dates from the late 1530s or the 1540s.

281. See also Letters 13, 14, 17, and 27.

282. Colonna, *Carteggio*, no. CXLIV. The only other letters from Colonna to use the address "Revered Father" were those addressed to the Benedictine friars Benedetto Canofilo and Feliciano (Colonna, *Carteggio*, no. XXVIII, LXXX, and LXXXI). As for the signature, "daughter" reappears in only two other letters, to father Feliciano (Colonna, *Carteggio*, no. XXVIII) and to sister Serafina Contarini (Colonna, *Carteggio*, no. CXLVII), while the term "disciple" is not used anywhere but here.

283. Colonna, *Carteggio*, no. CXLV.

284. Edited in Simoncelli, *Evangelismo italiano*, 423–28; Pagano and Ranieri, *Nuovi documenti*, 119–27; Cargnoni, *I frati cappuccini*, 2:251–59; Jung-Inglessis, "Il *Pianto della Marchesa*," 115–47; an English translation is in Haskins, *Who is Mary?*, 53–65.

285. Chemello, "Vittoria Colonna's Epistolary Works," 28.

286. See Cargnoni, *I frati cappuccini*, 3:2115–305.

faith, what she calls "the sacred papers" (the Scriptures) and "the book of the cross" (S1:165). Her personal meditation on biblical episodes leads Colonna to visualize each event, in an intense process of identification with the protagonists of the holy stories which is driven by an overwhelming desire to *see* the gestures and emotions at play, almost as if via a kind of interpenetration of the words, gestures and feelings. As a consequence, in her poetry and prose reflecting on biblical events or on the lives of the saints, she has frequent recourse to verbs such as *veggio* (I see), *mi parea* (it seemed to me), *scorgo* (I make out; see for example Letter 26).[287] Over the course of the meditation, questions arise over details that are left out of the biblical account: how did the Virgin feel as she fed the Christ child with her milk? Or as she witnessed Christ's death on the cross? Or when she laid her head upon his breast? To answer such questions, Colonna must pass from vision to imagination. This is an active form of contemplation, and the verbs therefore change to the hypothetical mood (*credo che*, I believe that; *penso che*, I think that): The letter below is constructed in just this way, as is the whole of Colonna's prose work the *Pianto sopra la Passione di Cristo*. First-person verbs of perception and imagination litter these texts as they do her poetry.

In this letter Colonna offers both a personal rereading of the gospel account of the adulterous woman, and one that is at the same time anchored in long-standing textual traditions. One of the elements of the story that particularly captures her attention is the impact of Christ's gaze on the crowd of onlookers. Christ bends over on the ground to write, and then stands up and looks around at the Pharisees and at the adulteress and speaks to them. Everyone present feels pierced by his gaze, but in Colonna's literary retelling of the event, the Pharisees "could not stand his gaze; . . . seeing how the sun in those beautiful eyes was overshadowed," while the adulteress saw "in those sainted eyes . . . a thousand rays of bright hope, and his face aflame with charity." In particular, the adulteress appears as the recipient of "a singular grace, probably one of the greatest that Christ ever gave on earth." After Christ absolved the woman, he made her "free from sin," "certain that she would never again be condemned, nor be capable of sinning in future." Sinlessness, in the spiritual literature of that period, was viewed as the culmination of the soul's journey towards God: "when the soul becomes at one with God, so that it places all its will in God, then it becomes capable of receiving the influx of divine grace and the fire of divine love."[288] The adulteress, as Colonna tells it, completed her journey to God all of a sudden: "She abandoned herself entirely to Christ and thought nothing of herself."

The doctrine according to which man, once justified by grace and elected to perfection, is rendered incapable of sin by that same grace, has as its corollary the denial of free will and negation of the virtue of constancy. Once man is pardoned,

---

287. Colonna, *Carteggio*, no. CLXIX and Letter 25.

288. Cordoni, *Dyalogo della unione spirituale*, fol. 112v. On this work see also Letter 39.

he is free to sin again. Ever since the Council of Vienna in 1311–1312, this doctrine had been condemned as heresy, but it had gained new traction in Colonna's lifetime thanks to the work of the Dominican Battista Carioni da Crema, the Benedictines Luciano degli Ottoni and Giorgio Siculo,[289] and of Bernardino Ochino himself.[290] In January 1547 the Council of Trent restated the impossibility of enjoying a state of freedom from sin on earth.[291] This letter therefore contains some of Colonna's most explicitly heterodox writing.

～

My Revered and Most Esteemed Father,

It occurs to me to write a simple meditation, with due humility, about the Gospel of the adulteress; thus I will leave aside the difficulties that have already been widely aired and discussed, to do with why Christ bent down and wrote on the ground, etc. [292] I will only say that the adulteress received a singular blessing, probably one of the greatest blessings that Christ ever gave on earth. Scripture tells us of Christ's two comings.[293] First he came in abundant sweetness, displaying only great goodness, clemency and mercy, and preached wherever he went that he had

---

289. See Massimo Firpo, *Nel labirinto del mondo: Lorenzo Davidico tra santi, eretici, inquisitori* (Florence: Olschki, 1992); and Adriano Prosperi, *L'eresia del Libro Grande: Storia di Giorgio Siculo e della sua seta* (Milan: Feltrinelli, 2000), 164–65.

290. See Veronica Copello, "Per un commento alle rime spirituali di Vittoria Colonna: Considerazioni a partire dal sonetto S1:52," *Schifanoia* 58–59 (2020): 165–71.

291. See Session VI, Chapter XIII, and the synthesis in Canon 22: "Si quis dixerit, justificatum vel sine speciali auxilio Dei in accepta justitia perseverare posse, vel cum eo non posse: anathema sit" ("If any shall say that a justified person, either can persevere in acceptable righteousness without the special assistance of God, or cannot do so with it; let him be accursed").

292. John 8:6: "Jesus autem inclinans se deorsum, digito scribebat in terra" ("Jesus, bowing himself down, wrote with his finger on the ground"). The Church Fathers and commentators over the centuries spent much time debating the significance of Jesus's actions in bending to write on the ground when questioned by the pharisees and teachers of the law; see, for example, Jerome, *Adversus pelagianos*, 2.17; Augustine, *In Evangelium Ioannis tractatus*, 33.5.

293. According to the Church Fathers, the first coming was when Christ was made flesh in order to save mankind, the second will be when he returns on the day of the Apocalypse to judge the living and the dead. See, for example, Augustine, *Enarrationes in Psalmos* (*Expositions on the Psalms*), 24:10: "Et ideo universae viae Domini, duo adventus Filii Dei, unus miserantis, alter iudicantis. . . . Intellegunt enim Dominum misericordem primo adventu, et secundo iudicem, qui mites et mansueti requirunt testamentum eius" (Psalm 25 in most English versions: "And therefore all the ways of the Lord are the two advents of the Son of God, the one in mercy, the other in judgment. . . . For they understand the Lord as merciful at His first advent, and as the Judge at His second, who in meekness and gentleness seek His testament." See also Augustine, *Enarrationes* 9.1.2 and John Chrysostom, *Homily on Psalm 49*.

come for all sinners, as doctor to the sick,[294] to minister, to bring peace, light, grace, all aflame with charity, clothed in humility, most sweet and merciful. When he comes again he will be armed, and he will demonstrate his justice, majesty, grandeur and infinite power, and there will be no time for mercy nor any place for blessings. This fortunate woman was blessed to be judged by the most just and truthful judge during his first, sweet coming when his words to us were kind; for, even though it was always his intention to judge the whole world, I do not think that his opponents elected him judge, nor did she, who was there and remained silent, but instead he freely assumed and executed the role of judge precisely in this act, that is by absolving her now and making her free from sin from that time forward beginning when he said: "Amplius noli peccare" ["Go and sin no more"].[295] And as he is immutable, and his true words infallible, it must be said that there was no need to judge her further. And since all those to whom Christ conceded particular grace can be considered to have been saved,[296] in her case it can be seen clearly, rather, (and it is an even greater thing), we should take it as certain that she lived a blessed life on earth, absolved from all past sins, and certain that she would never again be condemned, nor be capable of sinning in future. No one has ever done anything more useful for their closest and most beloved friend than did her enemies for her: they went to test Christ and do her injury, and instead they were confounded and overwhelmed, while she was left absolved and secure. Wishing to propel her into evil, instead they led her to the living font of all goodness, they positioned her midway between their darkness and Christ's true light; and they presented the law of Moses[297] to the founder of all laws,[298] the creator of all nature, bestower of faith and grace, believing either that he would transgress the law or that he would fail in his mercy. But the stones that in their wicked harshness they would hurl against her, and their malign intent, reached the heart of this woman which was, however, armed against them by constant faith in Jesus Christ, and with greater force they were hurled back upon her accusers. Thus I think that, hearing the phrase "He that is without sin among you, let him first cast a stone at her,"[299] they examined their consciences, and finding that they were full of infinite sins they saw every sin as a great stone that was launched upon each one of

---

294. See Mark 2:17: "Hoc audito Jesus ait illis: 'Non necesse habent sani medico, sed qui male habent: non enim veni vocare justos, sed peccatores'" ("Jesus hearing this, saith to them: They that are well have no need of a physician, but they that are sick. For I came not to call the just, but sinners").

295. John 8:11.

296. This is a reference to the elected souls to whom grace has been granted.

297. John 8:5: "In lege autem Moyses mandavit nobis hujusmodi lapidare. Tu ergo quid dicis?" ("Now Moses in the law commanded us to stone such a one. But what sayest thou?").

298. This expression derives from the Roman context, and was used to refer to Jesus.

299. John 8:7: "Qui sine peccato est vestrum, primus in illam lapidem mittat" ("He that is without sin among you, let him cast the first stone at her").

them, and so they fled. What is more, I believe that when Christ "erexit se"[300] and in his majesty looked down upon them as reprobates and convicts, they could not stand his gaze; rather, seeing that his bright eyes grew dark and the hailstorm of the stones of their sins rained down upon them, they saw that it was time to flee. "Incipientes a senioribus,"[301] because the elders had been the first to launch the perfidious plan to trap Christ with his own words, added to which old people are greedier so that they were more fearful of losing their riches, and more ambitious, so that they were more careful to preserve their status. And I also believe that, caught in this confusion as their own sins hailed down on them, they saw hell opening before them and Lucifer, full of blindness and error, summoning them down; for Christ was moving in judgment on them for the sin that they had committed against the glorious Stephen.[302] So that truly they were stoned inwardly, and to take greater revenge on themselves, they wished to transform the reason for their sin into a blessing and so they left that fortunate woman alone with Christ, so that she could well say: "O felix culpa, que tantum ac talem meruit habere Redemptorem!"[303] And what an honorable dishonor was hers: to have her evil accusers depart and leave her alone with the merciful judge! Oh what sweet solitude, to be abandoned by her cruel enemies, sinners and not only subject to death but dead forever, and to be alone with the true and most merciful Son of God, rather with mercy itself, both free from sin and divine! Some say that she trembled and commended herself to the Lord etc. But I dare to suggest the opposite: I believe instead that, when the others left, she felt as if all heavy burdens had been lifted from her shoulders and a great faith was born within her that this merciful Lord would forgive her; and in his sainted eyes she saw a thousand rays of bright hope, and his face aflame with charity. And when he said to her "Woman, who accused you?,"[304] I think he wished to reassure her so that her faith might grow stronger; and then he said to her "where are they?" as if to say "they are mere shadows, those invidious and cruel accusations are nothing, even if they are true. Born from evil roots, they do not bear fruit in the ear of the honest judge. I do not accept them. It is enough that they could not condemn you, because those who have sinned cannot condemn us, and you have repented for your own sins. And therefore I wish to bestow mercy upon you." Thus she took heart, with love enflamed and living faith, and said, "My Lord, no one

300. "Lifted himself up."

301. John 8:9 ("Beginning at the eldest").

302. See Acts 7. Stephen was the first Christian martyr, who was stoned to death for blasphemy by the authorities, witnessed by the Pharisee Saul of Tarsus who later became the apostle Paul (see Acts 7).

303. "Oh happy fault that earned for us so great, so glorious a Redeemer!" from the liturgical hymn *Exsultet* (Easter proclamation), delivered before the paschal candle during the Easter Vigil. The Church defines the sin of Adam as *felix* (happy) because its result was the incarnation of Christ. Notably, Colonna regenders the praise originally directed at Adam's sin, which brought about mankind's salvation, and offers the same words in praise of the sin of the adulteress.

304. John 8:10: "Woman, where are they that accused thee?"

has condemned me, you who are Lord of the world, Son of God, true Messiah, are the one to condemn or forgive me. I stand firm before you: I throw myself into your arms; do with me what you will."[305] And she did not boldly ask him for anything, but instead, like a true convert, illumined and perfected, she abandoned herself entirely to Christ and thought nothing of herself; she molded her will to the Lord's.[306] And this is truly a great thing to consider: to see that the judge who could condemn or absolve her instead speaks to her, asks her if she is condemned, almost as if giving her the strength to respond, and she recognizes him as her Lord and says to him "Nemo, Domine,"[307] stating clearly: "Lord, it is for you to say." And she is so abandoned to Christ that, confessing his power, she does not contest his law or his judgment, equally content to serve him and to honor his Majesty. And, in God's mercy, he not only wishes to absolve her and judge her so mercifully, but he even made her free from sin. To this grace may his mercy guide us all.

Most obedient daughter and disciple of Your Reverency,
The Marchioness of Pescara

⤳

[Letter 27]
Reverendo osservandissimo Padre mio,
Io pensarò di scriver così humilmente sopra lo Evangelio della adultera qualche meditation simplice, però lassarò star le difficultà tanto discusse et ventilate, cioè che li scrivesse il Signor et perché s'inclinasse, etc. Dirò solo che costei hebbe una singular gratia, et forse delle maggiori che Christo concedesse in terra. Due adventi si leggon di Christo: l'uno tutto dolce, ove solo mostrò la sua gran bontà, clementia et misericordia, nel qual disse in molti luoghi che veniva per li peccatori, per medico delli infermi, per ministrare, per dar la pace, la luce, la gratia, tutto infocato di carità, vestito d'humiltà, soavissimo et pietoso; l'altro tutto armato per molti, ove mostrarà la sua giustitia, la maestà, la grandezza, la infinita potestà, né ci sarà tempo di misericordia, né loco di gratia. Hor questa felice donna hebbe gratia d'esser giudicata dal giustissimo vero giudice nel suo advento dolce et nella sua benigna conversation fra noi; perché, anchor sempre stesse in sua volontà il giudicar tutto il mondo, io non trovo che dalla propria parte adversa et da lei, che era presente et taceva, fosse constituito giudice, et esso liberamente assdumesse et esseguisse lo uffitio del giudicare, se non in questo atto, dunque assolvendola

---

305. Colonna puts in the mouth of the adulteress the phrase uttered by Mary in response to the Archangel Gabriel: "Fiat mihi secundum verbum tuum" ("Be it done to me according to thy word"); Luke 1:38.

306. See the *Pater Noster* (Lord's Prayer): "fiat voluntas tua" ("Your will be done").

307. John 8:11 ("No man, Lord").

adesso et facendola impeccabile d'allhora innanzi che disse: "Amplius noli peccare." Et essendo, come è, immutabile, et le sue vere parole infallibili, bisogna dire che non fu necessario giudicarla più. Et benché di tutti quelli ai quali Christo concesse gratia particulare si creda che sian salvi, pure a costei si vede chiaramente, anzi, ch'è più, si deve tener per fermo che facesse vita beata in terra, assoluta del passato et certa di non esser più condannata, né poter peccar nel futuro. Mai niuno fece tanto utile al più intimo suo cordial amico come gli inimici feron a costei: andarono per tentar Christo et offender lei, et essi se ne andarono confusi et superati, et ella rimase assoluta et sicura. Volendo precipitarla ne i mali, la condussero al fonte vivo di ogni bene, la fecero star in mezzo fra essi tenebre et Christo vera luce, et allegarono Moisè al conditor delle leggi, anzi fattor della natura et dator della fede et della gratia, pensando o che trasgredesse la legge, o mancasse della sua misericordia. Ma le pietre della loro iniqua durezza giunte con la pessima lor volontà nel cor di questa donna, già armata della constante fede di Christo Giesù, con maggior impeto ritornarono sopra di loro. Et però penso che, udendo dire "Chi è di voi senza peccato, getti in lei la prima pietra," si considerarono, et vedendosi pieni d'infiniti peccati gli parve ogni peccato una grossa pietra gittar sopra ciascun d'essi, et ne andarono. Anzi credo che quando Christo "erexit se" et mostrò in maestà di guardarli come reprobi et condannati, non sostennero quella vista; anzi, vedendo il sol de gli occhi belli obnubilato et la grandine delle pietre de' lor peccati venirgli addosso, gli parve tempo da fuggire. "Incipientes a senioribus," perché quelli eran stati i primi a far il discorso perfido di prendere Christo nelle parole, oltra che i vecchi son più avari et temevan più di perdere le loro ricchezze, et più ambitiosi, però havevan più cura di conservarsi le degnità. Et credo anchora che, trovandosi in questa confusione che i peccati loro stessi gli lapidavano, li paresse veder l'inferno aperto et Lucifero che li chiamava alla sinistra piena di cecità et di errore, facendo allhora Christo in essi la giustitia del peccato che poi commisero nel glorioso Stephano. Sì che veramente furono lapidati costoro interiormente et, per far maggior vendetta di se medesmi, volsero far beata la cagion de i lor danni et lassarono sola con Christo la benedetta donna, la qual poteva ben dire: "O felix culpa, que tantum ac talem meruit habere Redemptorem!" Et che honorato disprezzo che fu il suo: partirsi gli iniqui accusatori et lassarla col pietoso giudice! O che dolce solitudine, essere abandonata da nemici crudeli, peccatori et sempre morti non che mortali, et star sola col vero Figliuol di Dio misericordissimo, anzi essa misericordia, et impeccabile et divino! Dicono alcuni che là restò tremando et raccomandò al Signor etc. Et io ardisco dire il contrario: anzi credo che, in partirsi coloro, gli parve che ogni grave peso se le togliesse dalle spalle et li nacque una grandissima fede che questo benigno Signore l'assolveria; et in quelli santi occhi vedeva mille raggi di viva speranza, l'aspetto tutto ardente di carità. Et quando gli disse "Mulier, ubi sunt qui te accusabant?," penso io che la volse assicurare per crescerli la fede et li disse "Dove sono?," quasi dicendo: "Sono un'ombra, non son niente le accuse invidiose et inique, se ben son vere. Nascendo da pessima radice, non fanno frutto nella orecchia del retto giudice. Io non le accetto. Basta che non t'han potuto condannare, perché i peccati d'altri non condannano, et del tuo sei pentita. Però ti voglio usar misericordia." Allhora ella, ripreso animo, con acceso amore et viva fede disse: "Signor mio, nessun m'ha condannata, et a te, che sei Signor del mondo, Figliuol di Dio, Messia vero, sta il mio condannarmi o l'assolvermi. Io sto sicura dinanzi a te; io mi butto nelle tue braccia; fa' di me quel che ti piace." Et non hebbe ardir di pregarlo di cosa alcuna, anzi, come veramente convertita, illuminata et perfetta, si lassò tutta in Christo et non riguardò se stessa; conformò la sua volontà con quella del Signore. Et è molto da considerar questo: veder quel giudice, che poteva condannarla et assolverla, li parla, le domanda se è condannata, quasi mostrando darli animo che lo pregasse, et ella lo riconosce per Signore et li dice "Nemo, Domine," dicendo chiaramente: "Signor, in te sta." Et è così abandonata in Christo che, confessando la potestà, non vuol turbar la sua legge et la sua determinatione, contentandosi egualmente di quanto fosse suo servitio et honor della sua Maestà. Et per la bontà di Dio non solo la volse assolvere et far di lei sì piatoso giuditio, ma la fece impeccabile. Alla qual gratia la sua misericordia ci conduca.

Figlia obedientissima et discepola di Vostra Reverentia,
La Marchesa di Pescara

Letter 28: Viterbo, 4 December [1542][308]
To Marcello Cervini

In August 1542, Bernardino Ochino failed to turn up in Rome, whence he had been summoned by the pope, and instead fled to Geneva (see Letter 27). The Catholic establishment was quick to condemn his actions, and it is therefore unsurprising that Vittoria Colonna felt herself to be in a compromising position when she received a book from him shortly thereafter. She immediately sent it to Marcello Cervini (1500–1555), who was a member of the newly-founded Congregation for the Doctrine of the Faith (informally known as the Holy Office).

Cervini had become a cardinal in 1539, had participated in the failed Diet of Regensburg in 1541, and had remained in contact with intellectuals, poets and artists. Although he belonged to the conservative wing of the Church, he was also on good terms with reformers such as Reginald Pole and Marcantonio Flaminio.[309] He was sent as a legate to the Council of Trent together with Pole

---

308. Facsimile of the autograph: BMF, Autografi Frullani, 384; Facsimile of the autograph: BPP, Palatino, *Carteggio* Lucca, 1 A–C; Facsimile of the autograph: BNCR, *Lettere* autografe di Vittoria Colonna, A.180/35; Facsimile of the autograph: BAV, Ferr. 433, fols. 180v–81r; Copy: BFF, Fondo Polidori 14: Colonna, *Carteggio*, no. CXLIX.

309. See Concetta Bianca, "Marcello Cervini e Vittoria Colonna," *Lettere italiane* 45 (1993): 427–39.

and another cardinal, Giovanni Maria Ciocchi Del Monte, later Pope Julius III.[310] In 1555 Cervini would become pope, taking the name Marcellus II, but died less than a month later.

From its very first publication this letter became a touchpaper for opposing views of Colonna's conduct.[311] Her nineteenth-century biographer, Alfred von Reumont, argued that it proved her unwavering faithfulness to the papacy.[312] An opposing opinion was offered by the collector Franz Kühlen, as well as by Pietro Ercole Visconti, editor of Colonna's *Rime*:[313] both thought she was seeking to distance herself from Ochino, fearing accusations of heresy. More than a century later, the question remains open: was Colonna sincere in writing this letter? She had always defended Ochino previously despite his many detractors (see for example Letters 14 and 15), but in this letter she distances herself from him and his drastic choice to flee. Was she playacting her disapproval? Or, despite her deep affection and admiration for the friar, was her love for the Church of Rome simply stronger, so that she viewed Ochino's flight as a grave sin?

The letter is constructed in two parts. The first part discusses Reginald Pole, as if Colonna were trying to prove that he is now her guide in place of Ochino. In the second part she turns to Ochino himself, and makes a show of scrupulous honesty in trying to provide the Inquisition with any additional information that might be useful. Finally, she draws on the well-established metaphor of St. Peter's storm-tossed boat, that had been prefigured, according to the Church Fathers, by Noah's ark: only by remaining within the boat of the church can a person save himself from the universal flood. Her use of this metaphor constitutes a strong affirmation of Catholic faith on Colonna's part. For Italian evangelicals and reformers, many of whom embraced the doctrine of justification by faith (*sola fide*) championed by Martin Luther, the institutional church stood in the way of the Christian's direct response to the word of God—a view from which Colonna may have retreated, if she ever held it. Ultimately, we can only hypothesize about the mixture of emotions that might have motivated Colonna, who must have been fully aware of the implications of her choice of metaphor, to write as she did to Cervini.

---

310. Colonna expressed her negative view of the trio of cardinals in a letter to Giovanni Morone; Colonna, *Carteggio*, no. CLXII, 20 May 1542.

311. Bianca, "Marcello Cervini," 429.

312. Alfred von Reumont, *Vittoria Colonna, marchesa di Pescara: Vita, fede e poesia nel secolo decimosesto* (Turin-Florence-Rome: Loescher, 1892), 238–39.

313. "A me pare che la lettera della V. C. a Santa Croce mostra evidente ch'era sviata, se non apostata e che la sua corrispondenza e letteratura fu sottomesso a una censura;" letter from F. Kühlen to P. E. Visconti; BAV, Ferr. 443, fol. 180r. Kühlen was in possession of the original letter. See also Vittoria Colonna, *Rime*, ed. by Pietro Ercole Visconti (Rome: Salviucci 1840).

ᕁ

Most Illustrious, Revered, and Esteemed Monsignor,
The more opportunities I have had to observe the behavior of the most Revered Monsignor from England,[314] the more I have come to believe that he is a true and sincere servant of God: so when he deigns out of charity to answer some of my questions,[315] I feel certain that I cannot err if I follow his advice. And since he told me that in his opinion, if any letter or other communication arrived from brother Bernardino [Ochino], I should send it to Your Most Revered Lordship without making any reply, unless I had been ordered to do so, I am sending you the attached letter with the little book you will find within,[316] received today. And it was all together in one packet conveyed here by a courier who came from Bologna, and there was no other note with it. I did not wish to use other means to send it except by one of my own men from Arpino. Thus I beg Your Lordship pardon me for this nuisance, since, as you can see, it has been printed. And may our Lord God preserve Your Most Revered person, together with the blessed life of His Holiness, which is the dear wish of all his servants.

From Santa Catarina in Viterbo, the fourth day of December.

Servant of Your Most Revered and Illustrious Lordship,
The Marchioness of Pescara

It pains me much that the more he thinks to excuse himself the more he condemns himself, and the more he thinks to save others from the shipwreck, the more he exposes them to the floods, since he is outside the boat that saves and protects.[317]

---

314. Reginald Pole.

315. Colonna's distress at Pole's failure to respond to her overtures is evident in this phrase; see also Letter 31.

316. We do not know which letter Colonna in fact attached; it is very unlikely that it was the one sent from Florence on 22 August, three and a half months earlier, as asserted in Cargnoni, *I frati cappuccini,* 2:264. As for the "little book" that she also specifies is in print, this was a copy of the *Prediche di Bernardino Ochino da Siena* (*Sermons of Bernardino Ochino da Siena*), printed on 10 October (probably in Geneva by Jean Gerard). The edition has a very significant frontispiece, citing John 15:20: "Si me persequuti sunt, et vos persequentur. Sed omnia vincit Veritas" ("If they have persecuted me, they will also persecute you. But truth conquers all").

317. Cargnoni, *I frati cappuccini,* 2:264 reminds us that "questa immagine è ripresa iconograficamente da un'incisione di Luca Bertelli, *Typus Ecclesiae Catholicae ad instar brevis laicorum catechismi,* Venice, 1574, in cui, insieme ad altri eretici, è raffigurato Ochino che sta annegando nel mare dell'eresia (Firenze, Gabinetto disegni e stampe degli Uffizi)." For the metaphor of the "navicula Petri" (St. Peter's boat), see also Massimo Firpo, and Fabrizio Biferali, *"Navicula Petri:" L'arte dei papi nel Cinquecento, 1527–1571* (Rome-Bari: Laterza, 2009).

On the reverse:

To my Most Illustrious, Revered, and Esteemed Monsignor, the Cardinal of Santa Croce

∾

[Letter 28]

Illustrissimo et Reverendissimo Monsignor observandissimo,

Quanto più ho hauto modo di guardar le actioni del Reverendissimo Monsignor de Inghilterra, tanto più me è parso veder che sia vero et sincerissimo servo de Dio: onde, quando per carità si degna resp[on]der a qualche mia domanda, mi par di esser sicura de no[n] poter errare seguendo il suo parere. Et perché me disse che li pareva che, se lettera o altro di fra Belardin mi venisse, la mandassi a Vostra Signoria Reverendissima senza responder altro se non mi fussi ordinato, havendo hauto ogi la alligata col libretto che vederà, ce lle mando. Et tutto era in un pligho dato alla posta qui da una staffetta che veniva da Bologna, senza altro scritto dentro; et non ho voluto usar altri mezzi che mandarle per un mio de Arpino. Sì che perdoni Vostra Signoria questa molestia, benché, come vede, sia in stampa. Et Nostro Signor Dio Sua Reverendissima persona guardi con quella felice vita de Sua Santità, che per tutti i suoi servi se desidera.

Da Santa Catarina di Viterbo, a' dì IIII di decembre.

Serva di Vostra Signoria Reverendissima et Illustrissima,

La Marchesa de Pescara

Mi dole assai che quanto più pensa scusarsi, più se accusa, et quanto più crede salvar altri da naufragii, più li exspone al diluvio, essendo lui fuor de l'arca che salva et assicura.

A tergo

A l'Illustrissimo et Reverendissimo Monsignor mio observandissimo, il Signor Cardinal Santa Croce

Letter 29: Viterbo, 25 August [1542][318]

To Alfonso de Lagni

The Neapolitan Alfonso de Lagni (d. 1558) was nominated ruler of Bassano, not quite twenty miles from Viterbo, by Pope Clement VII, who wished to thank him for economic help received in 1527 in defense of papal territories against imperial troops. Lagni's political alliance with the pope made him an official enemy of the

---

318. Original, autograph: ASR, Ospedale S. Spirito - Priorato di Bassano d'Orte, n. 14, fol. 834r–v: Tacchi-Venturi "Nuove lettere," 313.

Colonna family and their Spanish allies.[319] Colonna, however, was always willing to enter into dialogue with her enemies, and it seems that an "ancient friendship" existed with Lagni, as is implied by the unusual title of "brother" that she gives him in two letters addressed to him.[320]

In the first paragraph of this letter Colonna refers to the entry into the convent of Santa Caterina in Viterbo of a young girl called Bernardina, daughter of Pulisena de Desidero from Bassano, about whom Colonna had already written to Lagni the previous July.[321] The girl's mother was supposed to sell some of her belongings and pay over the profits to the convent, but she had failed to do so, and as a result "certain good people" in Viterbo had been obliged to take in Bernardina for a long period. This letter lets Lagni know that the story has had a positive conclusion. This is not the first time that Colonna concerned herself with the convent entry of a young girl. In 1536 a girl named Angeletta, a Roman prostitute, expressed a wish to enter the convent of the Convertite, only a few meters from the Convent of San Silvestro in Capite where Colonna often lodged. The girl's many lovers tried by all possible means to dissuade her from this choice, until "the Lady Marchioness of Pescara, who held her firmly by the hand, took her and went into the convent together with her."[322]

The second paragraph of this letter is concerned with Colonna's stay in Viterbo, which she justifies in relation to the recent Salt Wars between her brother Ascanio and the pope, which had made it uncomfortable for her to remain in Rome. It is striking here to note the manner in which Colonna distances herself from the "controversy" which seems to concern her brother alone; she declares that she herself has left Rome as a favor to the pope and in order to obey him, in stark contrast to Ascanio.

In this letter, as in other examples,[323] we witness the manner in which worldly events insert themselves dramatically and continually into the longed-for life of prayer, peace and silence that Colonna seeks, despite her plea: "the less I know of the world, the better I like it."

❧

319. For more information see Tacchi-Venturi, "Nuove lettere," 309–11.

320. See Tacchi-Venturi, "Nuove lettere," 313 as well as Letter 30.

321. See Tacchi-Venturi, "Nuove lettere," 313.

322. Letter from Carlo Gualteruzzi to Pietro Carnesecchi, 19 August 1536; see Ornella Moroni, *Carlo Gualteruzzi (1500–1577) e i corrispondenti* (Vatican City: Biblioteca Apostolica Vaticana, 1984), 226: "la Signora Marchesa di Peschara, che tuttavia la teneva per mano, la prese et s'entrò dentro [al monastero] insieme con lei."

323. See for example Letter 17 as well as Colonna, *Carteggio*, no. CXXXVIII: "sto in questi travagli consolatissima, et rengratio Dio che con perder li beni della fortuna me sia occasion de acquistar quelli del animo;" letter to Ercole II d'Este, Duke of Ferrara, 28 May [1541].

Most Magnificent and Excellent Lord Alfonso,

I thank Your Lordship for your action in ensuring that the girl's mother and her other family members agreed to honor her desire to be in God's service: today with God's grace she took the nun's habit, and the convent was paid in full and the nuns comforted her and received her with great charity. May Our Lord God grant her constancy and may he bless Your Lordship.

As for my presence here, the reason was the controversy between my brother and His Holiness. And since I was entirely obedient and much obliged to His Holiness, I saw that my departure from Rome was what he desired. And thus I remain obedient to him in this holy place where I feel healthy and the air is good for me, and the less I know of the world, the better I like it. I have put my territories in the care of my brother-in-law the Marquis of Guasto,[324] and I take care to steer my soul toward the Lord God who created it. And I offer my services to Your Lordship if I can do anything for you.

From Santa Caterina of Viterbo on the twenty-fifth day of August.

At Your Lordship's command,
The Marchioness of Pescara

On the reverse:
To the Excellent Signor, the Signor Alfonso de Lagni etc.

❧

[Letter 29]

Molto Magnifico et Excellente Signor Alfonso,

Rengratio Vostra Signoria de l'opera fatta in far che la madre et parenti della giovene che qui ha voluto esser al servitio de Dio siano venuti a satisfarla, et ogi con gratia del Signor si è vestita et hanno quietato il monasterio, et le suore hanno consolata l[ei] di receverla con gran carità. Nostro Signor Dio li dia perseverantia et contenti Vostra Signoria.

Circa il mio star qui, le cagion furno le controversie di mio fratello con Sua Santità. Et essendo io stata obedientissima della Santità sua et molto obligata, viddi che 'l mio absentarmi da Roma li parve allora al pro[po]sito. Et così mi sto sotto la sua obedientia i[n] questo santo loco ove mi trovo sana et l'aire mi è proficuo, et quanto meno intendo del mondo più mi piace. Le mie terre detti in governo al Signor Marchese del Guasto mio cognato, et io attendo a governare

---

324. Alfonso d'Avalos. Ferrante d'Avalos named him universal beneficiary of his will, although Colonna was granted usufruct.

l'anima a quel Signor che la creò. Et mi offero a Vostra Signoria si cosa alcuna posso per lui.

Da Santa Catarina di Viterbo, a' dì XXV di agosto.

Al Comando di Vostra Signoria,
La Marchesa di Pescara

A tergo
A l'Excellente Signor, il Signor Alfonso de Lagni etc.

Letter 30: Viterbo, 22 December [1542][325]
To Giovanni Morone

Giovanni Morone became papal nunzio to the emperor in Gand [Ghent, Belgium]. He participated in the Diets of Worms (1540), Regensburg (1541), and Speyer (1542), and thus came into close contact with Lutheran Protestants. Morone became a cardinal in June 1542 and in October of the same year, when it was anticipated that the Council of Trent was about to begin, he was sent to Trent as papal legate together with cardinals Reginald Pole and Pierpaolo Parisio. Morone was linked to the circle of the Spirituals from Viterbo, and he was put on trial in 1557, accused of heresy, exonerated in 1559, and once again elected papal legate to Trent in 1563, during the final sessions of that Council.

Only ten letters from Colonna to Morone are extant, all of them transcribed by inquisitors as part of his heresy trial. Written between 1542 and 1546, Colonna's letters to him testify to the importance of her relationship with "sweet Morone"[326] in the final years of her life. She even named him as executor to her will, along with Pole and Jacopo Sadoleto.[327]

In her endless search for a spiritual guide, "for my body was in continual motion searching for tranquility and my mind in agitation for peace," as she says in this letter, Colonna distills an idealized image of her friends Morone and Pole: the two cardinals, "quenching your thirst together" at the divine fountain, will irrigate all of the church, which has become a "too sterile vine," with holy water.

---

325. Copy: ACDF, Stanza Storica, N 4-d, fasc. 1, fols. 161v–62v; Copy: the same, R 5–b, fols. 63r–64r; Copy: AGSc, Processo del card. Morone, fols. 419v–23r: Colonna, *Carteggio*, no. CLXI. The text given here is based on the copy in ACDF, Stanza Storica, N 4-d, which is more authoritative than the corrupted and censored copy of the same trial in AGSc. The mention of the Council of Trent in this letter, which Pole and Morone are attending together, allows the dating of this letter to 1542: see Firpo and Marcatto, *Il processo inquisitoriale del cardinal Giovanni Morone*, 1:1018.

326. Letter from Pole, from Rome, 1544, ed. in Pagano and Ranieri, *Nuovi documenti*, 98–99, and in Firpo and Marcatto, *Il processo inquisitoriale del cardinal Giovanni Morone*, 3:551–52.

327. Bruto Amante, *La tomba di Vittoria Colonna e i testamenti finora inediti della poetessa* (Bologna: Zanichelli, 1896), 52, and Donati, *Vittoria Colonna*, 418.

The first to receive the water from them is Colonna herself: Pole has acted as an instrument in God's hands to give her light and freed her from the "chaos of ignorance" and the "labyrinth of errors" into which she had strayed. Colonna is endlessly thankful, and struggles to contain the "overabundance of my heart." She is not ashamed to confess to Morone that she longs for Pole to leave the Council of Trent and return to Viterbo. The love between Colonna and Pole, which both of them defined as "maternal"[328] but which was criticized by other members of their circle,[329] is defended here by Colonna: in Pole the "spirit of Christ" rings loud and "I have never seen anything in His Lordship but Christ."

&

Most Illustrious, Revered and Esteemed Monsignor,
The letter from Your Lordship will be enough to revive consolation where it was entirely dead; and I am led to consider how great is the consolation I feel for the same reason, for if on my small and mean heart and on my narrow mind it has such an incredible impact, then what will its effect be on Your Most Revered Lordship's expansive heart and ample mind? And I am no less thankful for the consolation aroused by Your Lordship in the Most Revered Monsignor,[330] for this fact demonstrates the reason that Your Lordship is writing to me, which is that you are not grudging at all with the grace and light that God has given you, and this is a clear sign that God has recognized that your blessed soul is so humble and generous that it does not allow one drop to spill of the living water that you have been given; on the contrary, you return it unaltered to its original source,[331] whence the Monsignor receives it, and thus, quenching your thirst together, you honor the Lord and delight his servants; and I hope that you will irrigate his by now too sterile vine,[332] about which Your Lordship in your humility at this moment seems almost to despair.

328. Pole in fact described Colonna as his mother; see Firpo, "Vittoria Colonna, Giovanni Morone," 250; Colonna, *Carteggio*, no CLXXIV; and Tordi, "Vittoria Colonna in Orvieto," 512. And Colonna referred to herself in the same way; see the sonnet "Figlio e signor, se la tua prima e vera:" S1:141; Colonna, *Sonnets*, 134; Colonna, *Carteggio*, no. CXLVII; and Brundin, "Vittoria Colonna and the Virgin Mary." These roles were also publicly acknowledged; see Firpo, *Nel labirinto del mondo*, 164; Colonna, *Carteggio*, no. CXLI; and Firpo and Marcatto, *I processi inquisitoriali di Pietro Carnesecchi*, 2.1:429.

329. See also the letter to Vincenzo Parpaglia dated 1545: "Se volemo spesso scriverne, in verità siano dalle nostre lettere escluse due cose: l'una, il burlar della mia debita servitù con monsignore [= Pole], l'altra, facende del mondo. Per amor vostro questa et per amor mio quella. Così dolcemente scriveremo;" in Abd-El-Kader Salza, *Lettere inedite di Vittoria Colonna e Benedetto Varchi, per le nozze Mancini-Achiardi* (Florence: pei Minori Corrigendi, 1898), 6–7, and Simoncelli, *Evangelismo*, 465.

330. Reginald Pole.

331. To God.

332. The "sterile vine" is the Church. The metaphor combines a number of biblical images, including: the thirsty deer of Psalms 41:2–3; the Samaritan woman at the well in John 4:7–13; the parable of the

I confess to Your Lordship that my happiness would have been far greater if I had been able to respond as I wished to, but every word from the Monsignor is for me, I will not say a law, for that reduces the spirit to servitude, but an infallible rule that frees me to walk along the straight path;[333] so that even though in his humility he will not command me, I am obliged by God to do what I think he wishes. And since he told me never to praise him, I must remain silent, but if on this most true matter, which is so very dear to me, I had been able to expand, Your Most Revered Lordship would have witnessed the chaos of ignorance wherein I dwelled and the labyrinth of errors where I walked with such certainty, clothed in the glittering, sparkling gold that is nothing compared to faith nor bears comparison to the fire of true charity, for my body was in continual motion searching for tranquility and my mind in agitation for peace. And God had Pole say to me "Fiat lux,"[334] and had him show me that I was nothing and that all things could be found in Christ. As Your Lordship will have understood so much better than I did, how different is my extreme need from your own quick and humble acceptance, and yet not so far etc.! And God knows how much effort it costs me to contain my overflowing heart so that it does not spill out upon these pages.

As concerns the other matter that Your Lordship raises, that you pray God to relieve you of the burden of your appointment to the Council, but not to separate you from the Monsignor, this is the exact prayer that I also wish to offer, for if Your Lordship were to return and were not separated from His Lordship, then the Monsignor would also be obliged to return. But in this too the means to serve him is very clear to me, for that same Signor [Pole] told me to ask God to make use of him by allowing him only as much grace as he needed to honor his divine Majesty. And finally on this matter, Your Lordship seems almost content in your letter, although due to your profound humility you believe it does harm where I hope it will be of benefit.

I will not bother Your Lordship any further, seeing that there is no need to thank you once again for the new and continuous proofs of affection that you make to the Monsignor, for I see that you are so much his that I pray you keep me in his favor and command me, for I am so very obliged to you; no less because of who you are than in my own interest, since Your Lordship from now on will be for me a firm and impenetrable shield against Master Luisi[335] and others who are sometimes disapproving of my servitude to the Monsignor and say that it is excessive, too maternally carnal and other such things, and I swear to Your Lordship that I have never in all

---

tenants of a vineyard in Matthew 21:33–43; and the true vine of John 15:1–17. These images were returned to by Colonna many times in her spiritual sonnets.

333. The allusion is to the "narrow gate and straight path" of righteousness cited in Matthew 7:13–14, which also occurs as a frequent image in Colonna's poetry.

334. Genesis 1:3: "Let there be light."

335. Luigi [Alvise] Priuli, who criticized Colonna's close attachment to Pole; see on the relations between Pole, Priuli, and Colonna, Thomas F. Mayer, *Reginald Pole: Prince and Prophet* (Cambridge: Cambridge University Press, 2000), 103–42.

my life said as much as Your Lordship says in this letter that you have written to me, and I have never seen anything in His Lordship but Christ, nor would I hold him in the high reverence that I do, since he is as humble as he is, if I did not sense the pure spirit of Christ in his words,[336] in his manner, and in all his actions. But for those who have the luxury of hearing him at all times, there is no need to show any desire for it. Most Revered Signor, I am extremely obliged to you, from the bottom of my heart, and desirous of serving you.

From Santa Catherina, on the twenty-second day of December.

Most dedicated to Your Lordship's service,
The Marchioness of Pescara

On the reverse:
To the Most Illustrious, Revered, and Esteemed Monsignor, the Cardinal Morone

☙

[Letter 30]
Illustrissimo et Reverendissimo Monsignor osservandissimo,
La lettera de Vostra Signoria saria sufficiente a resuscitare la consolatione dove fusse in tutto morta; et de quella ch'io sento per la medesima causa, considero quanto sia grande, perché se nel mio core piccolo et restretto et nella mia mente angusta fa incredibile effetto, hor che farà nel cuor dilatato et nella mente amplissima di Vostra Reverendissima Signoria? Et non meno mi allegro di quella che in Vostra Signoria Monsignor Reverendissimo sente, il che mi testifica la ragione che la Signoria Vostra mi scrive, cioè che non li è niente parco delle gratie et lumi che Dio li ha donati, che è manifesto segno che ha cognosciuto esser sì humile et capace il suo benedetto animo che non lassa cadere una minima stilla de l'acqua viva che li è data; anzi, senza alterarla punto la remanda al primo fonte donde Monsignor la receve, et così, satiandose insieme, ne honorano il Signore et ne allegrano i servi suoi, et spero ne inrigaranno la sua ormai troppo steril vigna, benché Vostra Signoria per humilità pare che di questo per hora quasi si desperi.

Confesso ben alla Signoria Vostra che saria stata la mia allegreza molto maggiore se havessi possuto respondere come mi pareva di esser mossa, ma ogni parola di Monsignor mi è non dico legge, che reduca lo spirito in servitù, ma regula infallibile, et libera mi fa andare alla dritta via; onde, se ben per humiltà non commanda, son da Dio constretta a osservare quanto vedo che li pare. Et havendomi ditto che non lo laudi mai, mi bisogna tacere, che se in questa

---

336. This is the same expression that Colonna used to describe Ochino (see Letter 14), echoing Romans 8:9 and 1 Peter 1:11.

materia verissima et a me tanto cara havessi possuto allargarmi, Vostra Signoria Reverendissima haveria visto il chaos di ignorantia ove io era et il laberintho et errori ove io passeggiava sicura, vestita di quel oro che luce et strida senza star saldo al paragon della fede né affinarsi al fuoco della vera carità, essendo continuo col corpo in moto per trovar quiete et con la mente in agitatione per havere pace. Et Dio volse che di sua parte mi dicesse "Fiat lux," et che mi mostrassi esser io niente et in Christo trovar ogni cosa. Come Vostra Signoria tanto meglio di me haverà compreso, quanto è differente la mia extrema necessità, qual ancor non è remota dalla sua quasi più presto humil accetation, etc.! Et sa Dio la fatica che ho di tenere la troppo abundantia del core, che non si sparga in questa carta.

Circa l'altro che Vostra Signoria mi dice, che faccia pregare Dio ch'el toglia dall'impresa del Concilio come impedimento, ma che non sia separato da Monsignor, questa è proprio la preghiera ch'io vorrei fare perché, tornando Vostra Signoria et non appartandosi da Sua Signoria, bisogneria che ancor Monsignor tornassi. Ma in questo similmente mi è preciso il modo da poterlo servire, perché ditto Signor mi disse che pregassi Dio che adempisci in esso ogni sua volontà con darli solo tanta gratia quanto li bisognava per honore della sua divina Maestà. Et di questo al fin quasi Vostra Signoria nella sua lettera si contenta, ma per profonda humiltà li pare di nuocere ove spero che giovarà.

Non sarò più molesta a Vostra Signoria, vedendo che non bisogna di novo rengratiarlo delle nove et continue demostrationi che fa a Monsignor, perché il vedo tanto suo che prego lei mi tenga in gratia sua et mi commandi come obligatissima che li sono; non meno per chi essa è che per mio interesse, essendomi Vostra Signoria da qui inanzi un saldo et impenitrabil scudo contra messer Luisi et altri che alcuna volta reprendono la mia servitù con Monsignor dicendo che è superchia, troppo maternamente carnale et simil cose, certificando Vostra Signoria che mai in tutta la vita mia ho ditto tanto quanto la Signoria Vostra dice in questa lettera che me scrive, né mai ho visto altro che Christo in Sua Signoria, né potria haverla la extrema reverentia che li ho, essendo lui di tanta humiltà come è, si non sentessi absolutamente lo spirito di Christo nelle parole, nel modo et in ogni sua actione. Ma quelli che natano nelle dolcezze di sempre odirlo, non bisogna mostrarvi desiderio. Sì che, Signor Reverendissimo, io vi sono di cuore extremamente obligata et desiderosa servirli.

Da Santa Catherina, a' dì 22 di decembre.

Al servitio di Vostra Signoria deditissima,
La Marchesa di Pescara

A tergo vero dictarum litterarum
A l'Illustrissimo et Reverendissimo Monsignor honorandissimo il Cardinale Morone

Letter 31: Viterbo, 15 July [1543][337]
To Reginald Pole

Reginald Pole was a descendant of the Plantagenet kings of England and related by marriage to the Tudor King Henry VIII, his benefactor, with whom nonetheless he fell into conflict when Henry moved to break with the Roman church. The conflict between the pair reached a climax in 1534, when by means of the Act of Supremacy Henry declared himself "Supreme Head of the Church of England," and they broke decisively in 1536, when Pole publicly called for the king's deposition.[338] Pole's friendship with Colonna probably began in 1536 when he was made a cardinal, but they grew much closer when he returned to Rome at the beginning of 1540, and their friendship developed further during the time they both spent in Viterbo, where Pole was sent as Legate of the Patrimony of St. Peter in August 1541. Giovanni Morone, during his Inquisition trial, described their friendship thus: Pole "often discoursed with that lady both in Rome and in Viterbo, and always, I believe, about godly matters, because both of them took more pleasure in that subject than in any other.... They spoke together without mediators and without witnesses."[339] In these intimate dialogues Pole took the role of spiritual guide to Colonna, replacing Ochino who had formerly occupied that position (see Letter 28). Inquisitorial records unanimously depict Colonna as Pole's disciple, and a constant if shadowy presence among the group of Spirituals in Viterbo.[340]

Nine letters between the pair exist today, although they no doubt wrote far more.[341] Colonna also addressed three sonnets to Pole ("Figlio e signor, se la tua prima e vera," "Perché la mente vostra, ornata e cinta," and "Questa imagin, signor, quei raggi ardenti"), and alluded to him by name in at least one other ("Il nobil vostro spirto non s'è involto").[342]

337. Copy: ACDF, Stanza Storica, N 4-d, fasc. 1, fol. 159r–v; Copy: the same, R 5-b, fol. 62r; Copy: AGSc, Processo del cardinale Morone, fols. 416v–19r: Colonna, *Carteggio*, no. CLIV. The text given here is based on the copy in ACDF, Stanza Storica, N 4-d, as with Letter 30. The dating of this letter is suggested by Colonna's mention of her ill health and Pole's prolonged absence (at this date he was in Bologna); see Firpo and Marcatto, *Il processo inquisitoriale del cardinal Giovanni Morone*, 1:1034.

338. On the deterioration of Pole's relations with Henry, see Mayer, *Reginald Pole*, 54–61.

339. "Havea spesso ragionamenti con quella signora et in Roma et in Viterbo et sempre, credo, delle cose di Dio, perché l'uno e l'altro se delettava più di questo che di niun altro subietto.... Parlavano insieme senza arbitri et senza testimonii;" Firpo and Marcatto, *I processi inquisitoriali di Pietro Carnesecchi*, 2.1:431.

340. Pagano and Ranieri, *Nuovi documenti*, 39. On the relationship between Colonna and Pole, see Brundin, *Vittoria Colonna and the Spiritual Poetics*, 68–73; Targoff, *Renaissance Woman*, 227–51.

341. Colonna, *Carteggio*, no. CXXXIX (mid 1541), CLIV (15 July 1543), and CLXXIV (4 October 1546); the other six letters are found in Pagano and Ranieri, *Nuovi documenti*: 21 June 1541; 19 August 1543; 1544; 25 December 1545; 27 March 1546; 28 July 1546.

342. S1:141 (Colonna, *Sonnets*, 135); S1:142; S1:143; S1:140.

In letters from this period there are frequent references to Colonna's ill-health, which would dog her from this date until her death in 1547. At the same time, her "longing to go to God" compelled Colonna to fast and castigate her flesh continually in a bid to reach a higher spiritual plane. Such actions went against the advice of her medics, who sought to bring her to a better state of health.[343] Although as early as 1541, Colonna had confirmed that she was "so indebted to his Most Reverend Lordship for the health of my soul and for that of my body" (Letter 24), this lesson did not appear to have been wholly absorbed, so that Pole was obliged, in the letter to which this one responds, to rebuke her once again for her self-neglect.

Pole left Viterbo in May 1543 when he was summoned to Bologna by the pope. From this time forward Colonna's longing for him grew ever more strident,[344] as did her pain at the loss of her spiritual guide. It was from Pole, as Colonna confessed to Morone, that she had learned "that I was nothing and that all things could be found in Christ" (Letter 30).

෧

My Most Illustrious, Revered, and Esteemed Monsignor,

I possessed both a longing to go to God and a duty to obey my doctor, since I heard from Your Lordship that this was necessary; but I did not understand how these two desires were brought together out of love for one sole cause. Now I thank God for inspiring Your Lordship to clarify it so well in your latest letter,[345] so that what I did before out of obedience I will now do in order not to stray into sin.

Our Lord knows that I long so much to talk with Your Lordship, for no other reason than because I see in you an order of spirit that only the spirit can detect, and it pulls me up so high towards that abundance of light that I am no longer confined to my miserable state; instead, it shows me the grandeur above and our own lowliness and nothingness using such high and weighty concepts that, seeing how we together with all created beings must make use of this, we must find ourselves only in him who is everything.[346] And however quickly I walk towards him, in his grace, so much greater is my need of conversation with Your Lordship; not out of anxiety, or doubt, or trouble that I have or fear I will have, thanks to the goodness of the one who saves me, but because every time Your Lordship speaks to me of the stupendous sacrifice

---

343. See the letter from Girolamo Fracastoro in August 1543 cited in note number 229.

344. See also the letter sent from Rome in 1544, cited in Pagano and Ranieri, *Nuovi documenti*, 98–99, and in Firpo and Marcatto, *Il processo inquisitoriale del cardinal Giovanni Morone*, 3:551–52, as well as Letters 24 and 39.

345. This letter has not survived.

346. Colossians 1:17.

that brought the eternal election of those who follow Christ; or tell of the reward and of that manna found hidden in those mountains, harbors and fountains,[347] while always directing the sword of the word against our presumption,[348] you give our souls wings to fly safely to the longed-for nest;[349] so that speaking with Your Lordship is for me like speaking with an intimate friend of the bridegroom,[350] who prepares me by these means and calls me to him, and wants me by talking of him to become enflamed and consoled. And the smaller I am, the greater is Your Lordship's humility, by which means God offers joy to you in return for the necessary grace that he offers to me. Thus may it please him that you get here soon and in good health, although your arrival together with His Holiness in these times causes me great anxiety, yet I trust in him in whom I must trust.

And in order not to cause you further annoyance I will write to Master Luisi[351] about the fact that Madam[352] has orders not to stay at the Rocca,[353] I believe out of

347. Firpo and Marcatto, *Il processo inquisitoriale del cardinal Giovanni Morone*, 1:1035, to be compared to a text attributed to Pole in which the soul's journey to God is described as one by way of "mountains," "valleys," and "fountains of eternal life" in order to reach the "port" of salvation. Contemplation of the Crucifixion makes the journey possible, as it reveals "la infinita dilettione di Dio con la quale ab aeterno amò ed elesse in lui tutti li membri suoi;" ed. in Fontana, "Documenti vaticani," 345–71. The verb *annichilarsi* (to annihilate oneself) appears a number of times in Pole's text and is taken up here by Colonna, with slight variations as well as in Letter 39, also to Pole, and Letter 25 to Costanza d'Avalos Piccolomini.

348. For the expression "sword of the word," see Hebrews 4:12: "For the word of God is living and effectual, and more piercing than any two edged sword; and reaching unto the division of the soul and the spirit, of the joints also and the marrow, and is a discerner of the thoughts and intents of the heart;" and Ephesians 6:17: "And take unto you the helmet of salvation, and the sword of the Spirit (which is the word of God)."

349. This passage could not fail to arouse the suspicion of the inquisitors, who note: "Polus arguitur male sentire de vocatione et praedestinatione, ex litteris marchionisse Piscariae ad eum" ("From the Marchioness of Pescara's letter to him, one can deduce that Pole erred on vocation and predestination"). See Firpo and Marcatto, *Il processo inquisitoriale del cardinal Giovanni Morone*, 1:1035.

350. The bridegroom is Christ, bridegroom of our souls and of the church. See Matthew 9:15; Matthew 25; Mark 2:19; Luke 5:34; 2 Corinthians 11:2. The expression *amicus sponsi* ("friend of the bridegroom") derives from John 3:29: "He that hath the bride, is the bridegroom: but the friend of the bridegroom, who standeth and heareth him, rejoiceth with joy because of the bridegroom's voice. This my joy therefore is fulfilled."

351. Luigi [Alvise] Priuli; see also Letter 24.

352. Margaret of Austria, natural daughter of the Emperor Charles V and wife of Ottavio Farnese, referred to again as "Madam" in Colonna, *Carteggio*, no. XCII. The identification is confirmed in Giampiero Brunelli, "Tra eretici e gesuiti: I primi anni di Margherita a Roma," in *Margherita d'Austria (1522–1586): Costruzioni politiche e diplomazia, tra corte farnese e monarchia spagnola*, ed. Silvia Mantini (Rome: Bulzoni, 2003), 82.

353. Firpo and Marcatto, *Il processo inquisitoriale del cardinal Giovanni Morone*, 1:1036: "A Viterbo, infatti, il Pole era solito risiedere nella Rocca, come risulta dalla lettera inviata da Viterbo, il 17 ottobre

respect for Your Lordship, and not because of the air, because she will take lodgings in town, since she cannot stay at S. Sisto,[354] where she really wanted to be.

And may our Lord God keep Your Lordship as I wish, and I kiss your hand in thanks for the cure that you sent and for the doctors' letters, but above all for your own letter and even more for your arrival, and may it please God to make it easy and safe. As for me I will say that I cannot claim to be in perfect health, in order not to contradict my doctor, but neither do I feel able to say that I am ill, so that I will say that I am very much better, all the more so thanks to the consolation offered by Your Lordship, which would be greater still if I did not fear for your journey. May God's goodness keep you safe.

From Santa Catharina, on the fifteenth day of July.

Your Most Illustrious and Revered Lordship's most dutiful servant,
The Marchioness of Pescara

On the reverse:
To the Most Illustrious, Revered, and Esteemed Monsignor, the Signor Cardinal from England

[Letter 31]
Illustrissimo et Reverendissimo Monsignor mio osservandissimo,
Il desiderio di andare a Dio et la advertentia di obedire il medico io l'haveva, havendo odito da Vostra Signoria che così conviene; ma come questi doi desideri stessino insieme per l'amor d'una istessa causa, no'l sapeva intendere. Hor rengratio Dio che inspirò la Signoria Vostra a chiarirlo tanto bene in questa sua lettera che quel che faceva per obedire farò hora per non peccare.

Et sa il Signor nostro che per altro non desidero excessivamente di parlare con Vostra Signoria se non perché vedo in lui un ordine di spirito che solo lo spirito lo sente, e sempre mi tira tanto in su a quella amplitudine di luce che non mi lassa troppo fermare nella miseria propria; anzi, con sì alti substantiosi concepti mi mostra la grandezza di là su et la bassezza et nichilità nostra che, vedendo noi stessi et tutte le cose create servirci a questo, bisogna trovarci solo in colui ch'è ogni cosa. Et quanto più io, per gratia sua, caminassi presto verso lui, tanto più bisogno ho di parlar alla Signoria Vostra; non per ansia, né dubii, né molestia che

1542, dal Priuli al Beccadelli (Oxford, BL, Ital. C. 25, fols. 251r–254v)."

354. Santo Sisto was the residence of the papal legates; Margaret of Austria could not stay there since Pole's predecessor, Cardinal Francesco Corner, still resided there.

habia né tema di havere, per bontà di colui che mi assicura, ma perché ogni volta che la Signoria Vostra parla di quel stupendissimo sacrificio della eterna electione, de l'esser premiati et di quel manna ascondito trovato su quelli monti, porti et fonte descrive, con sempre convertir il gladio del verbo contra ogni confidentia nostra, fa stare l'anima su l'ali, sicura di volare al desiderato nido; sì che tanto è a me parlare con Vostra Signoria come con un intimo amico del sposo, che mi prepara per questo mezzo et mi chiama a lui, et vole che ne ragioni per accendermi et consolarmi. Et quanto son io minor cosa, tanto maggior è la humiltà di Vostra Signoria, per il cui mezzo Dio concede gaudio a lui per la necessaria gratia che concede a me. Così li piaccia che presto et sano sia qui, che 'l venir con Sua Santità in questi tempi mi dà grand'ansia, ma in colui che soglio sperare spero.

Et per non fastidirlo più scrivo, a messer Luisi come Madama ha ordine di non allogiar in Rocca, credo per rispetto di Vostra Signoria, non già per l'aire, perché piglia casa nella terra, non havendo possuto in S. Sisto, ove molto desiderava.

Et nostro Signor Dio guardi Vostra Signoria come io desidero, et li baso la mano del remedio che fece mandare et delle lettere di medici, ma più della sua lettera et più assai della venuta, qual piaccia a Dio fare che sia lieta et sicura. Di me li dico che non posso dire essere in tutto sana per non contradire al medico, né manco mi sento di modo che possa dire che sto male, sì che dirò che sto assai assai meglio, massime con questa consolatione di Vostra Signoria, qual saria suprema se non temessi il viaggio. La bontà di Dio lo guardi.

Da Santa Catharina, a' dì 15 di luglio.

Serva obbligatissima di Vostra Signoria Illustrissima et Reverendissima, la Marchesa di Pescara

A tergo
A l'Illustrissimo et Reverendissimo Monsignor osservandissimo, il Signor Cardinal d'Inghilterra

Letter 32: Viterbo, 25 September 1543[355]
To Alfonso di Lagni

The affection that Colonna felt for the nuns of the convent of Santa Caterina in Viterbo is evident in her concern that they should not lack for wine. This letter makes clear how she sometimes demanded and expected immediate action from her correspondents. While she was immersed in the mystical conversations among the group of Spirituals in Viterbo, she still found time to pick up her pen

---

355. Original, autograph postscript and signature: ASR, Ospedale S. Spirito—Priorato di Bassano d'Orte, n. 14, fols. 836r–37v: Tacchi-Venturi, "Nuove lettere," 314.

to write to Alfonso de Lagni (see Letter 29) and ask him to source a large quantity of barrels of wine for the convent, specifying that the wine must be donated to them—they could not be expected to pay for it.

෧෴

Most Excellent and Magnificent Lord like [a brother],[356]
Since the grape harvest at the convent of Santa Caterina in Viterbo has been very scarce, the poor nuns are forced to seek what they need elsewhere in order not to run out. I came to know that they would be provided with good wines from Your Lordship's land. I pray you, out of love for me, please do me the favor of filling fifty or sixty barrels, which both they and I will understand to be a donation, and not that the nuns will pay for it. I recommend it to you as much as I can.

From Viterbo, on the twenty-fifth day of September 1543.

I beg Your Lordship most warmly, for I will be very obliged to you, even more than our longstanding friendship already warrants.

At Your Lordship's command,
The Marchioness of Pescara

On the reverse:
To the Most Excellent and Beloved Signor, the Signor Alfonso de Lagnino, mine like a beloved brother
In Bassano

෧෴

[Letter 32]
Molto Eccellente et Magnifico Signor come,
Per esser poco il recoglier del vino in lo monasterio di Santa Catherina di Viterbo, son forzate le pover suore cercar la lor bastanza altrove per non caderne in necessità. Intendo che costì ne la terra di Vostra Signoria sariano servite di bon vini. La prego, per amor mio, li voglia conceder gratia di farcine extraere da cinquanta o sessanta barili, che io et lor reputaremo che Vostra Signoria c'el doni, non ch'el paghino. C'el recomando al possibile.
Da Viterbo, a' dì 25 di settembre 1543.

---

356. Tacchi-Venturi, "Nuove lettere," 314, hypothesizes that the missing word here is "brother," as it occurs in other letters to Alfonso de Lagni.

Molto ne prego Vostra Signoria, che me causarà gran obligo, ultra quello che l'antica amicitia porge.

Al comando de Vostra Signoria,
La Marchesa de Pescara
A tergo
Al Molto Eccellente et Amatissimo Signor, il Signor Alfonso de Lagnino, suo da fratello charissimo
In Bassano

Letter 33: [Rome, Autumn 1543][357]
To Michelangelo Buonarroti

Colonna probably met Michelangelo for the first time in 1536, and their spiritual friendship gave rise to poems, letters, drawings and paintings, all of which focused on Christ.[358] Michelangelo famously made images of the *Pietà*, the *Crucifixion*, and the *Samaritan Woman* for Colonna, which have generated a sizable bibliography and extensive scholarly discussion as well as disagreement. Only seven letters between Colonna and Michelangelo survive, although they must have exchanged many more, and the majority are concerned with these images.

Letter 33 contains Colonna's precious first reaction on seeing the *Crucifixion* that her friend had made for her. Ascanio Condivi, Michelangelo's first biographer, described it thus: "He also made, out of love for her, a drawing of Jesus Christ on the cross, not in an attitude of death, as is common, but as if alive with his face raised towards the father, and he seems to be saying 'Heli, heli.' And one sees his body not abandoned drooping in death, but as if alive, contorted and twisted in bitter torment."[359] Amazed and delighted, Colonna studied the work

---

357. Original, autograph: BLL, Additional 23139, fol. 10: Colonna, *Carteggio*, no. CXXIII. The chronology proposed in *Il carteggio di Michelangelo*, as well as in Michelangelo Buonarroti, *Rime e lettere*, ed. Antonio Corsaro and Giorgio Masi (Milan: Bompiani, 2016) relating to Michelangelo's letters on the commissioning of the *Crucifixion* dates them to 1538–1541. More recently, Donati, *Vittoria Colonna*, 121–74, has suggested that the letters concerning the images of the *Crocifisso* (*Crucifixion*) and *Pietà* prepared for Colonna can be dated later, to 1543.

358. For recent contributions on the friendship between Colonna and Michelangelo, see Forcellino, "Vittoria Colonna;" Veronica Copello, "Il dialogo poetico tra Michelangelo e Vittoria Colonna," *Italian Studies* 62, no. 3 (2017): 271–81; and Targoff, *Renaissance Woman*, 176–207.

359. "Fece anco, per amor di lei [la Colonna], un disegno di Giesù Cristo in croce, non in sembianza di morto, come communemente s'usa, ma in atto di vivo col volto levato al padre, e par che dica: 'Heli, heli'; dove si vede quel corpo non come morto abbandonato cascare, ma come vivo per l'acerbo supplizio risentirsi e scontorcersi;" in Ascanio Condivi, *Vita di Michelagnolo Buonarroti pittore scultore architetto e gentiluomo fiorentino pubblicata mentre viveva dal suo scolare Ascanio Condivi* (Florence: Gaetano Albizzini all'insegna del sole, 1746), 53. Christ's exclamation from the cross, rendered by

as closely as she could with painstaking attention: "an analysis of the page at ever closer range, first with her naked eye, then with the help of a light . . . , then with a lens," and finally with a mirror.[360]

Colonna had a particular attachment to images of the Crucifixion, one that she shared with many contemporaries—the Franciscans, the Capuchins, Ochino, as well as the circle of the *Spirituali*. She dedicated a large number of her poems and prose to Christ on the cross, and these meditations allowed her to come to an understanding of her own sins and to recognize God's love. Alluding to the biblical texts of Matthew 11:25 and Luke 10:21, Colonna states that "he who can fix his eyes upon God, / not he who better understood or who read more / books on earth, will be blessed in heaven."[361] It is not intellectual understanding but devoted contemplation that leads to God. And it is not enough merely to gaze at carved or painted crucifixes or to make the sign of the cross with one's hands: the "clear eyes of the heart" must be raised "to the book of the cross."[362] Nonetheless, material images play an important role as a recall to the soul's memory: "his living, powerful effigy / must be sculpted in the soul, before its virtue / we must always bow down, and its painted effigy / must always be before my eyes."[363]

❧

Unique master Michel Angelo and my most singular friend,

I received your letter and I have seen the *Crucifixion*, which has certainly crucified in my memory every other picture I have ever seen. One could not hope to see a better executed, livelier, and more finished image. Certainly I will never be able to express how subtly and wonderfully it is done, and thus I am resolved not to have it by any other hand. And so explain something to me: if this is by another hand, so be it; but if it is yours, I want it from you at all costs. But if it is the case that it is not yours, but you wish your assistant[364] to complete it, let's discuss it first because I know how difficult it will be to imitate it, and I would prefer him to make something

---

Condivi in Italian as "Heli, heli," is recorded in the gospel of Mark 15:34: "And at the ninth hour, Jesus cried out with a loud voice, saying: Eloi, Eloi, lamma sabacthani? Which is, being interpreted, My God, my God, why hast thou forsaken me?"

360. "L'ansia della scoperta si esprime in un'analisi sempre più ravvicinata del foglio, prima ad occhio nudo, con l'aiuto di un lume . . . , poi con una lente;" in Ragionieri, *Vittoria Colonna e Michelangelo*, 165.

361. "Quel ch'avrà in lui le luci fisse, / Non quel ch'intese meglio o che più lesse / Volumi in terra, in ciel sarà beato;" S1:78; Colonna, *Sonnets*, 119.

362. "Del cor le luci chiare / Al libro de la croce;" in "Doi modi abbiam da veder l'alte e care," S1:165.

363. "L'effigie Sua viva e possente / Sculta esser de' ne l'alma, al cui valore / Sempre s'inchini, e la dipinta fore / Esser de' ognor al veder mio presente;" in "Simile a l'alta imagin Sua la mente," S2:38.

364. Probably Marcello Venusti; see Donati, *Vittoria Colonna*, 155.

else and not this. But if this is by your hand, then forgive me if I never return it.[365] I have looked at it closely with a lamp and a lens[366] and a mirror,[367] and I have never seen such an exquisite thing.

Signor,
At your command,
The Marchioness of Pescara

❧

[Letter 33]
Unico maestro Michel Agnelo et mio singularissimo amico,
Ho hauta la vostra et visto il *Crucifixo*, il qual certamente ha crucifixe nella memoria mia quante altre picture viddi mai; non se pò veder più ben fatta, più viva et più finita imagine, et certo io non potrei mai explicar quanto sottilmente et mirabilmente è fatta, per il che son risoluta de non volerlo de man d'altri, et però chiaritemi: se questo è d'altri, patientia; se è vostro, io in ogni modo v'el torrei. Ma in caso che non sia vostro et vogliate farlo fare a quel vostro, ce parlaremo prima perché, cognoscendo io la dificultà che ce è de imitarlo, più presto mi resolvo che colui faccia un'altra cosa che questa; ma se è il vostro questo, habbiate patientia che non son per tornarlo più. Io l'ho ben visto al lume et col vetro et col specchio, et non viddi mai la più finita cosa.
Signor,
Al comando vostro,
La Marchesa de Pescara

Letter 34: [Rome, 1544][368]
To Michelangelo Buonarroti
This letter weaves together art and spirituality.[369] It is God who confers genius upon the artist (see Letter 40), who must therefore turn to the deity for sufficient

365. For a discussion of this complex passage, see Nagel, "Gifts for Michelangelo," 653.

366. A magnifying glass. In another letter Colonna promises to obtain some "spectacles" for Michelangelo: "quel vetro verde che vene da Venetia, che vorrei fare guarnire bene con piede d'argento dorato et intorno per la vista nel depingere che se lli fatica forte nella cappella che fa di S. Paulo;" Maria Forcellino, *Michelangelo, Vittoria Colonna e gli "spirituali:" Religiosità e vita artistica a Roma negli anni Quaranta* (Rome: Viella, 2009), 79.

367. On the use of mirrors for the contemplation of holy images, see Abigail Brundin, Deborah Howard, and Mary Laven, *The Sacred Home in Renaissance Italy* (Oxford: Oxford University Press, 2018), 78–80.

368. Original, autograph: ABF, IX, fol. 508: Colonna, *Carteggio*, no. CXXIV.

369. For discussion of this letter see Charles de Tolnay, "Michelangelo's Pietà Composition for Vittoria Colonna," *Record of the Art Museum, Princeton University*, 12, no. 2 (1953): 47; Michael Hirst,

"grace" to produce a miraculous work. This relationship can also be reversed, in that the miracle flows from the work back to God. From the materiality of the artwork, embodied in the paper and pencil strokes observed with our human eyes, we enter via the eyes of faith into a real dialogue with the sacred subject that is depicted. By looking at the image we come closer to God and are enabled to pray "to this sweet Christ, whom you have depicted so well and so perfectly," as Colonna says below.

The brevity of Letter 34, and the absence of any formal opening salutations as well as of a date, are signs that this missive was just one element of an ongoing and active relationship between Colonna and Michelangelo in this period in which they were both in Rome: the letter is a means of rapid communication between individuals who were constantly in touch, both in person and in writing.

∽

Your works of art forcibly excite the judgment of those who look at them: and to intensify the experience I spoke of adding greater perfection to things that are already perfect, for I have seen that *omnia possibilia sunt credenti*.[370] I had absolute faith that God would grant you the preternatural grace needed to complete this Christ; then I saw it was so marvelous that it surpassed all my expectations in every way. Thus inspired by your miracles, I wished for precisely that which now I see marvelously accomplished, which is that it is so perfect in every part that one could not wish for anything more, nor even desire so much. And I tell you that it makes me very happy that the angel on the right hand side is by far the more beautiful, for the Archangel Michael will place you, Michel Angelo, on the right hand side of the Lord on Judgment Day. In the meantime I do not know how to serve you in any other way than by praying to this sweet Christ, whom you have depicted[371] so well and so perfectly, and praying that you will command me as your servant in all matters.

At your command,
The Marchioness of Pescara

Michelangelo and His Drawings (New Haven: Yale University Press, 1988), 117–18; Maria Forcellino, *Michelangelo*, 86–97; Maria Forcellino, "Vittoria Colonna," 305; and Donati, *Vittoria Colonna*, 165.

370. Mark 9:22; "All things are possible to him that believeth."

371. The use of the term *dipinto*, translated here neutrally as "depicted," has generated a good deal of scholarly debate between those who interpret it literally, as "painted," and those who consider this work to be a drawing. See for example Hirst, *Michelangelo*; Nagel, "Gifts for Michelangelo;" Antonio Forcellino, *La pietà perduta*; Maria Forcellino, "Vittoria Colonna;" Bambach, "Spiritual Poetry and Friendship with Vittoria Colonna: Drawings for Vittoria Colonna," in Bambach, *Michelangelo: Divine Draftsman*, 191–99; and most recently Donati, *Vittoria Colonna* and the bibliography therein.

❧

[Letter 34]

Li effetti vostri excitano a forza il giuditio de chi li guarda, et per vederne più exsperientia parlai de accrescer bontà alle cose perfette, et ho visto che *ommia possibilia sunt credenti*. Io ebbi grandissima fede in Dio che vi dessi una gratia sopranaturale a far questo Christo; poi il viddi sì mirabile che superò in tutti i modi ogni mia expettatione. Poi, fatta animosa dalli miraculi vostri, desiderai quello che hora maravegliosamente vedo adempito, cioè che sta da ogni parte in summa perfectione et non se potria desiderar più, né gionger a desiderar tanto. Et ve dico che mi alegro molto che l'angelo da man destra sia assai più bello perché il Michele ponerà voi, Michel Angelo, alla destra del Signore nel dì novissimo; et in questo mezzo io non so come servirvi in altro che in pregarne questo dolce Christo che sì bene et perfettamente havete depinto, et pregar voi mi comandiate come cosa vostra in tutto et per tutto.

Al vostro comando,
La Marchesa de Pescara

Letter 35: Rome, 28 August [1544][372]
To Antonio Bernardi della Mirandola

The philosopher Antonio Bernardi della Mirandola (1502–1565) studied with Pietro Pomponazzi (1462–1525) at the university in Bologna and there taught commentaries on Artistotle. In 1540, he was invited to the Roman court of the pope's nephew, cardinal Alessandro Farnese (1520–1589), where he spent the next twenty years engaged in a notable ecclesiastical and diplomatic career. In Rome he was a successful professor at La Sapienza University, where he taught Aristotle's *Ethics*. In 1544, he was entrusted with the Prepositure (the role of provost) of the collegial church of Santa Maria Maggiore in Mirandola, a turn of events which elicited this letter from Colonna. He was in contact with Marcantonio Flaminio and Paolo Giovio, and over the following years published a number of philosophical treatises.

Just as she did for Pietro Bembo when he became a cardinal (see Letter 19), Colonna is concerned here with offering the new priest some words of advice. Her message is clear: study the Holy Scriptures. But Bernardi's treatment of the Scriptures will need to move beyond the purely intellectual (through "human reason"); now he will need to "join" them with faith. If he does so, they will reveal many new secrets to him. The philosopher will need to submit his reason to his faith, the latter a "supernatural intelligence," but not one that is antithetical

---

372. Original, autograph: PML, 106376, MA 2641; Copy: BAV, Vat. Lat. 9069, fols. 44v–45v: Colonna, *Carteggio*, no. CLXV.

to reason or to philosophy: "Travel via Aristotle," but only "for a while." Once Bernardi arrives at the point where every action is governed by the Holy Spirit, Aristotle will once again become relevant, provided that philosophy is kept "in its place." The human search for comprehension (via philosophy) is not dismissed by Colonna, but merely put into a new perspective.

Conscious of his intellectual status and of the novelty of his interpretation of Aristotelian texts, Colonna writes to Bernardi in a philosophical vein, using terms from the discipline (*potentia, atto*) and casting her own arguments in the lexical field of consciousness, including in her citations from the Scriptures (*cognovit, revelare*). Faith is insistently presented as an instrument of consciousness, a concept that would be of interest to a philosopher. The same theme runs through Colonna's spiritual poetry.[373] Faith is God's gift: man retains the freedom to submit to God (*captivare*), in imitation of illustrious models from the past.[374] Abandonment to the actions of the Spirit is expressed a number of times in this letter via the choice of particular verbs of sacrifice.[375] Colonna's fundamental message is the same one expressed in the biblical passage of Matthew 16:24: "If any man will come after me, *let him deny himself*, and take up his cross, and follow me." The denial of the self renders the Christian happy, as Colonna makes clear: "you were never so happy with your high intellect as you will be now by harnessing it *ad obsequium fidei*" (in the service of faith). There is no evidence to suggest that Bernardi, immersed as he was in the political, diplomatic and careerist machinations of the Farnese court, paid much heed to Colonna's advice.

❧

Most Revered Master Antonio,

I was very pleased to learn that you are about to set out for your church to celebrate your first Mass: now you will need to spend a bit of time studying the Epistles and the Gospels, so that God can give you illumination and the grace to understand his word in a new way by joining it with faith, rather than with human reason; thus we will see a divine philosopher join with the celestial man, and the spirit in which you walk without even realizing it, in the sensitive way that you will perceive now that you must perforce study the Sacred Scriptures. And the Omnipotent Father, in his divine and supernatural wisdom, draws you wondrously to feel his goodness more inwardly, and you will recognize that paternal power which leads you to consider Christ as your intimate friend, far more than he is to you now when you have not read his

---

373. See for example the sonnet "Questo vèr noi maraviglioso effetto" (S1:78; Colonna, *Sonnets*, 119). On the difference between faith and reason, see also "A la durezza di Tomaso offerse" (S1:118; Colonna, *Sonnets*, 115); and "Fuggendo i re gentili il crudo impero" (S1:81; Colonna, *Sonnets*, 125).

374. See the sonnets "La innocenzia da noi pel nostro errore" (S1:59; Colonna, *Sonnets*, 110), and "Il Ciel, la terra, ogni elemento rende" (S1:11; Colonna, *Sonnets*, 74).

375. The verbs are "mactando," "abbatuto," and "sacrificare."

sweet words, for Christ said "nemo potest venire ad me," and he said "nisi Pater, qui misit me, traxerit eum, et nem[o] venit ad Patrem nisi per me."[376] And he said "nemo cognovit Patrem nisi Filius, et cui voluerit Filius revelare."[377] And he does not reveal himself to mighty intellects like you unless you seek him in his own words,[378] for even if as a Christian you know and love him, he will reveal to you the sweetness of his wondrous secrets in a new way, just as he gave you the grace to satisfy your reason and your human intellect in investigating the words of Aristotle. Thus you were never so happy with your high intellect as you will be now by harnessing it *ad obsequium fidei*,[379] feeling yourself clothed in that supernatural intelligence which the true faith only reveals in this most excellent Master.[380] Blessed are you who are able to make such a great sacrifice to God by offering up your great intellect, which, already sated with natural learning, must now be torn down by God to offer it a new, divine cause. And this effect is already so close to actuality in you that it cannot remain only in potentiality: you must sacrifice all your earthly self to God who became a man to sacrifice himself for you. Travel via Aristotle for a while, so that when divine supernatural things have become principal master of all your actions, putting philosophy in its place it will serve you perfectly. How is it possible that, if you recognize all the graces God has given you as coming from him, you can say that you do not wish to revel in his divine law "secundum interiorem hominem"?[381] There is certainly no reason, so that I hope that in his infinite goodness he will say to you that "durum est tibi contra

376. John 6:44: "No man can come to me, except the Father, who hath sent me, draw him; and I will raise him up in the last day."

377. Matthew 11:27: "And no one knoweth the Son, but the Father: neither doth any one know the Father, but the Son, and he to whom it shall please the Son to reveal him."

378. See Matthew 11:25: "At that time Jesus answered and said: I confess to thee, O Father, Lord of heaven and earth, because thou hast hid these things from the wise and prudent, and hast revealed them to the little ones."

379. 2 Corinthians 10:4–5: "Nam arma militiae nostrae non carnalia sunt, sed potentia Deo ad destructionem munitionum, consilia destruentes, et omnem altitudinem extollentem se adversus scientiam Dei, et in captivitatem redigentes omnem intellectum in obsequium Christi" ("For the weapons of our warfare are not carnal, but mighty to God unto the pulling down of fortifications, destroying counsels, and every height that exalteth itself against the knowledge of God, and bringing into captivity every understanding unto the obedience of Christ").

380. See also line 10 of the sonnet "Di vero Lume abisso immenso e puro:" "and clothed in you alone with living faith" (S1:93; Colonna, *Sonnets*, 59). The metaphor of clothing derives from Saint Paul; see Galatians 3:27: "For as many of you as have been baptized in Christ, have put on Christ;" and Romans 13:14: "But put ye on the Lord Jesus Christ." Ochino often made use of the same metaphor; for instance, "tutto vestito di fede viva," cited in Cargnoni, *I frati cappuccini*, 3:2155, a phrase also found in the *Beneficio di Cristo*, in which one chapter has the title "Come il cristiano si veste di Cristo" ("How the Christian clothes himself in Christ").

381. Romans 7:22: "Condelector enim legi Dei secundum interiorem hominem" ("For I am delighted with the law of God, according to the inward man").

stimulum calcitrare,"[382] above all because in your case there is no need for conversion nor for remaking you anew as God's servant, but only that you no longer need to resist the many spurs that he gives you inwardly as we do outwardly.[383] And thus I beg of you, and I declare that I only meant to write two words, but it is fitting that this letter should be long as it is in replying to so many of yours, since you demonstrate the usual courtesy and I the certainty that I have of your steadfast affection.

From Santa Anna, on the twenty-eighth day of August.

At your command,
The Marchioness of Pescara

On the reverse:
To the Most Reverend Signor, Master Antonio de Bernardi della Mirandola

∾

[Letter 35]
Molto Reverendo messer Antonio,
Ho hauto gran piacer de intender che siate per andar alla vostra chiesia et cantarvi la prima Messa, sì che bisognarà pur studiar un poco la Epistola et l'Evangelio, et così Dio vi darrà lume, gratia de intender con altra renovation la sua parola aderendo a essa con la fede, non con la ragione humana; et vederemo un divino philosopho con l'homo celeste, col qual spirito caminate senza che hora ve ne accorgiate, in quel sensibil modo che ve ne accorgereti studiando hora per forza la Scrittura Sacra. Et così l'onnipotente Padre con la divina et sopranatural sua sapientia vi tira in ottimo modo a sentir più internamente la sua bontà, et cognoscereti quella paterna forza de condurvi a veder Christo per più vostro intimo amico che hora senza legger le sue dolci parole par di haverlo, che "nemo potest venire ad me," dice lui, "nisi Pater, qui misit me, traxerit eum, et nem[o] venit ad Patrem nisi per me," et "nemo cognovit Patrem nisi Filius, et cui voluerit Filius revelare." Et lui non se revela alli grandi ingegni come voi se nelle sue parole no'l cercate, che, se ben come christiano il cognosceti et l'amate, altramente vi mostrarà la dolcezza delli suoi mirabili secreti, come ve ha dato gratia per satisfar la ragione et intellecto humano de ben investigar quelli de Aristotile. Et però non fusti mai tanto alegro del vostro alto intellecto quanto serreti hora lieto de captivarlo "ad obsequium fidei," sentendovi vestir di quella intelligentia sopranatural qual solo

382. Acts 26:14: "It is hard for thee to kick against the goad." This is the phrase that Saint Paul heard God speak to him just before his conversion.

383. Here Colonna insists on the need for companions—as Pole and the Viterbo circle of Spirituals were for her—who will work on behalf of divine grace to continually urge one to attend to one's faith.

mostra la vera fede in questo sì ottimo Maestro. Beato voi che posseti fare a Dio sì gran sacrifitio mactando il v[ostro] sì grande intellecto, il qual, ormai satio delle cose naturali, deve esser abbattuto da Dio per d[ar]li altra divina impresa. Et questo effetto è già in voi sì vicino a l'atto che non pò più stare in potentia: bisogna sacrificare tutto il vostro homo terreno a Colui che si fece humano per sacrificarsi per voi. Vada via Aristotile per un pezzo, che poi quando questo divin sopranaturale serrà principal signor di ogni vostra actione, mettendo la philosophia nel suo loco vi servirà ottimamente. Hor come è possibile che, se tutte le gratie che vi ha date Dio le recognosceti da lui, possiate dir che non voleti condelectarvi della sua divina legge "secundum interiorem hominem"? Per certo non ce è causa alcuna, sì che spero ne l'infinita sua bontà che vi dirrà che "durum est tibi contra stimulum calcitrare," maxime che in voi non è necessaria conversione né farvi de novo bon servo de Dio, ma solo che non più habbiate a resistere a tanti speroni che lui interiormente et noi exsteriormente vi damo. Et così ve ne prego, et vi certifico che pensai scriver doi parole, ma è giusto che sia longa respondendo a molte et molte vostre con questa, mostrando voi la solita cortesia et io la sicurtà che ho nella vostra incomutabil affection.

Da Santa Anna, a' dì XXVIII di agosto.

Al comando vostro,
la Marchesa de Pescara

A tergo
Al molto Reverendo Signor, Messer Antonio de Bernardi della Mirandola

Letter 36: Rome, 2 September [1544][384]
To the Mother Superior and the nuns of Santa Caterina in Viterbo

Colonna's entire life was conditioned by her continuous search for a guide to lead her on the path of faith, and she was always on the lookout for a reflection of

---

384. Copy: BAP, 479 G 68, fols. 252r–53r: Salza, *Lettere inedite*, 5–6. We can concretely date this letter to between 1544 and 1546, following Colonna's stay in Viterbo (1541–1543). The hypothesis that it dates from 1544 is based on the closing line: "This coming April it will be more likely, and I hope, God willing, to stay for the whole summer." It seems that Colonna's return to the peace of the Viterbo convent, which the nuns awaited eagerly, was prevented by some obligation that kept her in Rome (probably the presence of Pole, who left for Trent in early April), or else by the undesirability of spending the winter in a location that she had left precisely on health grounds. See the letter from Alvise [Luigi] Priuli to Beccadelli, 23 November 1543: "La signora Marchesa di Pescara è già 15 giorni qui in Rome, venuta per consiglio dei medici, per rispetto della sua indisposizione di cataro sotile, della quale per gratia di Dio sta meglio;" cited in Pagano and Ranieri, *Nuovi documenti*, 96. Whatever the reason, Colonna postponed her return to Viterbo to the following spring, and finally arrived in mid-May, as we learn from letters sent on 10 May 1545 from Rome (Pagano and Ranieri, *Nuovi documenti*, 116–18), and on 20 May from Viterbo (Colonna, *Carteggio*, no. CLXXII).

some kind of authentic religious experience in the people she met. She offered her financial and political support to those she considered to possess a true faith that they turned outwards towards the world, those who "make faith here out of the divine / light from above."[385] God has designated certain elect souls to blaze more brightly than the rest. In them his light shines so that it is visible to others. Anyone who gazes at them is raised towards heaven, because he recognizes in them the power of God.

In 1544, as she wrote this letter with great affection to the nuns of Santa Caterina in Viterbo who had housed her and comforted her, Colonna felt very distant from such sources of spiritual inspiration. Far from that place of comfort and from the circle of Spirituals, she felt very alone in Rome, "a city that seems to me to be surrounded by the flood." She longed for the company of her spiritual guides, above all Reginald Pole, her most important interlocutor on matters of faith. The English cardinal had distanced himself from his most passionate disciple and their relationship had grown cold (see Letters 24 and 39). In Colonna's moments of trial, Christ is the only stable point and her sole source of consolation: thus, the keyword of this letter, deriving from a biblical source in 2 Corinthians 1:3–7, is "consolation."

Revered and most beloved Sisters,

May Christ who is the only consolation for the afflicted be your medicine,[386] just as he alone is absolutely mine. And if, on the human level, we commonly say that it is a joy in our suffering to have fellow sufferers,[387] then how much more comfort must it bring in our Christian happiness (for we must define all our trials in this way) to see our companions in the same state! You, as you cannot see me, will see Christ ever sweeter; and I, as I cannot see you and cannot be among those who make me happy, you know how much, hope to share in that same sweetness which that infinite source of all tenderness will pour into our hearts for the same reason. Oh, so many words from the Scriptures come to mind now to comfort you! But the truth that I feel in my heart does not allow me to tell you things that I cannot learn on my own behalf, even though I know I should learn them and be most consoled and happy, since there is no firmer joy than the one we find in him who never abandons us.[388] And even if God's servants show us this and live it for us, nothing brings the

---

385. "Fede fan qui de la divina / Luce là su" ("Par che 'l celeste Sol sì forte allume," S1:177).

386. See 2 Corinthians 1:5: "per Christum abundat consolatio nostra" ("By Christ doth our comfort abound").

387. Colonna is paraphrasing the common Italian proverb "mal comune, mezzo gaudio," which corresponds to the English one, "a trouble shared is a trouble halved."

388. See Matthew 28:20: "and behold I am with you all days, even to the consummation of the world."

message more alive and closer to our experience than suffering, although certainly I am almost ashamed to call it by that name. But since no affliction could be greater for us than these absences, then I call it suffering, for the loss of belongings is a way to unburden ourselves and make us feel as light as pilgrims;[389] the loss of our earthly attachments makes us run without impediments, and our own death leads us to the true harbor with Christ,[390] for the mere hope of him fills us with joy. But the absence of those who guide us to him, who through their example show us his footprints and through their words his light and through every action make the road sweet and easy, this alone is the true grief that a Christian can experience, above all when he has long been used to deriving great benefit from receiving their charity. Thus, sisters, I, who am left alone and deprived of this support in a city that seems to me to be surrounded by the flood, I deserve your compassion. But you, who can only be irritated by me, although thanks to your great charity you think it useful, you can console yourselves with our beloved common father Master Luigi Priuli, and with Signor Flaminio,[391] and I dare say even more with the true father and Lord, the Most Revered Legate,[392] from whom I am sure that all your and my true consolation flows.

This coming April it will be more likely, and I hope, God willing, to stay for the whole summer; for right now I had to come back as quickly as possible. I commend myself always to your prayers.

From Santa Anna in Rome, on the second day of September.

Your Sister, at your command,
The Marchioness of Pescara

ᕀᕖ

[Letter 36]
Sorelle Reverende et amatissime,
Christo unica consolation de gli afflitti sia vostro rimedio, come esso solo assolutamente è mio. Et se, humanamente parlando, si suol dire che è solazzo a' miseri haver li compagni afflitti, or quanto deve esser conforto nelle felicità christiane (che così dovemo chiamar tutte le tribolationi) veder le compagne nel medesimo grado! Voi, per il non vedermi, vedrete il Signore più dolce; et io, per non vedervi

---

389. This may be a reference to the fact that during the Salt Wars of 1541, the Colonna family lost all their feudal territories south of Rome; see Letters 21 and 22.

390. See the sonnet "Beati voi, cui tempo né fatica," addressed to souls in Paradise: "Per labirinti o reti non s'intrica / il vostro pie', ma sta sicuro e franco / in porto" (S1:130; Colonna, *Sonnets*, 85).

391. The humanist Marcantonio Flaminio. He was responsible for revising the *Beneficio di Cristo*, the famously heretical text written by Benedetto da Mantova. He, too, like Priuli, visited Colonna on her deathbed; see Colonna, *Sulla tomba*, 16.

392. Reginald Pole, legate at the Council of Trent from 16 October 1542.

et non esser dove sono quelli che sapete quanto mi allegrano, spero participar della istessa dolcezza che per una egual causa quell'infinito fonte di ogni soavità instillarà ne' cuori nostri. O quante parole della scrittura mi occorrono hora per consolarvi! Ma la verità che 'l cor mio sente non mi fa dire ancora a voi quello che in tutto non piglio per me ma cognosco che dovrei pigliarlo et star consolatissima et allegra, non ci essendo altro stabil gaudio che quello di colui che non mai da noi si parte. Et se ben li servi di Dio ce lo mostrano et rappresentano, pur niuna cosa c'el mostra più vivo et c'el fa abbracciar più stretto che la tribulatione, benché certo par vergogna chiamarla così. Ma perché niuna afflitione può esser più grave a noi che queste absenze, però la chiamo così, perché la perdita delle robbe è uno alleggerir la persona, che si sente peregrina; quella de' parenti terreni è un farne correr senza impedimento, et il proprio morire è un condurci al vero porto con Christo, la speranza solo del quale ci fa tanto liete. Ma l'assenza di quelli che ne guidano a lui, che con gli essempi ne mostrano le vestigie, con le parole la luce et con ogni effetto ne fanno la via soave et espedita, questo solo è quanto di affanno può intervenire a un christiano, massime quando per longa esperienza si prova grandissimo profitto ricevere dalla loro charità. Sì che, sorelle, io che resto sola et priva di questi sussidii, in una città che mi par c'habbia intorno il diluvio, merito compassione da voi. Ma voi, che da me solo molestia potevate ricevere et per abondanza d'amor vi pareva utilità, potete consolarvi col carissimo commun padre messer Luigi Priuli et col Signor Flaminio, et ardisco dire ancor col più vero padre et Signore il Reverendissimo Legato, dal qual certo non è rimasto ogni giusta vostra et mia consolatione.

Questo aprile sarà più al proposito, et starò poi, piacendo a Dio, tutta la state, che così hora bisognava tornarmene prestissimo. All'orationi vostre di continuo mi raccomando.

Da Santa Anna di Roma, a' dì II di settembre.

Sorella al comando vostro,
La Marchesa di Pescara

Letter 37: Viterbo, 20 July [1545][393]
To Michelangelo Buonarroti

The existence of a loving relationship between Michelangelo and Vittoria Colonna (albeit a platonic one) has been a long-held assumption. In this letter, Colonna defines their relationship in rather different terms, as a "stable friendship and Christian bond secured by our affection." The "bond" (literally "knot") between them is defined as "Christian," and it is worth noting that the letters and poems

---

393. Original, autograph: ABF, IX, fol. 510: Colonna, *Carteggio*, no. CLVII.

the pair exchanged talk exclusively of Christ: "our Lord, of whom with such ardent and humble heart you spoke to me."[394]

Colonna establishes a symmetry in this letter between her own visits to the chapel in the convent of Santa Caterina in Viterbo and Michelangelo's visits to the Capella Paolina (Pauline Chapel) in Rome where he was working on a commission. Both of them, in these places, find themselves indirectly in the service of Christ, engaged in a dialogue that refers to him. The contemplation of sacred images is thus assimilated with an act of prayer: frescoes "speak" just as much as "living beings." Art assumes a spiritual function as a means of dialogue with God. As in the earlier Letter 34, a continuous virtuous circle is established between the material representation of God and the intimate act of praying to God, who is represented. One can pray to an image (see Letter 33), or one can pray that the image of God will shine forth in one's friend just as it shines forth in an image.

This is the only extant letter between Colonna and Michelangelo that was not sent from Rome, and thus it carries an address.

∽

Magnificent Master Michel Angelo,
I did not reply before to your letter, since it was, one might say, a reply to mine, and since I thought that if you and I carry on writing according to my duty and your courtesy, I will have to leave the chapel of Santa Caterina[395] without joining the sisters at the appointed Hours,[396] and you will have to leave the chapel of San Paolo[397] without turning up before dawn to spend the whole day in sweet dialogue with your paintings—which with their living voices do not fail to speak to you just as the living beings that I have here around me do to me—and so I would disappoint the brides of Christ and you his vicar. But, given our stable friendship and Christian bond secured by our affection, I don't think it is necessary to endorse each of your letters with one of my own, but I will wait with my soul ready for a more weighty opportunity to serve you. I pray to our Lord, of whom with such ardent and humble heart you spoke to me before I left Rome, that I will find you on my return with his image renewed and

---

394. See Colonna, *Sonnets*, 31: "the friendship between Michelangelo and Colonna was embedded in a shared interest in just such spiritual issues;" and Targoff, *Renaissance Woman*, 187.

395. The Dominican convent of S. Caterina at Viterbo, no longer standing. Colonna stayed there from September 1541 to November 1543, and again from May to October 1545.

396. The Liturgy of the Hours that ordered monastic life.

397. The Pauline Chapel in the Vatican, frescoed by Michelangelo between 1542 and 1550.

revived by true faith in your soul, just as you depicted him in my Samaritan Woman.[398]
And I commend myself to you as always, and also to our friend Urbino.[399]

From the convent of Viterbo, on the twentieth of July.

At your command,
the Marchioness of Pescara

On the reverse, in Colonna's hand:
To my more than magnificent and more than beloved Master Michel Agnelo Buonaruoti

❧

[Letter 37]
Magnifico messer Michel Agnelo,
Non ho resposto prima alla lettera vostra, per esser stata si pò dire resposta della
mia, pensando che se voi et io continuamo il scrivere secondo il mio obligo et la
vostra cortesia, bisognarà che io lassi qui la cappella de Santa Catarina senza tro-
varmi alle hore ordinate in compagnia di queste sorelle, et che voi lassate la cappella
di San Paulo senza trovarvi, dalla matina innanzi giorno, a star tutto il dì nel dolce
conloquio delle vostre dipinture, quali con li loro naturali accenti non manco vi
parlano che facciano a me le proprie persone vive che ho de intorno, sì che io alle
spose et voi al vicario di Christo mancaremo. Però, sapendo la nostra stabile amicitia et ligata in christiano nodo sicurissima affectione, non mi par procurar con le
mie il testimonio delle vostre lettere, ma aspettar con preparato animo substantiosa
occasione di servirvi, pregando quel Signore, del quale con tanto ardente et humil
core mi parlaste al mio partir da Roma, che io vi trovi al mio ritorno con l'imagin
sua sì rinovata et per vera fede viva ne l'anima vostra, come ben l'avete dipinta nella
mia Samaritana. Et sempre a voi mi raccomando et così al nostro Urbino.
Dal monesterio di Viterbo, a' dì XX di luglio.

Al comando vostro,
la Marchesa di Pescara
A tergo, autografo
Al mio più che magnifico et più che carissimo messer Michel Agnelo Buonaruoti

398. The image of the *Samaritan Woman*, made by Michelangelo for Colonna, is only known to
us via copies; see Ragionieri, *Vittoria Colonna e Michelangelo*; Rovetta, *L'ultimo Michelangelo*; and
Bernadine Barnes, "The Understanding of a Woman: Vittoria Colonna and Michelangelo's Christ and
the Samaritan Woman," *Renaissance Studies*, 27 (2013): 633–53.

399. Francesco Amadori detto Urbino, employee of and collaborator with Michelangelo. He assisted in
the painting of the Pauline Chapel by erecting the scaffold, preparing the walls and grinding the colors;
see Anna Maria Luzietti, "Amadori, Francesco, detto l'Urbino," in *Dizionario biografico degli italiani*,
Vol. 2 (1960), <treccani.it/enciclopedia/amadori-francesco-detto-l-urbino_(Dizionario-Biografico)/>.

Letter 38: [before 24 November 1545][400]
To Pope Paul III

This is not the only letter from Colonna to Pope Paul III that adopts a severe tone (see Letter 17): at times she almost seems to express annoyance, and she is not afraid to contradict the pope, especially when the fate of the Capuchins is at stake.[401] Her familiarity with her addressee emerges from these few lines, a familiarity which permitted her to send him such a brief note, lacking any of the rhetorical formulae that generally characterized sixteenth-century letters. Colonna is not shy of reminding the pope that he promised a donation to the nuns of the convent of Santa Caterina in Viterbo, where she is resident at the time of writing. A papal brief dated 24 November 1545 approves her request, as is noted at the foot of the document: "Marchionissa Piscariae dicit impetrasse a Sanctitate Vestra" ("The Marchioness of Pescara says she obtained Your Holiness's agreement").[402]

Colonna adopts a dual strategy in this letter: first, her spiritual argument is that the pope's donation would be well directed and therefore pleasing to God; second, the worldly implication, less overtly stated, is that, as the request comes from her, with all that her name implies, the pope should do his best to satisfy it.

❧

Our Most Holy and Blessed father and Lord,
Your Holiness's saintly desire to make a splendid donation to the sisters of Viterbo has not yet been carried out, despite your having deigned to approve it for me twice now. And since I am certain that it could not be better directed, I therefore dare to beg once again that your true charity act to expedite it, in accordance with my hopes and with their devotion. Since Your Holiness is so generous with infinite donations, greater than any other pontiff, I believe this one will be especially pleasing to God, and in addition it will be an enormous favor to me, your most devoted servant. I wish for nothing, of course, that is not of service to Your Holiness, and may God allow you to prosper with all happiness.

From Your Holiness's most humble servant, who kisses your most holy feet,
The Marchioness of Pescara

❧

---

400. Original, autograph: AAV, Concilio Tridentino, XXXVII, fol. 171r: Colonna, *Carteggio*, no. CLXXVII.

401. See for example the letter dated 16 September 1538; Tacchi-Venturi, "Vittoria Colonna e la riforma cappuccina," 32; and the letter-cum-pamphlet of January/February 1536, for which see D'Alencon, *Tribulationes*, 27–31; Cargnoni, *I frati cappuccini*, 2:200–8; Copello, "Aggiornamenti: Parte II," 110–18.

402. AAV, Arm. XLI, 34, fol. 258r–v.

[Letter 38]

Santissimo et Beatissimo patre et Signore nostro,

La santa volontà di Vostra Beatitudine ne l'ottima elimosina fatta alle suore di Viterbo non è stata ancor posta in effetto, benché doi volte se sia degnata di dirme de sì. Et perché son certa che meglio non potria esser collocata, ardisco di suplicarla di novo che con la sua vera charità sia servita di exspedirla conforme alla mia speranza et alla loro devotione, che, de tante infinite elimosine che la Santità Vostra forsi più larghe che niuno altro pontifice ha fatte, questa credo sia nel numero delle più grate a Dio, ultra di fare a me, sua devotissima serva, grandissima gratia; non volendo, però, né desiderando se non quel che è servitio di Vostra Beatitudine, qual Dio si degne prosperar con ogni felicità.

De Vostra Santità humilissima serva, che li piedi suoi santissimi basa,
La Marchesa di Pescara

Letter 39: [Rome], 25 December [1545][403]
To Reginald Pole

As already seen in Letter 31, Colonna returns here to the comparison between her own smallness versus Christ's "great merit." This is a common theme among the Spirituals: mankind's salvation can only depend on Christ's merits, obtained through his sacrifice on the cross, and our own works contribute nothing—to consider our works meritorious would be to detract from Christ's own merits. Pole is once again essential to Colonna, as the one person who can help her "to understand myself . . ., to humble myself, almost to force me onto the road of self-annihilation where I see myself as nothing and live only in him, he who is all our good, all consolation, joy and happiness." The expression "road of self-annihilation" is reminiscent of the doctrine of *nichil*, deriving from the fourteenth-century works of Marguerite Porete and Ugo Panziera and adopted by the Franciscan Observant Bartolomeo Cordoni in his *Dyalogo della unione spirituale di Dio con l'anima*, one of the foundational texts of the Capuchin movement.[404] Cordoni includes self-annihilation as one of the six ways to union with God.[405] Making reference to the assertion in John 15:5, "apart from me, you can do nothing," he

403. Original, autograph: ACDF, Stanza Storica, E 2-e, fasc. 9, fols. 594r–95v; Copy: the same, N 4-d, fasc. 1, fol. 175r: Pagano and Ranieri, *Nuovi documenti*, 99–101. This letter can be dated securely to 1545 thanks to the reference to Pedro Pacheco's cardinalate.

404. See Paolo Simoncelli, "Il *Dialogo dell'unione spirituale di Dio con l'anima* tra alumbradismo spagnolo e prequietismo," *Annuario dell'istituto Storico Italiano per l'età moderna e contemporanea* 29 (1977): 565–601; and Camaioni, "Libero spirito."

405. See Chapter XXIV: "Come l'homo si può unire a Dio per via di abnegatione di se medesimo, cioè per annihilatione della propria volontà."

confirms that all the initiative and merits necessary for salvation reside in God: man must provide only a readiness to have an encounter with grace and to submit his freedom to divine will. This doctrine was adopted by Bernardino Ochino,[406] by the group of Spirituals,[407] and ultimately by Colonna herself.

In this letter, Colonna's wish to see and talk with Pole becomes urgent and her sense of abandonment is intense: "I lack only Your most Revered Lordship, I desire only you." Her nostalgia pervades the whole text: she begs Pole to remain in good health so that he can continue to perform his function as her example of a perfect spiritual life, and she prays that God may enter the depths of his heart so that he will be obliged—because his heart will overflow—to write back to her. Despite her overwhelming emotion, however, Colonna manages to weave this plea into a highly literary text that is linguistically, syntactically, and stylistically complex, replete with rhetorical questions, metaphors, emphatic repetitions, and parallelisms.[408]

❧

Most Illustrious, Revered and Esteemed Monsignor,
Master Josia, a scribe from the post in Trento, came to me to ask most kindly if I needed anything as he will be taking the cardinal's hat to Pacheco.[409] And since I wrote only yesterday at length to Signor Priuli,[410] I dare not bother him again today, so instead I pray that Your Most Revered Lordship will accept my overtures in his place, so that Josia does not make the journey without carrying any of my letters, and

---

406. "Eleggo per amore di farmi intima cordiale alle tre Divine Persone, et di mancar tutta a me stessa, et a tutte le creature, et viver sola a Dio, eleggo anchora di esser in me medesima innihilata, et in Dio tutta trasformata;" Bernardino Ochino, *Dialogi sette del reuerendo padre frate Bernardino Occhino* [sic] *senese generale di frati Capuzzini* (Venice: per Nicolo d'Aristotile detto il Zoppino, 1542), vol. VII, fol. 51r–v.

407. "O felice quella anima, la quale per dono di Dio viene a tanta annichilatione di sé stessa et, conoscendosi povera di meriti et carica di difetti et di debiti, s'attrista in sé medesima et si consola in Dio! Et quanto più si diffida della propria giustitia tanto più si confida in quella del suo diletto sposo Iesù Christo:" Marcantonio Flaminio, *Apologia del* Beneficio di Christo *e altri scritti inediti*, ed. Dario Marcatto (Florence: Olschki, 1996), 97.

408. See Claudio Scarpati, "Le rime spirituali di Vittoria Colonna nel codice Vaticano donato a Michelangelo," in Claudio Scarpati, *Invenzione e scrittura: Saggi di letteratura italiana* (Milan: Vita e pensiero, 2005), 153: "La confessione, pur recando il timbro di un'autenticità indiscutibile, non disdegna torniture retoriche e simmetrie costruttive, quasi che i modi della scrittura poetica scendano a sostanziare una prosa di altissima qualità letteraria."

409. Pedro Pacheco became a cardinal on 16 December 1545.

410. Alvise [Luigi] Priuli.

with the same I only pray to the infinite goodness of him who is our only Easter[411] that true joy will so reveal itself and be felt in the depths of your heart that you will be obliged to share some part of it with me through your letters. And I beg you, take care, by our faith in salvation, to stay healthy, so that, with the continual benefit of such redemption, you show us in your writings and in your actions the down payment to be made along the way in order to enjoy perfect salvation once we reach our homeland.

Certainly when he came I was thinking about how the Lord sometimes scourges us and sometimes caresses us; and how, as regards myself, when he scourges me his justice is merciful, and how, as regards Christ, when he bestows favors and blessings his mercy is just ! For what pain can I experience out of ingratitude that should not instead seem sweet, since I deserve all punishments, and what sweetness can he concede to me that out of Christ's great merit, by which God views me, should not seem to me to be wholly warranted, since he wishes good for all of his members? Therefore I wish for nothing in this world, considering this world, and I lack nothing since I am certain of my salvation, considering Christ. I lack only Your Most Revered Lordship, I desire only you, for you always helped me to understand myself (more than any living creature could), to humble myself, almost to force me onto the road of self-annihilation where I see myself as nothing and live only in him, who is all our good, all consolation, joy and happiness.[412] May he grant me this service on behalf of Your most Revered Lordship, because on my own behalf I say nothing, as I am a creature sustained in his kingdom almost by the prayers of others; and I kiss your hand, and commend myself to Signor Luisi, Signor Flaminio and the Revered Vigornia.[413] Please, Your Lordship, forgive my hasty closing lines, for I have no more time.

Today, Christmas Day.

Most dutiful servant of Your Most Illustrious and Revered Lordship,
The Marchioness
On the reverse:
To the most Illustrious, Revered, and Esteemed Monsignor, the Signor Cardinal from England

---

411. This expression echoes 1 Corinthians 5:7: "Etenim Pascha nostrum immolatus est Christus" ("For Christ our Passover [lamb] is sacrificed for us").

412. In a letter sent to Colonna in 1541, Pole confirmed that Jesus is "fons omnis verae et solidae consolationis" ("The source of all true and sure consolation;" Colonna, *Carteggio*, no. CXXXIX), for in the midst of trials "quid restat, nisi ut in Christo me consoler?" ("What else remains, if not that I am consoled in Christ?").

413. Richard Pate, archbishop of Worcester, who stayed in Pole's house in Trent in 1542–1543, together with Luigi [Alvise] Priuli, Marcantonio Flaminio, and Apollonio Merenda. Pate returned to Trent in May 1545; Firpo and Marcatto, *Il processo inquisitoriale del cardinal Giovanni Morone*, 3:553.

[Letter 39]

Illustrissimo et Reverendissimo Monsignor observandissimo,

Messer Josia, scrivano della posta di Trento, me è venuto con molta cortesia a dir se voglio cosa alcuna perché lui porta la barretta al Pacieco. Et io, per haver scritto hieri al Signor Luisi longamente, non ardisco darli oggi nova molestia, ma pregar Vostra Signoria Reverendissima che la pigli per lui, acciò costui non vada vacuo delle mie lettere, con le quali solo prego l'infinita bontà di colui che è sola nostra Pascua et vero gaudio che tanto se mostri et si faccia sentire dentro ne l'intimo del cor suo che sia sforzato mandarne parte a me con le sue lettere. Et la suplico procuri, in fede di questa nostra salute, conservarsi sano, acciò, continuamente godendo di tanto salutare in via, ne mostri nelli suoi scritti et nel suo exempio l'arra di goder della compita salute in patria.

Et certo, quando costui venne, considerava quando il Signor ne flagella et quando ne fa carezze: come, riguardando in me stessa, mi pare misericordiosa la sua giustitia nel tempo del flagello, et come, riguardando in Christo, mi par giusta la sua misericordia nel tempo delli favori et delle gratie! Perché qual amaritudine me pò dare che a l'infinite ingratitudine mia non debbia parer dolcezza, meritando sempre ogni male, et qual dolcezza mi pò concedere che al grandissimo merito di Christo, nel qual Dio mi guarda, non mi debbia parer conveniente, meritando lui sempre ogni bene per tutti i membri suoi? Sì che niente desidero in questo mondo considerando il mondo, et niente mi manca per sicurità di goder quell'altro considerando Christo. Solo Vostra Signoria Reverendissima mi manca, sola lei desidero, perché continuo (più che mai potessi far creatura) mi aiutava a cognoscer me stessa, a humiliarmi, a farmi quasi constretta andar per questa via de annichilarmi et vedermi niente et viver tutta in colui che è ogni bene, ogni consolatione, gaudio et felicità nostra. Qual con suo servitio si degni exaudirmi de Vostra Signoria Revederendissima, perché de me, come cosa che nel suo regno quasi per le oration d'altri son sostenuta, niente li dico; et, basandoli le mano, al Signor Luisi, Signor Flaminio et Reverendo Vigornia me recomando. Et perdoni Vostra Signoria questa mala creanza, che non ho tempo.

Ogi, il dì de Natale.

Serva obligatissima de Vostra Signoria Illustrissima et Reverendissima,
La Marchesa

A tergo
A l'Illustrissimo et Reverendissimo Monsignor observandissimo, il Signor Cardinal de Inghilterra

Letter 40: [Rome, 1546][414]
To Michelangelo Buonarroti

The "divine light" has now illuminated Michelangelo and caused him to understand the vanity of "earthly glory." Colonna therefore invites her friend in this letter to look at the work done by his own hands and see there the original imprint of the Creator: his art is a gift from God ("His goodness who made you art's only master;" see also Letter 33). In the same way, in contemplating her own poetry Colonna must rise up towards God, as he is its true source. In Colonna's poetry there are many references to the divine inspiration for her verses which she has chosen to obey with humility,[415] conscious of the limitations of her poetic talent.[416] Her poetry is an instrument played by God: he "moves her thoughts,"[417] the fire that inflames the poet's mind, sending out sparks that become poetry, is made by him.[418] In the same way in this letter Colonna thanks God for her poetry, because it was a lesser sin to respond to that divine inspiration, as she does now, than to fail to respond.

The detachment from any aspiration to glory thanks to her "virtue" and her divinely inspired works was a familiar *topos* for Colonna, who describes precisely this trajectory in the poem with which she opens her gift manuscript for Michelangelo in 1539–1540:[419] a desire for fame had once inspired her, but from now on every part of her writing would be dedicated to Christ: its inspiration, its contents, its form, its aim.[420] Now, however, that poetic experience is over (Colonna refers to her "dead works"). A new path opens on the horizon, and Colonna seems in this letter to be promising to devote herself to the production of "future works" (of what kind remains unclear), and these too will form part of her lifelong attempt to offend God a little bit less.

ᵔᕔ

---

414. Original, autograph: ABF, IX, fol. 509: Colonna, *Carteggio*, no. CLXXXII.

415. See for example the sonnets "Parrà forse ad alcun che non ben sano" (S1:1; Colonna, *Sonnets*, 103); "S'in man prender non soglio unqua la lima" (S1:4; Colonna, *Sonnets*, 137); and "L'alto Signor, del cui valor congionte" (S1:2).

416. See for example the sonnets "In forma di musaico un alto muro" (S1:64; Colonna, *Sonnets*, 113); and "Quasi rotonda palla accesa intorno" (S1:65; Colonna, *Sonnets*, 115).

417. See the sonnet "Parrà forse ad alcun che non ben sano" (S1:3; Colonna, *Sonnets*, 103).

418. See the sonnet "S'in man prender non soglio unqua la lima" (S1:4; Colonna, *Sonnets*, 137).

419. See Brundin's bilingual edition of this manuscript gift in Colonna, *Sonnets* as well as Colonna, *La raccolta*.

420. See the sonnet "Poi che 'l mio casto amor gran tempo tenne" (S1:1; Colonna, *Sonnets*, 57).

Magnificent Master Michel Angelo,

Your virtue affords you such great fame that you might never have believed that, subject to time and chance, it was merely a mortal state, if that divine light had not come into your heart to show you that earthly glory, however long it lasts, has its second death. Your sculptures bear witness to his goodness who made you art's only master, and thus you will understand that I thank only God for my nearly dead works, for I sinned less against him in writing them than I do now in my idleness. And I ask you to accept my desire as down payment on future works.

At your command,
The Marchioness of Pescara

On the reverse, in another hand:
Letter from the Lady Marchioness of Pescara

∾

[Letter 40]

Magnifico messer Michel Angelo,

Sì grande è la fama che vi dà la vostra virtù che mai forsi haveresti creso che per il tempo né per cosa alcuna fussi stata mortale, se non veniva nel cor vostro quella divina luce che ve ha dimostrato che la gloria terrena, per longa che sia, ha pur la sua seconda morte. Sì che, riguardando nelle vostre sculpture la bontà de colui che ve ne ha fatto unico maestro, cognoscerite che io de' miei quasi già morti scritti ringratio solamente il Signor perché l'offendeva meno scrivendoli che con l'otio hora non fo. Et ve prego vogliate aceptar questa mia voluntà per arra de l'opere future.

Al vostro comando,
La Marchesa de Pescara

A tergo, di altra mano
Poliza della Signora Marchesa di Pescara

Bibliography

Primary Sources

Manuscript

Italy

Brescia, Biblioteca Queriniana, E VIII 16, fasc. 2.

Fano, Biblioteca Federiciana, Fondo Polidori 14.

Florence, Archivio Buonarroti, IX.

Florence, Archivio di Stato, Ducato di Urbino, classe I, b. 266.

Florence, Biblioteca Moreniana, Autografi Frullani.

Lucca, Archivio di Stato, Fondo Anziani al tempo della libertà, 546.

Mantua, Archivio di Stato, Archivio Gonzaga, b. 1880.

Mantua, Archivio di Stato, Archivio Gonzaga, b. 1904.

Mantua, Archivio di Stato, Archivio Gonzaga, b. 1906.

Mantua, Archivio di Stato, Archivio Gonzaga, b. 3000.

Milan, Archivio Gallarati Scotti, Processo del card. Morone.

Milan, Biblioteca Ambrosiana, E 32 inf.

Milan, Biblioteca Ambrosiana, H 245 inf.

Modena, Archivio di Stato, Cancelleria ducale, Carteggio principi esteri, b. 1248/4.

Montecassino, Archivio dell'Abbazia, caps. LXVII, fasc. XVIII.

Naples, Archivio di Stato, Carte Farnesiane, fasc. 252.

Parma, Biblioteca Palatina, Palatino, Carteggio Lucca, 1 A–C.

Perugia, Biblioteca Augustea, 479 G 68.

Rome, Archivio di Stato, Ospedale S. Spirito – Priorato di Bassano d'Orte, n. 14.

Rome, Biblioteca Nazionale Centrale Vittorio Emanuele II, Lettere autografe di Vittoria Colonna, A.180/35.

Subiaco, Biblioteca di Santa Scolastica, Archivio Colonna, Corrispondenza di Ascanio Colonna, Sottoserie 2.

Venice, Biblioteca Nazionale Marciana, Cons. Ven. 160.4.1.

Verona, Biblioteca Capitolare, ms 810.

Vatican City

Archivio Apostolico Vaticano, Armadio XLI, 34.

Archivio Apostolico Vaticano, Concilio Tridentino, vol. XXXVII.

Archivio della Congregazione per la Dottrina della Fede, Stanza Storica, E 2-e, fasc. 9.

Archivio della Congregazione per la Dottrina della Fede, Stanza Storica, N 4-d, fasc. 1.

Archivio della Congregazione per la Dottrina della Fede, Stanza Storica, R 5-a, I.5.

Archivio della Congregazione per la Dottrina della Fede, Stanza Storica, R 5-b.
Archivio della Congregazione per la Dottrina della Fede, Stanza Storica, R 5-b, II.5.
Archivio della Congregazione per la Dottrina della Fede, Stanza Storica, R 5-c.
Biblioteca Apostolica Vaticana, Chigiano, L III 58.
Biblioteca Apostolica Vaticana, Ferrajoli, 433.
Biblioteca Apostolica Vaticana, Ferrajoli, 886.

Spain
Madrid, Real Academia de la Historia, A-42.
Madrid, Real Academia de la Historia, A-43.

United Kingdom
London, British Library, Additional 23139.
Oxford, Bodleian Library, Ital. C. 25.

United States
Boston, Massachussetts, Isabella Stewart Gardner Museum, n. 34.
New York, Pierpont Morgan Library, 106376, MA 2641.

Printed

Alamanni, Luigi. *Lettere.* In *Lettere di L. Alamanni, B. Varchi, V. Borghini, L. Salviati e d'altri autori citati dagli Accademici della Crusca per la più parte fin qui inedite,* edited by Francesco Zambrini. Lucca: Tip. Franchi e Maionchi, 1853.
Aretino, Pietro. *Lettere.* Edited by Paolo Procaccioli. *Edizione nazionale delle opere di Pietro Aretino,* vol. 4 in 6 parts. Rome: Salerno, 1997–2002.
———. *Lettere scritte a Pietro Aretino.* Edited by Paolo Procaccioli. *Edizione nazionale delle opere di Pietro Aretino,* vol. 9 in 2 parts. Rome: Salerno, 2002–2003.
Bembo, Pietro. *Lettere.* Edited by Ernesto Travi. 3 vols. Bologna: Commissione per i testi di lingua, 1987–1993.
———. *Prose e rime.* Edited by Carlo Dionisotti. Turin: UTET, 1960. Second edition, Turin: UTET, 1966.
Cargnoni, Costanzo, ed. *I frati cappuccini: Documenti e testimonianze del primo secolo.* 6 vols. Perugia: Edizioni Frate Indovino, 1988–1993.
Castiglione, Baldassarre. *Lettere famigliari e diplomatiche.* Edited by Guido La Rocca, Angelo Stella, and Umberto Morando. 3 vols. Turin: Einaudi, 2016.
———. *Il libro del cortegiano.* Edited by Amedeo Quondam. Rome: Bulzoni, 2016.

———. *La seconda redazione del* Cortegiano *di Baldassarre Castiglione: Edizione critica.* Edited by Ghino Ghinassi. Florence: Sansoni, 1968.

Colonna, Vittoria. *Carteggio.* Edited by Ermanno Ferrero and Giuseppe Müller. Turin: Loescher, 1889. Second edition, with "Supplemento" edited by Domenico Tordi, Turin: Loescher, 1892.

———. *Litere della divina Vetoria Colonna marchesana di Pescara ala duchessa de Amalfi sopra la vita contemplativa di Santa Caterina et sopra de la activa di Santa Madalena non piu viste in luce.* Venice: Alesandro de Viano Venetian, ad instantia di Antonio detto el Cremaschino, 1544.

———. *La raccolta di rime per Michelangelo,* edited and commented by Veronica Copello. Florence: SEF, 2020.

———. *Rime.* Edited by Alan Bullock. Bari: Laterza, 1982.

———. *Le rime.* Edited by Pietro Ercole Visconti. Rome: Salviucci, 1840.

———. *Rime de la diuina Vittoria Colonna marchesa di Pescara novamente stampate con privilegio.* Parma: [A. de Viottis], 1538.

———. *Sonetti: In morte di Francesco Ferrante d'Avalos, marchese di Pescara: Edizione del ms. XIII.G.43 della Biblioteca Nazionale di Napoli.* Edited by Tobia R. Toscano. Milan: Mondadori, 1998.

———. *Sonnets for Michelangelo: A Bilingual Edition.* Edited and translated by Abigail Brundin. Chicago: University of Chicago Press, 2005.

Condivi, Ascanio. *Vita di Michelagnolo Buonarroti, pittore, scultore, architetto e gentiluomo fiorentino pubblicata mentre viveva dal suo scolare Ascanio Condivi.* 2nd ed. by Girolamo Ticciati, Pierre-Jean Mariette, Domenico Maria Manni, and Antonio Francesco Gori. Florence: Gaetano Albizzini all'insegna del sole, 1746. English translation by Alice Sedgwick Wohl, edited by Helmut Wohl, *The Life of Michelangelo,* 2nd edition, University Park: University of Pennsylvania Press, 1999.

Cordoni, Bartolomeo. *Dyalogo della unione spirituale de Dio con l'anima dove sono interlocutori l'amor divino, la sposa anima, et la ragione umana.* Milan: Francesco Cantalupo e Cicognara Innocenzo, 1539.

Corso, Rinaldo. *Dichiaratione fatta sopra la seconda parte delle rime della divina Vittoria Collonna* [sic]. 1542.

———. *Dichiaratione fatta sopra la seconda parte delle* Rime *della divina Vittoria Collonna* [sic] *marchesana di Pescara: Da Rinaldo Corso alla molto illust. Mad. Veronica Gambara . . . et alle donne gentili dedicata . . .* Bologna: Gian Battista de Phaelli, 1543.

D'Alençon, Edouard, ed. *Tribulationes Ordinis Fratrum Minorum Capuccinorum primis annis pontificatus Pauli III, 1534–1541: Haec brevis illustratio monumentorum, editorum vel ineditorum, quae ad dicti ordinis historiam spectant, correcta et ampliata secundo prodit.* Rome: Tip. Manuzio, 1914.

D'Arcano Grattoni, Maurizio. "Lettere inedite di Vittoria Colonna, Giulia Gonzaga e Laura Sanvitale Rangoni a Gian Mauro d'Arcano." *Ce fastu?* 2 (1982), 291–313.

Ferrari, Monica, Isabella Lazzarini, and Federico Piseri. *Autografie dell'età minore: Lettere di tre dinastie italiane tra Quattro e Cinquecento.* Rome: Viella, 2016.

Fiamma, Gabriele. *Rime spirituali.* Venice: Francesco de' Franceschi Senese, 1570.

Firpo, Massimo, and Dario Marcatto, eds. *I processi inquisitoriali di Pietro Carnesecchi, 1557–1567.* 2 vols. in 4. Vatican City: Archivio Segreto Vaticano, 1998–2000.

———. *Il processo inquisitoriale del cardinal Giovanni Morone: Edizione critica.* 6 vols. in 7. Rome: Istituto storico per l'età moderna e contemporanea, 1981–1995.

———. *Il processo inquisitoriale del cardinal Giovanni Morone.* New critical edition. 3 vols. Rome: Libreria editrice vaticana, 2011–2015.

Flaminio, Marcantonio. *Apologia del* Beneficio di Christo *e altri scritti inediti.* Edited by Dario Marcatto. Florence: Olschki, 1996.

Fontana, Bartolomeo. "Documenti vaticani di Vittoria Colonna, marchesa di Pescara, per la difesa dei Cappuccini." *Archivio della società romena di storia patria* 9 (1886): 345–71.

Foscolo, Ugo. *Epistolario.* Edited by Mario Scotti. *Edizione nazionale delle opere di Ugo Foscolo,* vol. 9, part 22. Florence: Le Monnier, 1994.

Fracastoro, Girolamo. *Hieronymi Fracastorii Veronensis, Adami Fumani canonici Veronensis, et Nicolai Archii comitis Carminum* [. . .]. 2nd ed. 2 vols. Pavia: [Giovanni Antonio Volpi et Gaetano Volpi], 1739.

Giovio, Paolo. *Notable Men and Women of Our Time.* Edited and translated by Kenneth Gouwens. Cambridge, MA: Harvard University Press, 2013.

———. *Le vite del gran capitano e del marchese di Pescara.* Translated by Lodovico Domenichi. Edited by Costantino Panigada. Bari: Laterza, 1931.

Guidiccioni, Giovanni. *Opere di monsignor Giovanni Guidiccioni.* Edited by Carlo Minutoli. Florence: Barbèra, 1867.

Haskins, Susan. *Who is Mary? Three Early Modern Women on the Idea of the Virgin Mary.* Chicago: University of Chicago Press, 2008.

Lettere di diuersi autori eccellenti: Libro primo: Nel quale sono i tredici autori illustri, et il fiore di quante altre belle lettere si sono uedute fin qui: Con molte lettere del Bembo, del Nauagero, del Fracastoro, et d'altri famosi autori non più date in luce. Venice: appresso Giordano Ziletti, all'insegna della Stella, 1556.

Lettere di XIII huomini illustri: Alle quali oltra tutte l'altre fin qui stampate di nuovo ne sono state aggiunte molte. Edited by Thomaso Porcacchi. Venice: presso Giorgio de' Cavalli, 1565.

Lettere scritte al signor Pietro Aretino da molti signori: Comunità, donne di valore, poeti, et altri eccellentissimi spiriti. 2 vols. Venice: per Francesco Marcolini, 1551.

Lettere volgari di diuersi nobilissimi huomini et eccellentissimi ingegni scritte in diuerse materie: Libro primo. Venice: In casa de' figlivoli di Aldo, 1542.

Michelangelo Buonarroti. *Il carteggio di Michelangelo.* Edited by Giovanni Poggi, Paola Barocchi, and Renzo Ristori. 5 vols. Florence: Sansoni-SPES, 1965–1983.

———. *Rime e lettere.* Edited by Antonio Corsaro and Giorgio Masi. Milan: Bompiani, 2016.

Molza, Francesco Maria. *Delle poesie volgari e latine di Francesco Maria Molza corrette, illustrate, ed accresciute colla vita dell'autore scritta da Pierantonio Serassi.* 3 vols. Bergamo: Pietro Lancellotti, 1754–1757.

Nuovo libro di lettere de i più rari autori della lingua volgare italiana, di nuovo, et con nuova additione ristampato. Venice: Paolo Gherardo, 1545.

Ochino, Bernardino. *Dialogi sette del reuerendo padre frate Bernardino Occhino* [sic] *senese generale di frati Capuzzini.* Venice: per Nicolo d'Aristotile detto il Zoppino, 1542.

Pagano, Sergio M., and Concetta Ranieri. *Nuovi documenti su Vittoria Colonna e Reginald Pole.* Vatican City: Archivio vaticano, 1989.

Pasolini, Pier Desiderio. *Tre lettere inedite di Vittoria Colonna, marchesa di Pescara.* Rome: Ermanno Loescher & C. (Bretschneider e Regenberg), 1901.

Piccolomini, Alessandro. *Lettvra del S. Alessandro Piccolomini Infiammato fatta nell'Accademia degli Infiammati, M.D.XXXXI.* Bologna: Bartholomeo Bonardo e Marc'Antonio da Carpi, 1541.

Ranieri, Concetta. "Lettere inedite di Vittoria Colonna." *Giornale italiano di filologia* 7 (1979): 138–49.

Rota, Berardino. *Delle poesie del signor Berardino Rota cavaliere napoletano.* Edited by Scipione Ammirato. 2 vols. Naples: Stamperia di Gennaro Muzio, 1726.

Thesauro de la sapientia euangelica. Milan: Gottardo da Ponte, 1525.

Valdés, Juan. *Commentario o declaracion breve y compediosa sobre la Epistola de S. Paolo Apostol a los Romanos.* Venise [Genève]: [Jean Crespin] Juan Philadelpho, 1556.

Varchi, Benedetto. *Lettere, 1535–1565.* Edited by Vanni Bramanti. Rome: Edizioni di Storia e letteratura, 2008.

Wickart, Michael, ed. *Bullarium Ordinis FF. Minorum s.p. Francisci Capucinorum, seu Collectio bullarum, brevium, decretorum, rescriptorum oraculorum, &c. quae a Sede apostolica pro Ordine capucino emanarunt.* Vol. 1. Rome: Typis Joannis Zempel austriaci prope Montem Jordanum, 1740.

Secondary Sources

Amante, Bruto. *La tomba di Vittoria Colonna e i testamenti finora inediti della poetessa.* Bologna: Zanichelli, 1896.

Armour, Peter. "Michelangelo's Two Sisters: Contemplative Life and Active Life in the Final Version of the Monument to Julius II." In *Sguardi sull'Italia: Miscellanea dedicata a Francesco Villari dalla Society for Italian Studies*, edited by Gino Bedani [and others], 55–83. Exeter: Society for Italian Studies, 1997.

Bambach, Carmen. "Spiritual Poetry and Friendship with Vittoria Colonna: Drawings For Vittoria Colonna." In Bambach and others, *Michelangelo: Divine Draftsman and Designer*, 191–99.

Bambach, Carmen, and others. *Michelangelo: Divine Draftsman and Designer*. New York: The Metropolitan Museum of Art; New Haven: Yale University Press, 2017.

Bardazzi, Giovanni. "Le rime spirituali di Vittoria Colonna e Bernardino Ochino." *Italique* 4 (2001): 61–101.

Barnes, Bernadine. "The Understanding of a Woman: Vittoria Colonna and Michelangelo's Christ and the Samaritan Woman." *Renaissance Studies* 27 (2013): 633–53.

Bianca, Concetta. "Marcello Cervini e Vittoria Colonna." *Lettere italiane* 45 (1993): 427–39.

Bianco, Monica. "Le due redazioni del commento di Rinaldo Corso alle *Rime* di Vittoria Colonna." *Studi di filologia italiana* 56 (1998): 271–95.

Bowd, Stephen. "Prudential Friendship and Religious Reform: Vittoria Colonna and Gasparo Contarini." In Brundin, Crivelli and Sapegno, *A Companion to Vittoria Colonna*, 349–70.

Brundin, Abigail. "Composition *a due*: Lyric Poetry and Scribal Practice in Sixteenth-Century Italy." In *Renaissance Studies in Honor of Joseph Connors*, edited by Machtelt Israëls and Louis Waldman, 2:496–504. Florence: Villa I Tatti, 2013.

———. "Poesia come devozione: Leggere le rime di Vittoria Colonna." In Sapegno, *Al crocevia*, 161–76.

———. "Vittoria Colonna in Manuscript." In Brundin, Crivelli and Sapegno, *A Companion to Vittoria Colonna*, 39–68.

———. *Vittoria Colonna and the Spiritual Poetics of the Italian Reformation*. Aldershot, UK: Ashgate, 2008.

———. "Vittoria Colonna and the Virgin Mary." *Modern Language Review* 96 (2001): 61–81.

Brundin, Abigail, Tatiana Crivelli, and Maria Serena Sapegno, eds. *A Companion to Vittoria Colonna*. Leiden-Boston: Brill, 2016.

Brundin, Abigail, Deborah Howard, and Mary Laven. *The Sacred Home in Renaissance Italy*. Oxford: Oxford University Press, 2018.

Brunelli, Giampiero. "Tra eretici e gesuiti: I primi anni di Margherita a Roma." In *Margherita d'Austria (1522–1586): Costruzioni politiche e diplomazia, tra corte farnese e monarchia spagnola*, edited by Silvia Mantini, 65–83. Rome: Bulzoni, 2003.

Bullock, Alan. *Domenico Tordi e il carteggio colonnese della Biblioteca Nazionale di Firenze*. Florence: Olschki, 1986.

———. "Four Published Autographs by Vittoria Colonna in American and European Libraries, Together with New Data for a Critical Edition of Her Correspondence." *Italica* 49 (1972): 202–17.

Cabani, Maria Cristina. "Ariosto e Castiglione." *Italianistica* 45 (2016), 27–50.

Camaioni, Michele. "Libero spirito e genesi cappuccina: Nuove ipotesi e studi sul *Dyalogo della unione spirituale di Dio con l'anima* di Bartolomeo Cordoni e sul misterioso trattato dell'*Amore evangelico*." *Archivio italiano per la storia della pietà* 25 (2012): 303–72.

———. "'Per sfiammeggiar di un vivo e ardente amore': Vittoria Colonna, Bernardino Ochino e la Maddalena." In *El orbe católico: Transformaciones, continuidades, tensiones y formas de convivencia entre Europe y América, siglos IV–XIX*, edited by Maria Lupi e Claudio Rolle, 105–60. Santiago de Chile: RIL, 2016.

———. *Il Vangelo e l'anticristo: Bernardino Ochino tra francescanesimo ed eresia, 1487–1547*. Bologna: Il mulino, 2018.

Campi, Emidio. "Vittoria Colonna and Bernardino Ochino." In Brundin, Crivelli and Sapegno, *A Companion to Vittoria Colonna*, 371–98.

Carinci, Eleonora. "Religious Prose Writings." In Brundin, Crivelli and Sapegno, *A Companion to Vittoria Colonna*, 399–430.

Castagna, Raffaele. *Un cenacolo del Rinascimento sul Castello d'Ischia*. Ischia: Imagaenaria, 2007.

Chemello, Adriana. "Vittoria Colonna's Epistolary Works." In Brundin, Crivelli and Sapegno, *A Companion to Vittoria Colonna*, 11–36.

Christopher Faggioli, Sarah. "Di un'edizione del 1542 della *Dichiaratione* di Rinaldo Corso alle *Rime spirituali* di Vittoria Colonna." *Giornale storico della letteratura italiana* 634 (2014): 200–10.

Collett, Barry. *A Long and Troubled Pilgrimage: The Correspondence of Marguerite d'Angoulême and Vittoria Colonna, 1540–1545*. Princeton, NJ: Princeton Theological Seminary, 2000.

Colonna, Fabrizio. *Sulla tomba di Vittoria Colonna*. Rome: Stabilimento tipografico dell'opinione, 1887.

Copello, Veronica. "Aggiornamenti sul carteggio di Vittoria Colonna: Parte I." *Nuova rivista di letteratura italiana* 22, no. 1 (2019), 149–81.

———. "Aggiornamenti sul carteggio di Vittoria Colonna: Parte II." *Nuova rivista di letteratura italiana*, 22, no. 2 (2019), 85–119.

———. "Per un commento alle rime spirituali di Vittoria Colonna: Considerazioni a partire dal sonetto S1:52." *Schifanoia* 58–59 (2020): 165–71.

———. "Costanza d'Avalos (1460–1541): 'Letras' e 'valor guerrero' alla corte di Ischia." *Mélanges de l'école française de Rome: Moyen Âge* 31, no. 2 (2019): 343–60. <https://doi.org/10.4000/mefrm.6397>.

———. "Il dialogo poetico tra Michelangelo e Vittoria Colonna." *Italian Studies* 62, no. 3 (2017): 271–81.

———. "'Locum gerit et tenet authoritate': Il volto politico di Vittoria Colonna tra lettere e documenti inediti." *Rinascimento* 61 (2021): 237–82.

———. "Nuovi elementi su Vittoria Colonna, i cappuccini e i gesuiti." *Lettere italiane* 69, no. 2 (2017): 296–327.

———. "Un problema di giustizia e di verità: Vittoria Colonna e la restituzione di Colle S. Magno." *Schede umanistiche* 31 (2017): 11–61.

———. "'La signora marchesa a casa': Tre aspetti della biografia di Vittoria Colonna: Con una tavola cronologica." *Testo* 73 (2017): 9–45.

———. "Vittoria Colonna a Carlo V: 6 dicembre 1538." *Studi italiani* 29, no. 1 (2017): 87–116.

Corsaro, Antonio. "Manuscript Collections of Spiritual Poetry in Sixteenth-Century Italy." In *Forms of Faith in Sixteenth-Century Italy*, edited by Abigail Brundin and Matthew Treherne, 33–56. Aldershot, UK–Burlington, VT: Ashgate, 2009.

Cox, Virginia. "The Exemplary Vittoria Colonna." In Brundin, Crivelli, and Sapegno, *A Companion to Vittoria Colonna*, 467–500.

Cox, Virginia, and Shannon McHugh, eds. *Vittoria Colonna (1490–1547): Poetry, Religion, Art, Impact*. Amsterdam: Amsterdam University Press, 2022.

Crivelli, Tatiana. "Fedeltà, maternità, sacralità: Reinterpretazioni del legame matrimoniale nell'opera di Vittoria Colonna." In *Doni d'amore: Donne e rituali nel Rinascimento*, edited by Patricia Lurati, 171–79. Cinisello Balsamo [Milan]: Silvana, 2014.

———. "The Print Tradition of Vittoria Colonna's *Rime*." In Brundin, Crivelli and Sapegno, *A Companion to Vittoria Colonna*, 69–139.

Cummings, Brian. *The Literary Culture of the Reformation: Grammar and Grace*. Oxford: Oxford University Press, 2002.

D'Alençon, Edouard. "Gian Pietro Carafa vescovo di Chieti e la riforma nell'Ordine dei Minori dell'Osservanza." *Miscellanea francescana* 13 (1911): 131–44.

De Dominicis, Claudio. *La famiglia di Domenico Jacovacci*. Rome: Accademia Moroniana, 2014. <accademiamoroniana.it/monografie/Famiglia%20Jacovacci.pdf>.

D'Elia, Anthony. *The Renaissance of Marriage in Fifteenth-Century Italy*. Cambridge, MA: Harvard University Press, 2004.

Di Leone Leoni, Aron. *La nazione ebraica spagnola e portoghese di Ferrara, 1492–1559: I suoi rapporti col governo ducale e la popolazione locale ed i suoi legami con le nazioni portoghesi di Ancona, Pesaro e Venezia*. 2 vols. Florence: Olschki, 2011.

Di Majo, Ippolita. "Vittoria Colonna, il Castello di Ischia, e la cultura delle corti." In Ragionieri, *Vittoria Colonna e Michelangelo*, 19–32.

Dionisotti, Carlo. "Appunti sul Bembo e su Vittoria Colonna." In *Miscellanea Augusto Campana*, 1, 257–86. Padua: Antenore, 1981.

Dizionario biografico degli italiani [DBI]. Edited by Alberto Maria Ghisalberti. 96 vols. Rome: Istituto della Enciclopedia Italiana, 1960–. Online: <www.treccani.it/biografico/index.html>.

Doglio, Maria Luisa. *Lettera e donna: Scrittura epistolare al femminile tra Quattro e Cinquecento*. Rome: Bulzoni, 1993.

———. "'L'occhio interiore' e la scrittura nelle lettere spirituali di Vittoria Colonna." In *Omaggio a Gianfranco Folena*, 2:1001–13. Padua: Editoriale Programma, 1993.

Donati, Andrea. *Vittoria Colonna e l'eredità degli spirituali*. Rome: Etgraphiae, 2019.

Eisenbichler, Konrad. *The Sword and the Pen: Women, Poetry and Politics in Sixteenth-Century Siena*. Toronto: University of Toronto Press, 2014.

Erdmann, Axel, Alberto Govi, and Fabrizio Govi. *Ars epistolica: Communication in Sixteenth-Century Western Europe: Epistolaries, Letter-Writing Manuals and Model Letter Books, 1501–1600*. Lucerne: Gilhofer and Ranschburg, 2014.

Fenlon, Dermot. *Heresy and Obedience in Tridentine Italy: Cardinal Pole and the Counter Reformation*. Cambridge: Cambridge University Press, 1972. Reprint 2008.

Ferguson, Gary, and Mary B. McKinley, eds. *A Companion to Marguerite de Navarre*. Leiden-Boston: Brill, 2013.

Firpo, Massimo. *Tra alumbrados e "spirituali": Studi su Juan de Valdés e il valdesianesimo nella crisi religiosa del '500 italiano*. Florence: Olschki, 1990.

———. *Nel labirinto del mondo: Lorenzo Davidico tra santi, eretici, inquisitori*. Florence: Olschki, 1992.

———. "Vittoria Colonna, Giovanni Morone e gli 'spirituali.'" *Rivista di storia e letteratura religiosa* 24, no. 1 (1988): 211–61.

Firpo, Massimo, and Fabrizio Biferali. *"Navicula Petri": L'arte dei papi nel Cinquecento, 1527–1571*. Rome-Bari: Laterza, 2009.

Forcellino, Antonio. *La Pietà perduta: Storia di un capolavoro ritrovato di Michelangelo*. Milan: Rizzoli, 2010.

Forcellino, Maria. *Michelangelo, Vittoria Colonna e gli "spirituali": Religiosità e vita artistica a Roma negli anni Quaranta*. Rome: Viella, 2009.

———. "Vittoria Colonna and Michelangelo: Drawings and Paintings." In Brundin, Crivelli and Sapegno, *A Companion to Vittoria Colonna*, 270–313.

Fragnito, Gigliola. "'Per un lungo e dubbioso sentero': L'itinerario spirituale di Vittoria Colonna." In Sapegno, *Al crocevia*, 195.

———. "Gli 'spirituali' e la fuga di Bernardino Ochino." *Rivista storica italiana* 84 (1972): 777–813.

Frajese, Vittorio. *Nascita dell'Indice: La censura ecclesiastica dal Rinascimento alla Controriforma.* Brescia: Morcelliana, 2006.

Fresu, Rita. *L'altra Roma: Percorsi di italianizzazione tra dame, sante, popolani nella storia della città (e della sua regione).* Rome: Edizioni nuova cultura, 2008.

———. "Educazione linguistica e livelli di scrittura femminile tra XV e XVI secolo: Le lettere di Giulia Farnese e di Adriana Mila Orsini." *Cahiers de recherches médiévales et humanistes* 28, no. 2 (2014): 105–52.

Friedensburg, Walter. "Der Briefwechsel Gasparo Contarinis mit Ercole Gonzaga nebst einem Briefe Giovanni Pietro Carafas mitgeteilt." *Quellen und Forschungen aus italienischen Archiven und Bibliotheken* 2 (1899): 161–222.

Fumagalli Beonio Brocchieri, Maria Teresa, and Roberta Frigeni, eds. *Donne e scrittura dal XII al XVI secolo.* Bergamo: Lubrina-LEB, 2009.

Furey, Constance. "'Intellects Inflamed in Christ': Women and Spiritualized Scholarship in Renaissance Christianity." *Journal of Religion* 84 (2004): 1–22.

Gattoni, Maurizio. "Pace universale o tregue bilaterali? Clemente VII e l'istruzione a Nicolaus Schömberg, arcivescovo di Capua, 1524." *Ricerche storiche* 30, no. 1 (2000): 171–96.

Ginzburg, Carlo, and Adriano Prosperi. *Giochi di pazienza: Un seminario sul Beneficio di Cristo.* 2nd ed. Turin: Einaudi, 1977.

Giustiniani, Lorenzo. *Dizionario geografico-ragionato del Regno di Napoli.* Vol. 8. Naples: Vincenzo Manfredi, 1804. Anastatic reprint Bologna: Forni, 1970.

Guerra Medici, Maria Teresa. "Intrecci familiari, politici e letterari alla corte di Costanza d'Avalos." In Fumagalli, Fumagalli, and Frigeni, *Donne e scrittura dal XII al XVI secolo,* 115–62.

Gui, Francesco. *L'attesa del concilio: Vittoria Colonna e Reginald Pole nel movimento degli spirituali.* Rome: Editoria università elettronica, 1998.

Hirst, Michael. *Michelangelo and His Drawings.* New Haven, CT: Yale University Press, 1988.

Jung-Inglessis, Eva-Maria. "Il *Pianto della Marchesa di Pescara sopra la Passione di Cristo*: Introduzione." *Archivio italiano per la storia della pietà* 10 (1997): 115–47.

Kirshner, Julius. *Marriage, Dowry, and Citizenship in Late Medieval and Renaissance Italy.* Toronto: University of Toronto Press, 2014.

Lazzerini, Luigi. *Teologia del* Miserere: *Da Savonarola al* Beneficio di Cristo, *1490–1543.* Turin: Rosenberg & Sellier, 2013.

Liguori, Marianna. "Vittoria Colonna e la riforma cappuccina: Documenti epistolari e un'appendice inedita." *Atti e memorie dell'Arcadia* 6 (2017): 85–104.

Longo, Nicola. "*De epistola condenda*: L'arte di 'componer lettere' nel Cinquecento." In Quondam, *Le "carte messaggiere,"* 177–201.

Luzietti, Anna Maria. "Amadori, Francesco, detto l'Urbino." In *Dizionario biografico degli italiani,* 2 (1960). <treccani.it/enciclopedia/amadori-francesco-detto-l-urbino_(Dizionario-Biografico)/>.

Luzio, Alessandro. "Vittoria Colonna." *Rivista storica mantovana* 1 (1885): 1–52.

Luzio, Alessandro, and Rodolfo Renier. "Cultura e relazioni letterarie di Isabella d'Este." *Giornale storico della letteratura italiana* 40 (1902): 289–334.

Mayer, Thomas F. *Reginald Pole: Prince and Prophet.* Cambridge: Cambridge University Press, 2000.

Moro, Giacomo. "Le commentaire de Rinaldo Corso sur les *Rime* de Vittoria Colonna: Une encyclopédie pour les 'tres nobles dames.'" In *Les commentaires et la naissance de la critique littéraire, France/Italie, XIVe–XVIe siècles: Actes du Colloque international sur le commentaire (Paris, 19–21 mai 1988),* edited by Gisèle Mathieu-Castellani and Michel Plaisance, 195–202. Paris: Aux amateurs de livres, 1990.

Moroni, Ornella. *Carlo Gualteruzzi (1500–1577) e i corrispondenti.* Vatican City: Biblioteca apostolica vaticana, 1984.

Nagel, Alexander. "Gifts for Michelangelo and Vittoria Colonna." *Art Bulletin* 79 (1997): 647–68.

Orano, Domenico. "Il diario di Marcello Alberini." *Archivio della società romena di storia patria* 18 (1895): 319–416.

Ordine, Nuccio. "Vittoria Colonna nell'*Orlando furioso.*" *Studi e problemi di critica testuale* 1 (1991): 55–92.

Peyronel Rambaldi, Susanna. *Una gentildonna irrequieta: Giulia Gonzaga fra reti familiari e relazioni eterodosse.* Rome: Viella, 2012.

Pignatti, Franco. "Margherita d'Angoulême, Vittoria Colonna, Francesco Della Torre." *Filologia e critica* 38 (2013): 122–48.

Prosperi, Adriano. *L'eresia del* Libro grande: *Storia di Giorgio Siculo e della sua setta.* Milan: Feltrinelli, 2000.

———. *Tra evangelismo e controriforma: G. M. Giberti (1495–1543).* Rome: Edizioni di storia e letteratura, 1969.

Quondam, Amedeo, ed. *Le "carte messaggiere": Retorica e modelli di comunicazione epistolare, per un indice dei libri di lettere del Cinquecento.* Rome: Bulzoni, 1981.

———. "Note sulla tradizione della poesia spirituale e religiosa (parte prima)." In *Paradigmi e tradizioni,* edited by Amedeo Quondam, 127–211. Rome: Bulzoni, 2005.

Rabitti, Giovanna. Review of Vittoria Colonna, *Rime,* edited by Alan Bullock. *Studi e problemi di critica testuale* 28 (1984), 230–39.

Ragionieri, Pina, ed. *Vittoria Colonna e Michelangelo: Firenze, Casa Buonarroti, 24 maggio–12 settembre 2005.* Florence: Mandragora, 2005.

Ranieri, Concetta. "Ancora sul carteggio tra Pietro Bembo e Vittoria Colonna." *Giornale italiano di filologia* 14 (1983): 134–51.

————. "Censimento dei codici e delle stampe dell'epistolario di Vittoria Colonna." *Atti e memorie dell'Arcadia* S. 3, vol. 7, no. 1 (1977): 123–63; 7, no. 3 (1979): 259–69; 7, no. 4 (1980–1981): 263–80; 8, no. 1 (1981–1982): 251–64.

————. "Descriptio et imago vitae: Vittoria Colonna nei biografi, letterati e poeti del Cinquecento." In *Biografia: Genesi e strutture*, edited by Mauro Sarnelli, 123–53. Rome: Aracne, 2003.

————. "Premesse umanistiche alla religiosità di Vittoria Colonna." *Rivista di storia e letteratura religiosa* 32 (1996): 531–48.

————. "'Si san Francesco fu eretico li suoi imitatori son luterani': Vittoria Colonna e la riforma dei cappuccini." In *Ludovico da Fossombrone e l'Ordine dei Cappuccini*, edited by Vittorio Criscuolo, 337–51. Rome: Istituto storico dei appuccini, 1994.

————. "Vittoria Colonna e Costanza d'Avalos Piccolomini: Una corrispondenza spirituale." In *Cum fide amicitia: Per Rosanna Alhaique Pettinelli*, edited by Stefano Benedetti, Francesco Lucioli, and Pietro Petteruti Pellegrino, 477–90. Rome: Bulzoni, 2015.

Re, Emilio. "Una missione di Latino Giovenale: Un disegno di matrimonio fra Vittoria Farnese e Francesco, duca d'Aumale." *Archivio della società romena di storia patria* 34 (1911): 5–33.

Reid, Jonathan A. *King's Sister—Queen of Dissent: Marguerite of Navarre (1492–1549) and Her Evangelical Network*. Leiden-Boston: Brill, 2009.

Reumont, Alfred von. *Vittoria Colonna: Leben, Dichten, Glauben in 16. Jahrhundert*. Herder: Freiburg im Breisgau, 1881. Italian translation by Giuseppe Müller and Ermanno Ferrero, *Vittoria Colonna: Vita, fede e poesia nel secolo decimosesto*, Turin: Loescher, 1883; 2nd ed., *Vittoria Colonna, marchesa di Pescara: Vita, fede e poesia nel secolo decimosesto*, Turin-Florence-Rome: Loescher, 1892.

Richardson, Brian. *Manuscript Culture in Renaissance Italy*. Cambridge: Cambridge University Press, 2009.

Robin, Diana M. *Publishing Women: Salons, the Presses, and the Counter-Reformation in Sixteenth-Century Italy*. Chicago: University of Chicago Press, 2007.

Romei, Danilio. "Le *Rime* di Vittoria Colonna." Review of Vittoria Colonna, *Rime*, edited by Alan Bullock. *Paragone-Letteratura* 34, no. 404 (1983): 81–84.

Ronchini, Amadio. "Mons. Ambrogio Recalcati." *Atti e memorie delle deputazioni di storia patria per le Provincie dell'Emilia* 2 (1877): 69–79.

Rosalba, Giovanni. "Un episodio nella vita di Vittoria Colonna." In Nicola Zingarelli, ed., *Nozze Pércopo-Luciani: 30 luglio 1902*, 125–41. Naples: L. Pierro, 1903.

Rovetta, Alessandro, ed. *L'ultimo Michelangelo: Disegni e rime attorno alla Pietà Rondanini: Milano, Castello Sforzesco, Museo d'Arte Antica, 24 marzo—19 giugno 2011*. Milan: Silvana, 2011.

Russell, Camilla. *Giulia Gonzaga and the Religious Controversies of Sixteenth-Century Italy*. Turnhout: Brepols, 2006.

Rutter, Itala T. C. "La scrittura di Vittoria Colonna e Margherita di Navarra: Resistenza e misticismo." *Romance Languages Annual* 3 (1991): 303–8.

Salza, Abd-El-Kader, ed. *Lettere inedite di Vittoria Colonna e Benedetto Varchi, per le nozze Mancini-Achiardi.* Florence: pei Minori Corrigendi, 1898.

Sanson, Helena. "Vittoria Colonna and Language." In Brundin, Crivelli, and Sapegno, *A Companion to Vittoria Colonna,* 195–234.

Sapegno, Maria Serena, ed. *Al crocevia della storia: Poesia, religione e politica in Vittoria Colonna.* Rome: Viella, 2016.

Saulnier, Verdun-Louis. "Marguerite de Navarre, Vittoria Colonna et quelques autres italiens de 1540." In *Mélanges à la mémoire de Franco Simone: France et Italie dans la culture européenne,* vol. 1 *Moyen Age et Renaissance,* 281–95. Geneva: Slatkine, 1980.

Scarpati, Claudio. "Le rime spirituali di Vittoria Colonna nel codice Vaticano donato a Michelangelo." In Claudio Scarpati, *Invenzione e scrittura: Saggi di letteratura italiana,* 129–62. Milan: Vita e pensiero, 2005.

Simoncelli, Paolo. "Il *Dialogo dell'unione spirituale di Dio con l'anima* tra alumbradismo spagnolo e prequietismo." *Annuario dell'istituto storico italiano per l'età moderna e contemporanea* 29 (1977): 565–601.

———. *Evangelismo italiano del Cinquecento: Questione religiosa e nicodemismo politico.* Rome: Istituto storico italiano per l'età moderna e contemporanea, 1979.

Tacchi-Venturi, Pietro. "Nuove lettere inedite di Vittoria Colonna," *Studi e Documenti di Storico e Diritto,* 22 (1901): 307–14.

———."Vittoria Colonna e la riforma cappuccina." *Collectanea franciscana* 1 (1931): 28–58.

———. "Vittoria Colonna, fautrice della Riforma Cattolic*a, secondo alcune sue lettere inedite,"* Studi e Documenti di Storia e Diritto 22 (1901): 153–79.

Targoff, Ramie. *Renaissance Woman: The Life of Vittoria Colonna.* New York: Farrar, Straus and Giroux, 2018.

———. "La volontà segreta di Vittoria Colonna: Una lettera smarrita a Clemente VII." In Sapegno, *Al crocevia della storia,* 217–24.

Thérault, Suzanne. *Un cénacle humaniste de la Renaissance autour de Vittoria Colonna, châtelaine d'Ischia.* Paris: Marcel Didier; Florence: Sansoni antiquariato, 1968.

Tolnay, Charles de. "Michelangelo's Pietà Composition for Vittoria Colonna." *Record of the Art Museum, Princeton University,* 12, no. 2 (1953), 44–62.

Tordi, Domenico. *Il codice delle* Rime *di Vittoria Colonna, marchesa di Pescara, appartenuto a Margherita d'Angoulême, regina di Navarra.* Pistoia: Flori, 1900.

———. "Luogo ed anno della nascita di Vittoria Colonna." *Giornale storico della letteratura italiana* 29 (1892): 1–21.

————. "Vittoria Colonna in Orvieto durante la Guerra del Sale." *Bollettino della società umbra di storia patria* 1 (1895): 473–533.

Toscano, Tobia R. "Due 'allievi' di Vittoria Colonna: Luigi Tansillo e Alfonso d'Avalos." *Critica letteraria* 16 (1988): 739–73.

————. "Per la datazione del manoscritto dei sonetti di Vittoria Colonna per Michelangelo Buonarroti." *Critica letteraria* 175 (2017): 211–37.

Valeri, Elena. *"Italia dilacerata": Girolamo Borgia nella cultura storica del Rinascimento.* Milan: F. Angeli, 2007.

Waddington, Raymond B. *Pietro Aretino: Subverting the System in Renaissance Italy.* Farnham, Surrey, UK–Burlington, VT: Ashgate, 2013.

Zarri, Gabriella, ed. *Per lettera: La scrittura epistolare femminile tra archivio e tipografia, secoli XV–XVIII.* Rome: Viella, 1999.

Zimmermann, T. C. Price. *Paolo Giovio: Uno storico e la crisi italiana del XVI secolo.* Edited by Franco Minonzio. Cologno Monzese: Polyhistor, 2012. Reprinted 2014. Italian translation of *Paolo Giovio: The Historian and the Crisis of Sixteenth-Century Italy* (Princeton, NJ: Princeton University Press, 1995).

Index

The Other Voice in Early Modern Europe:
The Toronto Series

SENIOR EDITOR Margaret L. King

SERIES EDITORS Jaime Goodrich, Elizabeth H. Hageman

Series Titles

MADRE MARÍA ROSA
Journey of Five Capuchin Nuns
Edited and translated by Sarah E. Owens
Volume 1, 2009

GIOVAN BATTISTA ANDREINI
Love in the Mirror: *A Bilingual Edition*
Edited and translated by Jon R. Snyder
Volume 2, 2009

RAYMOND DE SABANAC AND SIMONE
ZANACCHI
Two Women of the Great Schism: The Revelations *of Constance de Rabastens by Raymond de Sabanac and* Life of the Blessed Ursulina of Parma *by Simone Zanacchi*
Edited and translated by Renate Blumenfeld-Kosinski and Bruce L. Venarde
Volume 3, 2010

OLIVA SABUCO DE NANTES BARRERA
The True Medicine
Edited and translated by Gianna Pomata
Volume 4, 2010

LOUISE-GENEVIÈVE GILLOT DE
SAINCTONGE
Dramatizing Dido, Circe, and Griselda
Edited and translated by Janet Levarie Smarr
Volume 5, 2010

PERNETTE DU GUILLET
Complete Poems: A Bilingual Edition
Edited with introduction and notes by
Karen Simroth James
Poems translated by Marta Rijn Finch
Volume 6, 2010

ANTONIA PULCI
*Saints' Lives and Bible Stories for the Stage:
A Bilingual Edition*
Edited by Elissa B. Weaver
Translated by James Wyatt Cook
Volume 7, 2010

VALERIA MIANI
Celinda, A Tragedy: *A Bilingual Edition*
Edited with an introduction by Valeria
Finucci
Translated by Julia Kisacky
Annotated by Valeria Finucci and Julia
Kisacky
Volume 8, 2010

Enchanted Eloquence: Fairy Tales by Seventeenth-Century French Women Writers
Edited and translated by Lewis C. Seifert
and Domna C. Stanton
Volume 9, 2010